HISTORY

of

OLD RAPPAHANNOCK COUNTY, VIRGINIA

1656–1692

Including the Present Counties of
Essex and Richmond, and Parts of
Westmoreland, King George, Stafford,
Caroline, and Spotsylvania

Thomas Hoskins Warner

HERITAGE BOOKS
2021

HERITAGE BOOKS
AN IMPRINT OF HERITAGE BOOKS, INC.

Books, CDs, and more—Worldwide

For our listing of thousands of titles see our website
at
www.HeritageBooks.com

Published 2021 by
HERITAGE BOOKS, INC.
Publishing Division
5810 Ruatan Street
Berwyn Heights, Md. 20740

International Standard Book Number
Paperbound: 978-1-58549-083-7

TABLE OF CONTENTS

DEDICATION

This book is dedicated to the memory of my mother, Kate Waring Hoskins Warner, wife of my dear father, Charles C. Warner. Both were interested in history and told their children many family tales about the past. A large proportion of the people named in this volume were in one way or another kinsmen of my mother. She loved the traditions they left, the high thinking that they evidenced, and shared with them their devotion to God and Virginia. She was descended from the Hoskins, Buckner, Ware, Waring, Vass, Aylett, Edmonds, Fox, Lowry, Ball, Cheney, Hockaday, Lawson, Macon, Payne, Rust, Broocke, Hudnall, Chilton, Walker and other families of this section of Virginia.

ACKNOWLEDGEMENTS

And I wish to acknowledge my debt to my dear wife, Pauline Pearce Warner, who not only constantly helped me in the research, but also, in the end, did all the work of publication, faithfully sided by our daughter, Pauline Baldwin Warner.

Thomas Hoskins Warner

ILLUSTRATIONS

Sidney E. King, of Milford in Caroline County, Virginia, nationally famous documentary artist, whose pictures are found at national monuments and in state and national parks across the nation, and who has illustrated many magazine articles and books on historical subjects, was so kind as to draw three of the illustrations for this book. His paintings on religious subjects are in many churches, as well as on exhibition at the New York World's Fair. He is also known locally for his fine portraits and for his paintings of natural scenery.

Mrs. John L. Motley, Jr. (Vivien Farish), of Port Royal, Virginia, drew the picture of Colonel Catlett's home above Port Royal. In her childhood it was the home of her grandparents, and before that of her great-grandparents. The last private owners of the property were Mr. and Mrs. James E. Carlton, who kindly furnished me with the pictures which guided Mrs. Motley in making the drawing. The house, on property now part of A.P. Hill Camp, was destroyed by the U.S. Army.

Mr. and Mrs. Joseph W. Chinn, of Wilmington, Delaware, and Richmond County, Virginia, cooperated with us in obtaining snapshots from which the picture of the old Fauntleroy house was drawn.

I particularly thank Mr. John L. Motley, Jr. of Port Royal, Virginia, for his care in printing the illustrations, and his cooperation, advice, and help with many details of publication.

Mr. John W. Dudley, Assistant Archivist of the Virginia State Library, has on many occasions been most helpful.

The drawing of Colonel Thomas Bowler's home was made from a painting owned by the author.

NOTE: The original mimeographed text has been retyped and reformatted in font Adobe Hebrew from the original by Wesley E. Pippenger. Be advised that page citations to the original text are modified in this edition.

ABBREVIATIONS and EXPLANATIONS

B	Book	N	Northumberland County
D or DB	Deed Book	O or OB	Order Book
E	Essex County	p or pp	page or pages
H	Hening's Statutes	PB	Patent Book
L	Lancaster County	R	Richmond County
MCGC	Minutes of the Council and General Court of Colonial Virginia	W or WB	Will or Will Book

References without a county initial identification are to be the records of Old Rappahannock County. The names Rappahannock County and Rappahannock River occur so frequently that they are not indexed. As the names in the North Farnham Parish Register are arranged alphabetically, they are not indexed [in the original text], except the names of the brides.

Spelling in quoted passages closely follows that of the original manuscripts except for a few words that have been modernized in order to make them comprehensible to the modern reader.

Rappahannock County lay on both sides of the Rappahannock River and included the territory from the ridge between the Mattaponi and the Rappahannock rivers to the ridge between the Rappahannock and Potomac rivers, and from the Middlesex and Lancaster County lines indefinitely north-westerly.

For each record book, typographical errors are corrected where they occur.

INTRODUCTION

Early Explorations and Adventures

The first settlement of white men in Virginia was apparently that made by the Spaniard, Menendez de Aviles Pedro, probably on the Potomac river. He commanded the Spanish Armada which carried Phillip the Second, back to Spain in 1559, and in 1560, he was commanded by royal order to examine the Atlantic coast north of Port Royal, South Carolina. When he went to Florida in 1570, he had, according to the records, established a mission at Axacon in the Chesapeake Bay region. The colony was massacred by the Indians on February 8, 1571. By the time of his return to it in 1572, all had perished. He captured and took off eight of the Indians known to have had a part in the massacre.

This might be regarded as closing a tragic incident were it not for the fact that Mosco, who appears to have been the descendant of one of these Spaniards, befriended the English, taught them military tactics effective on the river against the savages in the wilderness, guided their explorations, and helped them to secure food supplies. He stands out as one of the Indians whose friendship made possible the permanence of the English occupation in Virginia.

Captain John Smith

When Captain John Smith, in the latter part of December 1608, went out on his long expedition in search of food for the colonists, he was taken prisoner by the Indians and carried to the Mattaponi river. "From hence," he wrote,

> this kind king [of the Mattaponies] conducted mee to a place called Topahanocke, a kingdome upon another River northward: the cause of this was, that the yeare before, a shippe had beene in the River of Pamaunke, who having beene kindly entertained by Powhatan their Emperour, they returned thence, and discovered the River of Topahanocke, where being received with like kindnesse, yet he slue the King, and tooke of his people, and they supposed I were hee. But the people reported him [Smith] a great man that was Captaine, and using mee kindly, the next day we departed.

> This River of Topahanock [Rappahannock] seemeth in breadth not much lesse than that we dwell upon. At the mouth of the River is a Countrey called Cuttata-women: upwards is Marraughtacum, Tapohanock, Appamatuck, and Nantaugs-tacum: Topmanahocks, the head issuing from many Mountaines. The next night I lodged at a hunting town of Powhatans, and the next day arrived at Werowocomoco upon the river of Pamauncke, where the great king is resident; by the way we passed by the top of another little river, which is betwix the two, called Payankatank. The most of this Countrey, though Desert, yet exceeding fertil; good timber, most hils and dales, in each valley a cristall spring.

Smith, in his *Description of Virginia*, says that the Toppahanocks had about one hundred fighting men.

Discoverers

According to the record of Walter Russell and Anas Todkill on "The second of June 1608, Smith [Captain John Smith] left the fort, to perform his discoverie [of Chesapeake Bay]: with this Company:

Walter Russell, Doctour of Physicke		Anas Todkill	}
Ralph Morton	}	Robert Small	} Sould
Thomas Momford	}	James Watkins	} [Soldiers]
William Cantrill	} Gent.	John Powell	}
Richard Fetherstone	} [Gentlemen]	James Read, blacke smith	
James Bourne	}	Richard Keale, fishmonger	
Michael Sicklemore	}	Jones Profit, fisher."	

After exploring the eastern shore of the Bay, the ship sailed down the western shore until it reached the mouth of the Rappahannock river. According to the old record,

Having finished this discovery (though our victuall was neare spent) he intended to have seene his imprisonment-acquaintances upon the river of Toppahannock. But our boate (by reason of the ebbe) chansing to ground upon a many shoules lying in the entrance, we spied many fishes lurking amongst the weedes on the sands, our captaine [Smith] sporting himselfe to catch them by nailing them to the ground with his sword, set us all a fishing in that manner, by this devise, we tooke more in an hour than we all could eat; but it chanced, the captain taking a fish from his sword (not knowing her condition), being much of the fashion of a Thornebacke with a longer taile, whereon is a most poysoned sting of 2. or 3. inches long, which shee strooke an inch and halfe into the wrist of his arme, the which in 4. houres, has so extreamly swolne his hand, arme, shoulder, and part of his body, as we all with much sorrow concluded his funerall, and prepared his grave in an Ile hard by (as himself appointed) which then wee called Stingray Ile, after the name of the fish. Yet by the helpe of a precious oile, Doctour Russell applyed, ere night his tormenting paine was so wel asswaged that he eate the fish for his supper, which gave no lesse joy and content to us, than ease to himselfe. Having neither Surgeon nor surgerie but that preservative oile, we presently set saile for James Towne; passing the mouth of Pyankatanck, and Pamaunke rivers, the next day we safely arrived at Kecoughtan.

Explorers

Nathaniell Powell and Anas Todkill record that on "The 20th of July, Captain Smith set forward to finish the discovery (of the Bay) with 12 men. Their names were:

Nathaniell Powell	}	Anas Todkill	}

Thomas Momford	}	Edward Pysing	}
Richard Featherstone	} Gent.	Richard Keale	} Sould.
Michael Sicklemore	} [Gentlemen]	Anthony Bagnall	} [Soldiers]
James Bourne	}	James Watkins	}
		James Ward and	}
		Jonas Profit	}

Coming down the Chesapeake Bay [1608], they found the Patawomecks tractable and civil, and promised to revenge them on the Massawomecks, but

Our purposes were crossed in the discoverie of the river of Toppahannock, for wee had much wrangling with that peevish nation; but at last, they became as tractable as the rest. It is an excellent, pleasant, well inhabited, fertill, and a goodly navigable river, toward the head thereof; it pleased God to take one of our sicke (called Master Fetherstone), where in Fetherstons bay we buried him in the night, with a volley of shot; the rest (notwithstanding their ill diet, and bad lodging, crowded in so small a barge, in so many dangers, never resting, but alwaies tossed to and againe) all well recovered their healthes; then we discovered the river of Payantank, and set saild for James Towne.

A much more complete account of this voyage of discovery into the Rappahannock River is to be found in the 1625 edition of *Purchas his Pilgrimes*, Book 4, pages 1715-1716. This also was written by Nathaniell Powell and Anas Todkill. They wrote:

In the discovery of this River, which some call Rapahanocke; we were kindely entertained by the people of Moraughtacun.

Here we encountred our old friend Mosko, a lustie Savage of Wighcocomoco, upon the River of Patawomecke. Wee supposed him some Frenchmans Sonne, because he had a thicke, blacke, bush Beard, and the Savages seldome have any at all, of which hee was not a little proud to see so many of his Countrie men. Wood, and water hee would fetch us, guide us any whether, nay cause divers of his Countie men helpe us to helpe us too, against winde or tyde, from place to place, till we came to Patawomeke. There he rested, till we returned from the head of the River, and then occasioned us conduct to the Mine, which we supposed Antimony.

Now in the place hee failed not to doe us all the good he could, perswading us in any case not to goe to the Rapahanocks, for they would kill us, for being friends with the Moraughlacuds, that but lately had stolne three of the Kings women.

This we did thinke was but that his friends might only have our trade, & so crossed the River to the Rapahanocks. There some twelve or sixteene standing on the shore, directed us to a little narrow cricke, where was good landing, and commodities for us, in three or foure Canoaes which we saw there.

.. *their arrowes*
  which were an armefull ..

The Trap

But according to our custome, we demanded to exchange a man, in signe of love, which after they had a little consulted foure or five came to the middles to fetch our man, and leave us one of them, shewing we neede not feare them, for they had neither Clubs, Bowes, nor Arrowes. Notwithstanding Anas Todkill being sent on shore to see if he could discover any ambuscadoes; desired to goe over the plaine to fetch some wood, but they were unwilling, except we would come into the creeke, where the Boate might come close ashore.

Todkill by degrees having gotten some two stones throwes up the plaine, perceived two or three hundred men as he thought behinde the trees, so that offering to returne to the Boate, the Savages assayed to carry him away perforce, he called to us, we were betraid, and by that he had spoken the word, our hostage was over-boord, but Watkins his keeper slew him in the water. Immediately we let fly amo[n]gst them so that they fled, & Todkill escaped, yet they shot so fast that he fell flat on the ground ere he could recover the Boate.

Here the Massawomecks Targets stood us in good stead, for upon Mosco's words we had set them about the forepart of our Boate like a fore-castell, from whence we securely beate the Savages from off the plaine without any hurt, yet they shot more then 1000 Arrowes, and then fled into the woods, arming our selves with those light Targets (which are made of little small sticks, woven betwixt strings of their hempe and silke grasse, as in our cloth, but so firmely, that no Arrow can possibly pierce them) we rescued Todkill, who was all bloudied by some of them who were shot, but as it pleased God, he had no hurt, and followed them up to the woods, we found some wounded, some slaine, & in divers places much bloud. It seemes all their Arrowes were spent, for we hard no more of them.

Their Canoas we tooke; the Arrowes which we found we broke, except those we kept for Mosco, to whom we gave the Canoaes for his kindnes, that entertained us in the best triumphing manner and warlike order in armes he could procure of the Moraughtacunds.

The rest of the day wee spent in accommodating our Boate, instead of tholes we made stickes like bedstaves, to which we fastened so many of our Massawomecke Targets, that invironed her as waistcloathes. The next morning we went up the River, and our friend Mosco followed us along the shoare, but at last desired to goe with us in our Boate. But as wee passed by Pisacacke, Machopeake, and Wecuppom, three Townes scituated upon high white clay Clifts, the other side all a low plaine marish, and the River there but narrow. Thirty or forty of the Rapahanockes had so prepared themselves with branches, as we tooke them for little Bushes growing amongst the Sedge: seeing their Arrowes strike the Targets and drop in the River, Mosco fell flat on his face, crying the Rapahanocks; which presently we espied to be the Bushes, which at our first Volley fell downe in the Sedge; when we were gone neere halfe a mile, they shewed themselves, dancing and singing very merrily.

The Kings of Pissassacke, Nandtaughtacund and Cuttatawomen, used us kindely, and all the people neglected not any thing to Mosco to bring us to them. Betwixt Secobecke and Massawtecke is a small Isle or two, which causeth the River to be broader than ordinary; there it pleased God to take one of our company, called M. [Master] Richard Fetherstone, that all the time hee had beene in the Country had behaved himselfe very honestly, valiantly, & industriously, where in a little Bay, called hereupon Fetherstones Bay [Green Bay], we buried him with a volly of shot, the rest notwithstanding their ill diet and bed lodging crouded in so small a Barge, in so many dangers never resting, but alwaies tossed to & againe, had all well recovered their healths.

The next day we sailed so high as our Boat would flote, there setting up Crosses and graving our names in the trees. Our Sentinell saw an arrow fall by him; though we had ranged up and downe more than an houre, in digging in the earth, looking at stones, herbs, and springs, not seeing where a Salvage could well hide himselfe.

Upon the alarum, by that we had recovered our armes, there was about an hundred nimble Indians skipping from tree to tree, letting fly their arrows so fast as they could: the trees here served us for Baricadoes as well as they. But Mosco did us more service then we expected; for having shot away his quiver of Arrowes, he ran to the Boat for more. The Arrowes of Mosco at the first made them pause upon the matter, thinking by his bruit and skipping, there were many Salvages. About halfe an houre this continued, then they all vanished as suddainly as they approached. Mosco followed them so farre as he could see us, till they were out of sight. As we returned there lay a Salvage as dead, shot in the knee; but taking him up we found he had life; which Mosco seeing, never was Dog more furious against a Beare, then Mosco was to have beat out his braines. So we had him to our Boat, where our Chirurgian [A. Bagnall] who went with us to cure our Captaines hurt of the Stingray, so dressed this Salvage that within an houre after he looked somewhat cheerfully, and did eate and speake. In the meane time we contented Mosco in helping him to gather up their arrowes, which were an armefull; whereof he gloried not a little.

Then we desired Mosco to know what he was, and what Countries were beyond the mountaines; the poore Salvage mildly answered, he and all with him were Hassininga, where there are three Kings more, like unto them, namely the King of Stegora, the King of Tauxuntania, and the King of Shakahonea, that were come to Mohaskahod, which is onely a hunting Towne, and the bounds betwixt the Kingdome of the Mannahocks and the Nandtaughtacunds, but hard by where we were.

We demanded why they came in that manner to betray us, that came to them in peace, and to seeke their loves; he answered, they heard we were a people come from under the world, to take their land from them.

We asked him how many worlds he did know, he replyed, he knew no more but that which was under the skies that covered him, which were the Powahatans, with the Monacans and the Massawomeks that were higher up in the mountaines.

Then we asked him what was beyond the mountaines, he answered the Sunne: but of any thing els he knew nothing; *because the woods were not burnt. (*They cannot travell but where the woods are burnt.)

These and many such questions wee demanded, concerning the Massawomeks, the Monacans, their owne Country, and where the Kings of Stegora, Tauxsintania, and the rest. The Monacans he sayd were their neighbours and friends, and did dwell as they in the hilly Countries by small rivers, living upon rootes and fruits, but chiefly by hunting. The Massawomeks did dwell upon a great water, and had many boats, and so many men that they made warre with all the world. For their Kings, they were gone every one a severall way with their men on hunting. But those with him came thither a fishing till they saw us, notwithstanding they would be all together at night at Mahaskahod.

For this relation we gave him many toyes, with perswasions to goe with us: and he as earnestly desired us to stay the comming of those Kings that for his good usage should be friends with us, for he was brother to Hassininga. But Mosco advised us presently to be gone, for they were all naught; yet we told him we would not till it was night. All things we made ready to entertain what came, and Mosco was as diligent in trimming his arrowes.

The night being come we all imbarked; for the river was so narrow, had it beene light the land on the one side was so high, they might have done us exceeding much mischiefe. All this while the King of Hassininga was seeking the rest, and had consultation a good time what to doe. But by their espies seeing we were gone, it was not long before we heard their arrowes dropping on every side the Boat; we caused our Salvages to call unto them, but such a yelling and hallowing they made that they heard nothing, but now and then [we shot off] a peece, ayming so neare as we could where we heard the most voyces. More then 12 myles they followed us in this manner; then the day appearing, we found our selves in a broad Bay, out of danger of their shot, where wee came to an anchor, and fell to breakfast. Not so much as speaking to them till the Sunne was risen.

Being well refreshed, we untyed our Targets that covered us as a Deck, and all shewed our selves with those shields on our armes, and swords in our hands, and also our prisoner Amoroleck. A long discourse there was betwixt his Countrimen and him, how good wee were, how well wee used him, how wee had a Patawomek with us [who] loved us as his life, that would have slaine him had we not preserved him, and that he should have his libertie would they be but friends; and to do us any hurt it was impossible.

Upon this they all hung their Bowes and Quivers upon the trees, and one came swimming aboord us with a Bow tyed on his head, and another with a Quiver of Arrowes, which they delivered our Captaine as a present: the Captaine having used them so kindly as he could, told them the other three Kings should doe the like, and then the great King of our world should be their friend; whose men we were. It was no sooner demanded but performed, so upon a low Moorish [marshy] poynt of Land we went to the shore, where those foure Kings came and received Amoroleck: nothing they had but Bowes, Arrowes, Tobacco-bags, and Pipes: what we desired, none refused to give us, wondering at every thing we had, and heard we had done: our Pistols they tooke for pipes, which they much desired, but we did content them with other Commodities. And so we left foure or five hundred of our merry Mannahocks, singing, dauncing, and making merry, and set sayle for Moraughtacund.

In our returnes we visited all our friends, and rejoyced much at our Victory against the Mannahocks, who many times had Warres also with them, but now they were friends; and desired we would be friends with the Rapahanocks, as we were with the Mannahocks. Our Captaine told them, they had twise assaulted him that came onely in love to doe them good, and therefore he would now burne all their houses, destroy their corne, and for ever hold them his enemies, till they made him satisfaction. They desired to know what that should be. He told them they should present him the Kings Bow and Arrowes, and not offer to come armed where he was; that they should be friends with the Moraughtacunds his friends and give him their Kings sonne in pledge to performe it; and then all King James men should be their friends.

Upon this they presently sent to the Rapahanocks to meete him at the place where they first fought, where would be the Kings of Nantautacund and Pissassac: which according to their promise were there so soone as we; where Rapahanock presented his Bow and Arrowes and confirmed all we desired, except his sonne, having no more but him he could not live without him, but in stead of his sonne he would give him the three woman Moraughtacund had stolne. This was accepted: and so in three or foure Canowes, so many as could went with us to Moraughtacund, where Mosco made them such relations, and gave to his friends so many Bowes and Arrowes, that they no lesse loved him then admired us.

The 3 woman were brought our Captain, to each he gave a chayne of Beads: and then causing Moraughtacund, Mosco and Rapahanock stand before him, bid Rapahanock take her he loved best, and Moraughtacund chuse next, and to Mosco he gave the third. Upon this, away went their Canowes over the water, to fetch their venison, and all the provision they could; and they that wanted Boats swam over the river. The darke [darkness] commanded us then to rest.

The next day there was of men, women, and children, and we conjectured, six or seaven hundred, dauncing, and singing; and not a Bow nor Arrow seene amongst them. Mosco changed his name Uttasantasough, which we interpret Stranger, for so they call us. All promising ever to be our friends, and to plant Corne purposely for us; and we do provide hatchets, beads, and copper for them, we departed: giving them a Volley of shot, and they us as loud shouts and cryes as their strengths could utter.

Discovery of Pyanketank River
and Back to Jamestown

After leaving the Rappahannock, Smith made a voyage of discovery up the Pyanketank River, thence along the shores of the Chesapeake Bay, thence up a narrow river to the country of Chisapeac, and so, after divers adventures, to James Towne.

Sir Samuel Argall to Master Nicholas Hawes, June 1613

Sir Samuel Argall in his letter written to Master Nicholas Hawes, June 1613, and recorded in *Purchas his Pilgrimes*, pp. 1764-1765, related touching his voyage to Virginia:

> After my returne from Sir Thomas Smiths Iland, I fitted my ship to fetch Corne from Patowomeck, by trading with the Indians, and so set sayle from Point Comfort the first of December [1612]: and being entered into Pembrooke River [Rappahannock], I met with the King of Pastancie a hunting, who went presently aboord with me, seeming to be glad of my coming, and told me that all the Indians there were my very good friends, and that they had good store of Corne for mee, which they had provided the yeere before, which we found to be true. Then I carried my ship presently before his Towne, and there built me a stout shallop, to get the Corne aboord withall, which being done, and having concluded a peace with divers other Indian Lords, and likewise given and taken hostages: I hasted to James Towne, beeing the first of January, and arrived at Point Comfort the first of February. In this voyage I got 1100 bushels of Corne, which I delivered into the several Store-houses ... besides the quantitie of 300 bushels, reserved for mine Company.

He also relates his second voyage to Pembroke [Rappahannock] River:

> On the 19th of March I returned with ship into Pembroke River and so discovered the head of it, which is about sixty-five leagues into the land and navigable for any ship, and then marching into the country I found great store of Cattle as big as Kine of which the Indians which were my guides, killed a couple which we found to be very good and wholesome meats, and are very easie to be killed in regard they are heavy, slow and not so wild as other beasts of the wilderness. In this Journie I likewise found a mine, of which I have sent a trial into England and likewise a strange kind of earth, the virtue whereof I know not but the Indians eat it for Physicke, alleging that it cureth the sickness and pains of the belly. I likewise fond a kind of water issuing out of the earth which hath an earth taste much like unto allum—Water—it is good and wholesome, for my men did drink much of it, and never found it otherwise. I also found found an earth like a Gumme, white and cleare; Another sort red like. Terra sigillate [the earth that swimmeth] another [earth] very white and of so light a substance that being cast into the water it swimmeth.

Argall Captures Pocohontas

Sir Samuel Argall, in the same manuscript, tells of his capture of Pocahontas, by which the English were able to bring Powhatan to terms. He wrote:

While I was in this business I was told by certain Indians, my friends, that the great Powhatans daughter Pokahontis was with the great King Patowomeck whether I presently repaired resolving to possess myself of her by any stratagem that I could use, for the ransoming of so many Englishmen as were prisoners with Powhatan; and also to get such arms and tooles as hee and other Indians had got by murther and stealing from others of our nation, with some quantities of Corne for the Colonies relief. So soon as I came to an anchor before the Towne I manned my boat and sent on shore for the King of Pastancy and Swift (whom I had left as a pledge of our love and truce the voyage before) who presently came and brought my pledge with him: whom after I had received I broke the matter to this King and told him that if he did not betray Pokahontis into our hands, wee would no longer be brothers and friends. He alleged that if he should undertake this business, then Powhatan would make wars upon him and his people, but upon my promise that I would joyne with him against him, he repaired presently to his brother the Great King of Patowomeck who being made acquainted with the matter, called his council together; and after some few hours of deliberation, concluded rather to deliver her in my hands then lose my friendship, so presently he betrayed her into my boat wherein I carried her aboard my ship. This done an Indian was dispatched to Powhatan to let him know that I had taken his daughter; and if he would send home the Englishmen (whoom he detained in slaverie) with such arms and tools as the Indians had gotten and stolen and also a great quantitie of Corne, that then he would then have his daughter restored, otherwise not. This news much grieved this great King, yet, without delay, he returned the message with this answer. That he desired me to use his daughter well, and bring my ship into his river and there he would give me my demands, which being performed I should deliver his daughter and we should be friends. Having received this answer I presently departed from Patowomeck, being the 13th of April, and repayred with all speed to Sir Thos. Gates to know of him upon what conditions he would conclude this peace and what he would demand to whoom I also delivered my prisoner towards whose ransome within few days, this king sent home seven of our men who seemed very joyful for they were freed from slavery and feare of cruel murther which they dayly before lived in. They brought also three pieces, one broad axe, one whip saw and a canoe of corne.

Second Attempted Settlement

The second attempted settlement associated with the Rappahannock appears to have been made by the Earl of Pembroke, who patented thirty thousand acres of land in 1612. Prior to this date the Rappahannock River was sometimes called Queen River in honor of Queen Ann Stuart, daughter of Frederick the Second, King of Denmark, and wife of James I of England. She died March 2, 1619. After the assignment of so large a tract to Pembroke, the name was changed to Pembroke River, and Argall so called it in 1612. The Council in England instructed Governor Wyatt to see to it that the Earl of Pembroke's thirty thousand acres be very good. The patenter was William Herbert, third Earl of Pembroke, born 1580.

If he ever succeeded in establishing a settlement here, it did not long endure; and no further record concerning it is now available.

Little is known about this river until about 1642 when permanent land patents were first taken.

HISTORY OF
OLD RAPPAHANNOCK COUNTY, VIRGINIA
1656-1692

CHAPTER 1

Early Settlement

The first English settlement at Jamestown was repeatedly in arms against the Indians. As the number of Indians at first far exceeded the number of English, the Virginia colony did not extend over much territory before 1630. After the number of English became commensurate with the number of Indians in the James River valley, year by year the English settlements spread outward to the York, the Nansemond, the Elizabeth rivers, up the Chesapeake Bay, across to the Eastern Shore, and finally into the Potomac and Rappahannock River regions.

However, the first habitation of white men on the Potomac River was built by settlers who came out of St. Mary's, Maryland

At a Grand Assembly of the Virginia burgesses at Jamestown on the 12th day of January 1641, an act was passed concerning the seating [settling] of the "Rapohanok River."

> This assembly does declare and be it so enacted that it is and may be free for any person or persons to seat the Rapohanock River the next year provided that the number that seat be not under 200 persons and not less than 6 able tithable persons in every family that there sit down and the authority aforesaid doth further declare and enact that all claims made to land heretofore in the said River be voyde, except such as have order heretofore and that no Clayme had to any land there shall be good except they shall enter their rights to the said land with the said Clayme, & the P'ties that there intend to seat are hereby commanded to Compound with the native Indians whereby they may live more securely.[1]

This order was drafted by men unfriendly to the idea of settling the river. Few individuals had the power or the wealth to command effective agreements with the Indians. As a result, no movement was launched to settle this river valley.

By June 1642, it was evident that this act was impracticable, and that another act relative to the seating of the Rappahannock River was needed, for in *Hening's Statutes*, Vol. 1, p. 274, Act LIX, is the record of the re-affirming of a second act at the March Assembly, 1642/3. It reads:

> Whereas it was enacted at a Grand Assembly in June 1642, That Rappa'k. river should remain unseated for divers reasons therein contained, notwithstanding it

---

[1] *Virginia Magazine of History and Biography, Vol. 9, p. 53.*

should and might be lawfull for all persons to assume grants there, Provided the same be first bounded, though not by a surveyor and to continue still their proper rights, till the seating thereof be admitted by a Generall Assembly, & then all dividents to be bounded by just surveyors, *which said act this present Grand Assembly to all intents and purposes ratifieth and confirmeth.*

It was under this act that John Carter, Richard Bennett, Capt. Daniel Gookin, and Mr. Durant came into the river and selected land that would be very desirable after the red man withdrew. Durant's land was definitely once an Indian habitation, where the Neincoucs then resided. Bennet's and Gookin's lands were probably also desirable because of Indian clearings to be found on them. They were not selecting lands for immediate seating, but lands that they would be able to seat after the Indians had moved out.

Capt. Daniel Gookin, Richard Bennett, and William Durant appear to have come into the Rappahannock River on the same ship. On November 4, 1642, they each patented land that was thirty-five miles up-river. Bennett's and Durant's lands adjoined, and the line between them later became known as the Essex-Middlesex county line. Gookin's lands were on the north side of the river opposite them.

These patents were followed by those of Bartholomew Hoskins and Robert Ayers on January 1, 1645. These patents were for land further up-river, Hoskins taking up the land where the town of Tappahannock now stands.

By this date, immigrants from Maryland had moved to the south side of the Potomac. They gave but little consideration to the Virginia government and its treaty agreements with the Indians. They settled, as it were, by squatters rights, and, until forced to do so by Berkeley, refused to recognize the authority of Virginia over them.

The encroachment on Indian territory as evidenced in the patenting by the English of lands on the Rappahannock and the inclusion of certain Indian towns in some of the patents and the seating of the fertile valley of the Coan River was doubtless the fire brand that caused the Indians of the section to join with Opecancanough, chief of the Powhatan Confederacy, in the great massacre of 1644. The white man had created a new enemy whose forces had not been spent by wars in the James River valley.

Apparently, this group of tribes in northern Virginia was not a part of the old Powhatan Confederacy. Evidence of this fact is found in the incident of the taking of Pocohontas by Argall in 1613. At that time the King of the Potomacs chose the friendship of the English in preference to the friendship of Powhatan. It was in complete disregard of Powhatan that the Potomacs betrayed Pocahontas.

By 1644, things were different. The spirit of tribal rivalry was changed to cooperative planning against a common foe. The white man was not claiming the daughter of a distant king, but their lands and the lands of their forefathers.

In the early years of the colony, they had, time and again, been friends to the English, had sold them grain and kept the colony alive when Powhatan was trying to starve it by refusing it aid. But now the white man, who had been Powhatan's enemy and was now the enemy of Opecancanough, his successor, had also made himself the enemy of the Indians of all the Rappahannock and Potomac valleys. Leading English, who had pretended to be their friends, had passed laws permitting the settling of their territory. Prominent citizens had patented their lands. It became plain to the Indians that the only way by which they could keep their territory was by fighting. For this reason it was easy for Opecancanough to persuade them to join him in a war to exterminate the English.

In the massacre of 1644, the life-blood of hundreds of settlers was spilt.

When it was over, Opecancanough, backed by the Indians of northern Virginia, demanded that all the country north of Charles [York] River be vacated by the white man. This condition was made a part of the treaty of peace. On October 21, 1646, Berkeley agreed that the territory north of the York and Pamunkey rivers should be given to the Indians. He ordered that all settlers in that territory should move back below the York. Those, however, who desired might go north until March 1, 1649, and fetch their cattle. It was made a felony for an Englishman to be seen north of the York after that date, and it was to be death to an Indian to be seen south of the York after that date unless he wore the striped suit of a messenger.

This treaty, had it been enforced, would have worked a considerable hardship on the settlers who survived in the Gloucester section. Yet it might have held had there not been a great influx of settlers into the colony. The royalists of England had been defeated by Cromwell in 1645. These followers of Charles I began coming to Virginia in large numbers. The treaty with Opecancanough had so limited the domain of the white man that the increase in population caused serious congestion. By many it was felt that there was not enough land to go around. It was bad to have the new settlers from England flocking into the restricted territory. It was no time at all to have the inhabitants of Chesapeakus or Chesapeake parish north of the York River move into the country about Jamestown or settle on the narrow strip of land on the south side of the James River.

In consideration of these conditions the governor extended the time of the settlers for moving, and ordered that all people north of the York might retain their land until December 20, 1647. On December 22, 1647, the governor issued a second extension of time, ordering "That those who had land on the north side of the York be allowed to inhabit for three more years." This order, however, while it permitted old settlers to continue their residence, did not allow new migration into the territory.

Two years later the treaty with the Indians was abrogated, for "After serious consideration, there being many planters south of the York with depleted lands, it is unanimously agreed that after September 1, 1649, planters could settle north of the Charles [York] and Rappahannock rivers."

Thus the treaty that Berkeley made with the Indians in 1646 was never carried out, the date for executing it being put off from time to time while the white men manoeuvered for advantage. On September 1, 1649, it was definitely broken, and the act that declared it a felony to go north of Charles River was repealed.

September 1, 1649, may thus be regarded as the beginning of the permanent settlement of the valley of the Rappahannock River and of the territory of old Rappahannock County.

To the Indian the English became a people who would not keep faith. Had there not, because of conditions in England, been an unusual increase in population, the treaty would have held for many years; but life in England was in confusion. In 1645, the main army of the royalists under Charles I was defeated in open battle against the supporters of Parliament. In 1649, Charles I was beheaded. Many thousands of his supporters, despairing of safety at home, took their families and remnants of their fortunes and fled to Virginia, declaring their friendship to the crown, and even inviting Charles II to come here and become king. It is little wonder that Virginia attracted the royalists to her shores. Not until 1652 did Virginia finally give allegiance to the Commonwealth.

The royalists who came here were men in the habit of owning land. When the act forbidding migration north of the Charles River was repealed, they had already, for five years, been flocking into the James River valley. Some of them bought land and settled along the banks of the James; but many of them, land hungry, established themselves in temporary domiciles south of the York until more extensive territory should be open to settlement. When the treaty with Opencancanough was broken in 1649, they moved into the new lands. One-half of the first settlers to patent land in Rappahannock valley and about one-half of the settlers in the Potomac valley were these royalists.

These new immigrant colonists did not rise to political power during the first few years of the settlement. The counties were organized and courts established by older settlers from the counties south of the York, more especially south of the James, and it was from this older group that the officers of the court prior to 1660 were usually chosen. The first court of Rappahannock County was made up almost entirely of men who came here from the south side of the James River before the time of the royalists.

During their administration of county affairs the courts were tolerant in matters of religion, and this had its influence on immigration. When Berkeley was restored to power, a great change took place in public affairs in Virginia.

While these royalists were coming into the Rappahannock valley, there came old settlers from the lower counties who wished more virgin land on which to grow tobacco, the one profitable crop of the colony. A little later there came a group of religious refugees and of supporters of the Commonwealth who left the oppression at home to cast their lot with that northern section of Virginia of which such glowing tales had for years been going to England.

By 1672, the part of Virginia north of the York and westward up the Mattaponi, the Pianketank, the Rappahannock, and the Potomac rivers for, perhaps, fifty miles from the Bay, housed almost as many white people as are to be found even now among the rural white population of that territory. In the year 1689, Rappahannock County was listed as the second largest tobacco producing county in Virginia.

There was no great Indian disturbance from 1645 through 1666, though during all that period the Indians constituted a menace to the settlers, and at times gave them much to worry about. Troubles increased after 1666, though not until 1675 did they actually crystallize into open warfare.

Few effective plans for protection against the Indians were made and carried out. In Virginia, planters did not settle in towns as did the settlers in New England. Homes were isolated. As soon as a county was formed and the government was functioning, troops of horse and foot, numbering at various times from ten to fifty, were stationed on the frontiers of the then inhabited territory to intimidate the Indians and to put down any sporadic disturbance. From 1660 to 1675, such troops were stationed in forts under the assumption that hostile Indians would attack the fort rather than the settlers. The soldiers, however, were not allowed to leave the fort to attack the Indians. This was forbidden by Berkeley. As a result of this unwise ruling, the Indians did much mischief among the inhabitants. If the settlers went to the forest, their homes were left to the torch. This unfortunate situation of the planters not being allowed to organize to fight the marauders or to protect their homes was one of the prime grievances which culminated in the rebellion against Berkeley in 1675. In the earlier days of the settlement, this problem of protection had been partially met by giving large tracts of land free of taxes for fourteen years to several prominent men in the county in return for their aid in defense against the Indians.

In the Rappahannock in 1654, Captain Henry Fleet and William Claybourne had, in return for such aid, acquired large tracts of land with all profits and furs free for fourteen years. In 1666, Lawrence Smith and Robert Taliaferro were given the privilege of establishing a town on the upper Rappahannock, the said town to be one mile long and one-quarter mile wide, in which town the said Smith and Taliaferro pledged to have fifty men in about a year's time settled and ready to answer a call to arms in twenty-four hours. Their services were to be over a territory extending twenty miles in all directions from their town.

In 1676, Colonel Augustine Warner seems to have entered into this same type of contract on the upper Mattaponi and extending toward the Rappahannock River. Captain William Peirce established such a program on or near the head of Rappahannock Creek between Rappahannock and Westmoreland counties, as did Captain William Claybourne also on the upper waters of Pianketank River and Dragon Swamp. Each of these men, though exempt from taxation for a season, brought over the usual quota of settlers for the land patented. Augustine Warner brought over two hundred and ten people to settle his claim. He was granted 10,100 acres of land. Smith and Taliaferro brought over one hundred and twenty-seven people, and were granted 6,300 acres of land.

After 1676, when foreign Indians had been pushed back by Bacon, permanent settlements were made further and further west and into the wilderness beyond the falls of the river. This process of pushing the Indian westward continued for another century and a half.

CHAPTER 2

Political Formation of Old Rappahannock County

Charles River County was the most northern of the original Virginia counties. In 1642 its name was changed to York County. As settlements sprang up north of the York River, the political domain of the county was extended. By 1642 land was being patented within the territory that later became Rappahannock County. In 1649 quit rents were being paid there. The territory lying between York and Rappahannock rivers was called, in 1642, Chesapeakus or Chespekus Parish. This large and sparsely settled country was too far from York County courts to have much part in the political life of the county.

The territory lying near Chesapeake Bay and between the Rappahannock and the Potomac rivers, perhaps ten miles up, was loosely designated Chicacoon. This also seems to have had no definite bounds, nor political organization, though after the formation of Northumberland County lands lying in the lower end of the Northern Neck were sometimes referred to as being in Chicakoon or Chicacoon. The name was derived from early Indians of that section.

The Northern Neck peninsula along the Potomac and opposite St. Mary's appears, as formerly stated, to have been settled by emigrants who left the Catholic colony of Maryland, established a more or less independent organization, but became a part of Northumberland County when it was formed.

By 1652, Lancaster County was organized and included lands on both sides of the Rappahannock River. This new county was found to be too long. In December 1656, there was presented to the General Assembly by Captain Moore Fantleroy a petition of some of the inhabitants of Lancaster County showing their vast distance from the county courts and setting forth their desire that the county be divided. This the Assembly ordered; and the bounds of the existing parishes were fixed as the bounds of the new counties: viz,

> The upper part of Mr. Bennett's land knowne by the name of *Naemhock* on the south side and the easternmost branch of Moratticock Creeke on the north side of the river be the lowermost bounds of the upper county; The lower county to retaine the name of Lancaster, and the upper county to be named Rappahannock county and notwithstanding this division both counties to be liable to the Burgess charge of this present assembly. (Rand. MS. Jef. MS.)[2]

This is the first mention of Rappahannock County. Even before this county was formed it was very common for a planter to designate himself as "of the Rappahannock" or "in the Rappahannock," meaning that he resided in the Rappahannock River valley. It was natural that the section, called after a strong

---

[2] Hening, Vol. 1, p. 427, December 1656.

Indian tribe, should be known as Rappahannock Parish and, in turn, officially named Rappahannock County.

This, the seventeenth county, formed in 1656, soon became one of the foremost counties of the colony. It endured as Rappahannock County for thirty-six years, during which time the Indians were subdued, a few paths widened, and travel made more practicable by land than by water. These developments, and the fact that during storms the river proved too treacherous to cross to the regular county courts ultimately led to the division of the county in 1692.

The county of old Rappahannock embraced the Rappahannock River valley upward from Moraticco Creek until 1664 when Stafford was carved from the upper part of Rappahannock and a part of Westmoreland, which paralleled it on the Potomac side. The bounds of Stafford and Westmoreland for that period are not definitely known, though patents in Rappahannock County continued to be recorded as high up as the falls. We do know that in 1652 old Lancaster, before Rappahannock was carved from it, extended to the head of the river on both sides, and back to the ridges between the rivers on both sides,[3] and that the Rappahannock River side of the present King George and Westmoreland counties was a part of the old county of Rappahannock, since that portion of King George was carved out of Richmond County in 1721, and that part of Westmoreland in 1722. Just where the lower bounds of Stafford were it is hard to say.

The political organization of the seventeenth century differed widely from that of the twentieth century. Virginia was divided into five necks of land lying between its great rivers, each having its own Escheator General, who collected land taxes for the king. There was first the Northern Neck, which later became the property of Lord Culpeper's family; second the neck between the Rappahannock and the York rivers in which Pamunkey Neck was included; third, the neck between the York and James rivers; fourth, the territory south of the James; and fifth, the Eastern Shore peninsula.[4]

John Weir was Escheator General on the south side of the Rappahannock River. In 1668, Colonel Isaac Allerton was Escheator General in the county [D6, p. 319].

The highest legal tribunal in the colony was the Quarterly Court at James City, which, however, met only three times a year, in September, November, and April, but the date, and even the month, of the meetings varied somewhat from year to year. In March 1661/2 the name of this court was changed to General Court. This court tried all cases of murder, of treason, all suits involving very large sums of tobacco or money, and all cases granted appeals from the county courts.

---

[3] Lancaster Co. Orders, Bk. 1, pp. 63-65.
[4] Beverley, p. 243

The people did not directly choose any of the county officials. The only public officers elected by them were their representatives in the House of Burgesses at Jamestown. The county court was composed of prominent citizens who were chosen and appointed by the governor to serve indefinitely, usually for life. New appointees were made on recommendation of active members of the court.[5] They were first known as Commissioners and later as Justices. In the days of the Commonwealth and earlier, the court was presided over by a commissioner especially appointed by the governor to act as "maior" of the court. Subsequently the maior of the court became known as "president." When Rappahannock County was organized, five commissioners and five of the quorum, for the most part younger men, were appointed with Col. Moore Fantleroy as maior. In the absence of the maior any three members of the court might hear a case, provided that the one who presided was a commissioner. All of the commissioners present usually sat in the court, but the members of the quorum were not called on except in the absence of several commissioners. The commissioners were sworn into office at the courthouse after taking oaths of allegiance and supremacy, and the justices of the quorum were sworn after taking the oath prescribed by Parliament. On one occasion, Mr. Lloyd, one of the justices present, having left the room, it was necessary to adjourn the regular county court for want of a sufficient number of justices [Orders 2, p. 95 (131)].

The county court had jurisdiction in all cases of common law and in equity. Juries were selected from the most able men in the county.

The great majority of cases were tried before the justices, who heard all the evidence, and then went over the case in court much as a jury in the jury room, finally rendering the verdict that represented the opinion of the majority. Occasionally, when some justice did not agree, it was so entered, for there occurs the expression [O1, p. 148], "It is the judgment of this court Col[o.] William Lloyd only discenting." This court tried many cases that now come before justices of the peace and trial justices. This system seems to have been very workable and to have had many attractive features.

Witnesses were required to take oath "in the name of the Holy Gospel of God and of the Evangelists" [O2, p. 324].

The whole court did not always sit in all cases, as sometimes, when there was a case involving the just division of property, it appointed two or three of its members to meet on the site of the property, hear the different claims, and make the division as appeared proper to them with the full power and authority of the county court [O1, p. 199, O2, p. 126]. It was a regular custom to order one of the justices to conduct the inventory and appraisal of a large estate. He was ordered to go to the house of the deceased, and to swear in all witnesses, including those who pointed out the goods and those who recorded and appraised them.

---

[5] Winder, Vol. 1, Virginia Manuscripts From British Record Office, p. 276.

Nor was the County Court clogged by small, petty disputes. A statute gave individual commissioners jurisdiction of cases involving under two hundred pounds of tobacco. A case was thrown out of court because "disputes involving less than two hundred pounds of tobacco must be tried by a single justice" [O1, p. 123].

Through most of the history of Rappahannock County, there were two courthouses in the county, one on each side of the river. These were established to help reduce the distance men had to travel to court. Even with this arrangement, court, on its second day, would met by eight in the morning or even as on a February day in 1688, by seven A.M., in order that it might close early and "people be able to reach their distant homes by night fall."

If jurors failed to appear in court they were fined—sometimes as much as three hundred pounds of tobacco. The court was, however, very considerate, for in one case it revoked a fine imposed on a man when it heard that he was sick and could not appear [O2, p. 183].

Occasionally the county court was visited by members of the General Court. On September 24, 1689, Col. John Alloway, Secretary to the General Court, appeared in Rappahannock County Court. Upon the rising of the court, Mr. Alloway made motion that his presence be recorded [O2, p. 169].

The only real executive officer of importance in the county was the high sheriff. The senior member of the commission was automatically, in his order, raised to this position to serve for one year.

> For as much as the commissioners of this county court are by laws of this county answerable for the levyes and escheatments of each County of which the sheriff is usually collector, be it therefore enacted that none but one of the Commissioners shall exercise that said office of sheriff successively as they hold their places in the commission every one a whole year and no longer, under-sheriff to serve only one year. The Governor only having power to pass by any magistrates he prefers in making appointments.[6]

The county had its land surveyor who in the beginning was commissioned by the Royal Governor, but later the county surveyor came under the control of the Surveyor General of the colony, who also held the position of dean of the College of William and Mary. The first clerk of Rappahannock County was also the surveyor, but this was not usual. The county surveyors were men who were "earned in the art of measuring land." They were among the more scholarly citizens, and occasionally rendered their countrymen valuable services with little profit to themselves.

For each parish in the county two justices of the county were commissioned coroners by the governor. These coroners usually held office for life. As for the

---

[6] Hening, Vol. 2, p. 78, March 1661/2, Act XLIV, Sheriffs to be chosen in the commission.

compensation of this office, a coroner was allowed one hundred and thirty-three pounds of tobacco for an inquest on a corpse [Beverley, p. 248].

There were in the county at all times three or more commissioned militia officers. These were usually justices of the county court, and their presence did not excite the people. Berkeley, however, frequently directed other officers of the militia, temporarily stationed in these parts, to sit with the court. Their presence occasioned such bitter feeling that he was petitioned to discontinue the practice.

In each county there were one or more parishes. The parishes were further divided into precincts. In each precinct the court appointed a constable and a surveyor of roads. The constable's duties were limited to his precinct and the single justice court. The surveyor of roads was not a land surveyor, but was one who surveyed or viewed the condition of the roads in his precinct and supervised the repairing and maintaining of them.

There existed also a parish court, but little appears in our records concerning it. This court looked after daily routine of discipline for the church, such as most cases of fornication, profanity, cursing, and the like. It was also charged with the welfare of orphans, widows, and the poor.

Four different types of juries served the courts: a grand jury of twelve men, which must serve for one year, usually separate grand juries on the north and the south sides of the river; a petty jury drawn from time to time to decide chases in chancery as well as criminal cases; a coroner's jury assembled on the summons of a coroner on the occasion of an inquest; and fourthly, a land jury chosen for each case involving a disputed line. Land juries were usually accompanied by the sheriff, who was present to establish the peace. Sometimes even a justice was present to represent the court. The most celebrated of these land disputes was regarding what is known as *Jackman's Folly*, a tract of 2,349 acres patented by Thomas Dyas, which embraced the peninsula lying between Totuskey and Richardson's Creeks. Though assigns of Thomas Dyas held title, much of the land was claimed by Anthony Jackman, who held later patents to it. The case hung for years in the courts, and there was so much feeling about it that the court finally informed the governor that it could not get together justices or juries to make the survey.

For the Northern Neck there was no Escheator General of the governor after 1672, since on that date it passed under the proprietorship of Lord Culpeper and later of his family. This included the portion of Rappahannock County on the north side of the river. There is recorded Lord Culpeper's letter appointing George Brent of Woodstock in the county of Stafford his steward and receiver general of all rents, issue, profits, and fines in the counties of Rappahannock and Stafford [D7, p. 50].

With its two courthouses and one court sitting alternately on each side of the river, the custom was to continue a case on the same side of the river on which it was opened. This so seriously deferred the execution of justice that in 1686 cases were ordered to be tried at the next succeeding court. This program, maintained for two years, in turn worked such a hardship on those who had to cross the river, that on August 1, 1688, the clerk of Rappahannock County wrote in behalf of the local court representing that, as by custom, cases commenced had been tried on the same side of the river, he pleaded that the practice might be revived [O2, p. 103, 107]. On October 18, 1688, the General Council restored the "practice in Rappahannock County, after two years trial otherwise, that cases opened on one side of the river be tried on the same side as hath been their custom in former years."[7] This delay of law enforcement was not regarded with favor by the legislators, and on April 16, 1691, it is again ruled that cases be taken across the river.

This dual problem of hardship in travel and delay in justice was the immediate reason for the division of the county, when the General Assembly met at James City, April 16, 1691, and passed the act dividing it:[8]

> Whereas sundry inconveniences attend the inhabitants of Rappahannock County and all others who have occasion to prosecute law suits there, by reason of the difficulty in passing the river. Bet it therefore enacted by their Majesties' Lieutenant Governor, Council & Burgess of the present General Assembly and the authority thereof and is therefore enacted that the county of Rappahannock be divided in two distinct counties so that the Rappahannock River divide the same, and that part which is on the north side thereof be called and known by the name of Richmond County and that part which is on the south side thereof be called and known by the name of Essex County, and for the administration of justice that the records belonging to the County of Rappahannock be kept in Essex County.

So it was that the new counties of Essex and Richmond were formed.

---

[7] *Executive Papers of the Colony of Virginia*, Vol. 1, pp. 98-99.
[8] Hening, Vol. 3, p. 104, April 1692, Act V, An act for dividing Rappahanoc county.

CHAPTER 3

Old Rappahannock County
Indian Affairs, Tribes and Settlements

Many fragments of information about the Indians of the Rappahannock valley are left, but few traces of their life here are now in existence. Groups of twenty to two hundred or more warriors with their families were usually known as tribes. These tribes had their own rulers, and each ruler had his council or "quinoquinson." Before the tribe entered into any agreement with its neighboring tribes or with the English, the king of the tribe called a meeting of his leading warriors. At this conference any serious problem was discussed and a final decision made upon it.

The smaller tribes were usually friendly allies of the larger tribes in the immediate section. In the Rappahannock River valley and in the county of old Rappahannock, the great Rappahannocks were the controlling tribe in the lower end of the county, and the Nansemons in the upper end. These two great tribes were usually friends. They gathered unto themselves all of the smaller tribes of the entire Rappahannock. In spite of their power, these northern Virginia Indians seem to have presented no materially united opposition to the encroachments of the English until about 1644. They appear to have been more friendly to the English than were the Indians of the James River section. To their credit it should be said that they seem rarely to have engaged voluntarily in aggressive warfare against the settlers. In the massacre of 1644, which was after the white man had begun to make claims and to patent land in the Rappahannock valley, they were persuaded by King Opecancanough to take part. In the hostilities against the English in 1675, preceding Bacon's Rebellion, the Seneca Indians, who roamed into the Rappahannock valley, were the inciting agents.

Before entering into a discussion of the military activities against the Indians of this section, let us consider this chapter the Indian tribes, their settlements, and the legislative enactments of the English concerning them.

On December 10, 1649, the Grand Assembly at James City ordered an apportionment of land among the Indians; that is to say, it ordered that the bounds of the Indian settlements be defined and marked. This order was not executed seriously here, probably due to the fear of the hostility of the Indians. The order was renewed on November 23, 1652. In compliance with this last act, Lancaster County Court ordered that on September 21, 1653:

> The several commissioners of the county, with six men each, sufficiently armed with a formidable gun, powder and shot, and with either a sword or a pistol, and a weeks supplies, meet at the house of Wm. Underwood, and for the several rendezvous to be appointed by each commissioner in his limits respectively

choosing places meet for their convenience and their limits as is hereafter expressed.

Each commissioner with his men must mark the bounds of all Indian towns within his district. The order describes the districts:

> Mr. Coxes limits from James Bourns upward to Mr. Burham's and Mr. Richard Loe's from Parot's Creek to Dedman's Creek. James Bagnall from Dedman's Creek to upper side of Puscaticon [Piscataway], and Mr. Andrew Gilson from Puscaticon to the head of the river. On the north side to Capt. Fleet's Plantation to be in Mr. George Taylor's limits, and Mr. Wm. Underwood on Totuskey from his own house to the upper side of Moraticond and David Fox below Moraticond Creek to Mr. Brier's. Mr. Brier from his house to the side of Corotoman and Dr. Rowland Lawson from the Corotoman to the mouth of the river.

Thus, at this time, the territories of the Indian tribes inhabiting these bounds were marked off by these several commissioners. The order here laid down was intended to cover all of the county, whether there were Indians on several parts or not. Indeed the existence of Indian tribes or settlements in all of these precincts is seriously doubted, but the following are known:

The Tacobwomen Indians at one time lived in the are above described as within Mr. Coxes limits. In Mr. Richard Loe's district, below the present town of Urbanna, were the old and new towns of Nyemcouc (variously spelled, as Niamcouk, etc.), the former near Burhan's and the latter near the present town of Urbanna. In Mr. Andrew Gilson's, a few years later, were the Mattaponies on the south side of Piscataway Creek swamp, and the Portobagoes on the north side of Portobacco Bay and Green Bay. The latter were a strong tribe. In Mr. Bagnall's district had been the tribe of Piscatocons. In Mr. Taylor's limits were the Nancemuns with several towns, and the Nanzaticons. Perhaps there were also some of the scattered Rappahannock who had resided in the hills back of what is now called Carter's Wharf, in the years about 1610-1613. The Doeges were in this territory and near the Nancemuns on what is now known as Doeges Run, above Leeds Town. In Mr. Underwood's precinct was the tribe called the great Rappahannocks on Rappahannock Creek just across the river above Tappahannock, now called Cat Point Creek. In Toby Smith's precinct was the new town of Morattico on Totuskey Creek, established just about this time, and sometimes incorrectly referred as the town of the Totuskeys. In Mr. Lawson's precinct were the Chicakoon Indians [L1, pp. 63-65]. Five of these precincts were in territory which later became Rappahannock County, and these Indians here named became at times menacing to the English of this county.

The Moratticoes

References to the Moratticoes are found as early as 1608 in the account of Anthony Bagnall, Nathaniel Powell [Poell] and Anas Todkill. It was the first tribe with whom they stopped on their trip up the Rappahannock River. With them they found their good friend Mosco. Until after the Massacre of 1644, this tribe was located in the vicinity of the Corotoman River.

Very early the English settled in this section. The oldest patent extant and recorded as being taken up in the Rappahannock River valley was taken by John Carter in 1642 near the Corotoman. In the Rappahannock valley, by 1652, the Corotoman section had become one of the more thickly populated regions by white men; and the Moratticoes, made uncomfortable by the proximity of the English, had already moved out of their old town, for on October 27 of that year Thomas Brice patented their deserted lands [P.B. 3, p. 167].

In 1665 some of these lands were repatented by Col. Edward Carter. His patent of 1,650 acres is described as "lying on the north side of Rappahannock River, it being part of an old Indian habitation called Moraticon." It was located on the peninsula between the mouth of Corotoman River and Carter's Creek, and is again described in part as follows [P.B. 5, p. 29]:

> Beginning on the side of a small branch called Harrises Creek near to line of E. Harris, thence n.n.e. 360 poles to southern side of the dividing creek, which belongeth to Corotoman River, thence to dividing point, thence 414 poles N. along dividing creek, thence S.W. to fair Water creek, thence south across land, thence along the river across Brice's Creek to the point of beginning.

In the early days the tribe of the Moratticoes was powerful. In 1608 it was strong enough not to fear the wrath of the Rappahannocks, who had two hundred warriors. At that time Mosco said they had stolen from the Rappahannocks several of their wives. After 1612 this tribe lost much of its strength. When the white man came to settle, it had become tractable and appears to have moved continually rather than contest its territory with the English. The old name Moratacond was corrupted by the English in their spelling. Soon after the white man actually moved into the Corotoman. The town of the tribe was spelled both Moratticond and Moratiquond.

When the Moratticoes moved from their old town and gave Thomas Brice the opportunity to patent their lands in 1652, they established a new town on the present Morattico Creek. But again they gave place to the white man, for we find that in 1658, Morattico town on Morattico Creek had been sold by the Indians to Col⁰· Moore Fantleroy [D2, pp. 39-40]. Fantleroy took up 5,350 acres of land, 2,600 acres of it being on Farnham and Morattico Creeks, and the residue back of it in the head of Totuskey Creek [P.B. 2, p. 230]. This vast plantation came to be known as *Farnham*. It was within the bounds of this tract that the Moratticoes had built their second town of Morattico, and it was from that the creek took its name.

Dwindling in numbers and becoming more and more amenable to the wishes of the English, the Moratticoes, after their sale to Col. Moore Fantleroy, established themselves on the east side of Totuskey Creek. Here they were assigned a reservation by act of Assembly at James City. By 1662 this was already being encroached upon. The order that follows, dated November 5, 1662, cites that the English were moving within the three-mile limit from the Indian town beyond which it was not lawful for the English to go, that they were allowing their hogs to run in the Indian king's corn, and were clearing his allotted lands [D2, p. 189].

Home of
Colonel Fountleroy
built about 1675

Orders Concerning the King of Moratticond

Whereas divers English are seated illegally near unto the King of Moratticond his Towne who being poor men, if they should be removed, might probably be thereby undone and whereas the King of Moraticond hath freely and Voluntarily consented to the continuance of their seating and providing his town be sufficiently seated and have also some small satisfaction for the land. It is therefore ordered by consent of both parties that the said English which have seated within three miles of the bounds of the said King and have no right and title thereunto, by surrender in quarter court or Assembly according to law, continue still seated with this proviso that is in the nature of a tenure whereby they hold their said lands that first they pay unto the said King one Match-coat for every hundred acres they clayme before December next. Also that they with the assistance of the said Kings Indians except 5 of the Great Men sufficiently fence to keep out hogs and cattle from the cornfields of the said King and Indians that reside there with him and also that they the said English with the said assistance always keep in repair the said fence. It is further ordered that there be no more intrenchments by the English upon the said Kings land by clearing any more lands of their dividends on that side which lyes towards the Indians land that is within a mile of the Kings lands. It is also ordered that Edward Lewis who hath built a little quarter between the Indians and the woods be removed. It is ordered by the court for Indian Affairs that the Moraticond Indians have 2000 acres of land for their towns and cornfields beginning at the upper bounds of Thomas Robinson and from thence extending upwards along the river and for the length of one mile into the woods and from these bounds three mile interval according to law within which interval several man are already seated by consent of the King of Moratticond and the great men they paying a matchcoat for every hundred acres within their --- limits and fencing according to the order passed by the said Council to that purpose. Mr. Moseley is also ordered to bound and measure the said 2000 acres by marked trees.

Match-Coat
A Match-coat was a loose, robe-like garment made of coarse wollen material.

By 1682 the Moratticoes had moved from the Totuskey reservation, deserting their third town. Just where they established their fourth town is not known.

When they moved from their Totuskey Creek location, the white man again clamored for their forsaken, cleared lands. Capt. John Hull patented a part of them. In 1672, he and his wife Eliza sold "Morattico Indian town" to John Sherlock, Jr. and Philip Davis [D4, pp. 528-9]. A little later Mr. Wm. Bendall bought 430 acres of the same town land "known as *Moratiquond.*"

This old town stood on the east side of Totuskey. The main village was on the slope of the hill just south of the present Totuskey bridge. The old road leading through Emmerton to the Totuskey near the present concrete bridge was originally an Indian trail leading to this town. An old trail also led from the north side of Totuskey opposite their town to what was known as the Middle Field well back of the reservation of the Rappahannock Indians. This middle field was the vicinity of Warsaw. From here the trail led to the Great Town of the Rappahannocks.

The Mattaponies

The small Mattaponi tribe is first known positively to have been located in Rappahannock County in 1657, when its bounds were ordered to be surveyed. The tribe had moved over from the Mattaponi River; and, in their new location, the Indians were soon again encroached upon by the English. Hence the need for the survey. It appears that Francis Brown had certain lands which were within the prescribed three-mile limit. To this the Mattaponies gave him a treaty deed. Others are mentioned as taking up their cleared land.

The location of the Mattaponi Indian town, as designated in this survey, was on the south branch of Piscataway Creek, between Routes 620 and 647 about one mile up the swamp known once as town marsh. There have been found a considerable quantity of broken flint and pieces of arrows in this section on the north bank of the marsh just where the sandy valley is well sheltered by the hills, about a mile and a half south of Dunbrooke. Immediately northwest from this spot is a narrow forsaken path-like road that leads northwest up and into the hills past Enon church. This is thought to be a segment of the long-forsaken Mattaponi Indian Path, later called the King's Highway, which is known to have passed by the town of the Mattaponi Indians.

This town seems sometimes to have been called "Tobicock Indian town." The path leading east from the town on the hill along the south side of Piscataway Creek was the "Lizzard Tree Path."

Governor Berkeley built the king of the Mattaponies an English house. A little later the king accused Col. Thos. Goodrich of burning the English house. At the same time several planters were accused at the General Court of stealing furs that belonged to the Mattaponies.

The house-burning was taken to the General Court.[9]

> It is ordered by the Assembly that Lieutenant Colonel Goodrich be summoned to appear before the honorable governor and council at next quarter court to answer the complaint of the king of the Mattaponi Indians concerning the burning of his English house, and that the said Indian king have notice given him to be present.

To settle the difference with the Indians in the matter of the appropriated lands and stolen furs, the court of old Rappahannock County commanded restitution as follows [D2, pp. 249-50]:

> It is ordered by consent of the king of the Mattapony and some great men of the Indians and Thomas Cooper, Francis Browne and James Vaughan that 50 Matchcoats be paid unto the said King to leave their old towne and adjacent parts belonging unto it and for the well and orderly payment thereof it is further ordered that the said Thomas Cooper, Francis Browne and James Vaughan equally proportion and collect the said match-coats of themselves and of others

---

[9] Hening, Vol. 2, p. 155, March 1661/2, At a Grand Assemblie.

that have taken up the said Indian Towne and adjacent parts, and any concerned in this order shall refuse these conditions that then it shall be lawful for the rest to enjoy the land paying the matchcoats, and Mr. Marsh and Lt. Col⁰· Goodrich are appointed to see these orders performed at the arrival of the second ship or else to issue fourth execution.[10] It is ordered that Francis Browne, Robert Armstrong, John Burnett and Jane Valentine pay unto Tappyocimoun, King of Mattapony, six matchcoats in consideration of several skins taken from the Quioulilise House, and it is further ordered that if there be any more had any of the skins that they recover of them their proportions, and Lt. Col⁰· Goodrich and Mr. Marsh authorized to sue for execution. August 9, 1662.

By March 3, 1668/9, the Mattaponies had forsaken for a new site their town near the head of the western branch of Piscataway swamp [D3, p. 425]. Available information as to where this new town was located is scarce, but in 1672, Col. Goodrich patented a large tract of land in Rappahannock and New Kent counties. This was re-patented by Col. Edward Hill. It embraced 2,770 acres of land. In 1683 this tract is described as lying upon the branches of the Mattaponi River and Piscataway Creek, and bounded in part as follows: Beginning [near Beulah Church] at a white oak standing on the north side of an Indian path that goes from Mattapony town that was at the head of Piscataway Creek into a new town now planted by those Indians on the 85

er, etc. The bounds of this survey also passed over this same path about a mile and three-quarters north 35 degrees west of the before-mentioned oak. This proves not only that they had removed from Piscataway, but indicated the general direction of the new town from the old one. Indian paths were, as a rule, rather straight. A road leading from Beulah Church through the present village of Newtown to the Mattapony River would have fulfilled the general requirements set forth in the description given in Col. Edward Hill's patent.

The patent also declared their new town to be on the Mattapony River. The above suggested road moving straight in Indian fashion would have arrived before it reached the Mattaponi, a large pocoson near the junction of Beverley Run and Marracassick Creek, close to the river. It must have been in this vicinity by the river that they established themselves.

In many respects the new site was sell suited to the needs of an Indian tribe. There are about ten miles of pocoson [wooded swamp] lying along Marracossick Creek and Beverley Run, which no doubt, at the time, teemed with ducks, geese, turtles, frogs and other game. The nearby streams furnished a greater abundance of fish than had Piscataway, which was already harnessed below their town by the water grist mill dam of old Piscataway Mill. Thus, at their new town, the undammed Mattaponi River and the extensive pocosons made fine fishing and hunting. Today the name, Newtown, is derived doubtless from the nearby "new

---

[10] The fact that they were to be given fifty matchcoats would imply that there were at least fifty Indian men in the town.

town" of the Mattaponi Indians. Living in that section today [1964] are many people who claim Indian descent.

The Mattaponi tribe was not large. The English finally requested that they united with the Moratticoes that the two might better defend themselves from the harassing northern Indians, who preyed on the smaller tribes in Virginia because these would not join in their war against the English.

The Rappahannocks

The Rappahannock Indians were the most influential tribe of the lower part of Rappahannock County. In 1658, they confirmed a treaty with Col. Moore Fantleroy. The fragmentary manuscript reads as follows [D2, pp. 39-40]:[11]

> To all to whom these presents shall Come greeting. Know ye that we the King & great [men of the] Rappahannock Indians remembring & calling to mind the words of Attapaugh King at his Decease ... ordered us & Either of us the great men & his relations to take speciall care & regard of hi ... Coll. More ffantleroy that he nor his substance sustain no harm nor injury by any of the ... [More]over that we nor none of us should any way obserent [obstruct?] nor hinder the said Coll. ffantleroy ... plant, live on & enjoy as well his Land at Mangorite as that of Morattaco both which ... valluable consideration assigned under the hand & seal of the said King & sundry [Great Men] ... of the said Coll. ffantleroy for soe long as the same moon should [ ] & now for and ... self end of Coll. ffleet misinforming & [existing] some others to joyne with him not only in ... Coll. ffantleroy but in Destroying the will, charge and command of our deced. King & present ... showing and fearing us the Indians to conforme unto ... of the English but now upon ... [ ] the present King & great men of Rapp[ ] the sallary of the said ffleet ... nor integrity to the English & our due observance ... & will of our said deced. King ... present know that we the King & great men [of the Rappahannock Indians do] gratify & fully confirme ... brother Coll. ffantleroy & his heirs ... them to have & to hold all ... according to the bounds of the ... not to stretch further into ... bounds in the said Ja ... suffer any other person or ... but only himself & ... the King & great [men] ... the said King grant with ... also hereby bind & oblige our heyres and Successors ... without any let hindrance ... done unto him or any assignes ... power and Authority to punish ... hereunto Signed & Sealed in the year ... the 27th Day of May 1658. Signed Sealed & Delivered in the presence of us, Ant. Stephens, John Woodington, William Clawson.

The bounds of the Rappahannock Indians extended from Rappahannock Creek, now often called Cat Point Creek, once called Fleet's Creek, to Totuskey Creek. Berkeley, in numbering the warrior hunters of the Indian tribes about 1670, said that there were about forty Totuskeys and thirty Rappahannock warriors; but as nearly half the Rappahannocks lived on the north bank of

---

[11] Ellipses indicate missing words from the fragmented document.

Totuskey, it is probable that Berkeley listed part of the Rappahannocks as Totuskeys. They occupied nearby towns, and became generally regarded as one tribe, the most powerful in lower Rappahannock County. Their town on Rappahannock Creek was referred to in 1652 as the town of the Great Rappahannocks [P.B. 3, p. 97].

One of these Indian quarters was called Matchymop Quarter, and was located on a point three miles up Totuskey on the north-west side of the creek [D8, p. 120]. There was also an Indian field on the east side of Totuskey Creek [D3, p. 399], and another in what is now known as Warsaw, and yet a third along Rappahannock Creek (Cat Point Creek).

The great Rappahannock Indians were first located on the northeast side of Rappahannock Creek (Cat Point) about two miles above its mouth and less than a mile above the point where Menokin Swamp flows into the creek. At this site the land slopes gradually southwest to the water. This town was strategically placed both for defense and for observation of craft on the river. Back of it was a high hill, from the summit of which a man might see down the creek almost to the river. If today a few trees on a small point of land across the creek were removed, one could see clearly out into the Rappahannock River. In fact, assuming it was cleared in those days, a vessel coming up the river would have been visible over the point. It was from this little hill that the Rappahannocks sighted the vessel bearing the little company of English explorers in 1608 and laid their plans for the trap that nearly succeeded in destroying Capt. Smith's party [see Chapter 1].

This hill from which the Indians could view the river is about 115 feet high, and is located Latitude 38° 15", and Longitude 76° 48' 50". On three sides it is cut off from sudden attack, on the west by a creek, on the south and east by a steep declivity, at the foot of which is a swamp and stream. The north is the only unprotected side.

On the north slope of this hill is an Indian relic that has aroused keenest interest. Near the top stands a twin cherry tree, the foot of which is about four feet below the level of the field. Here under the brow of the sloping hill just above the cherry tree is a level space circular in shape and more than thirty feet in diameter. Some hand has dug away the dirt from the edge of the field, and definitely shaped it. Around this entire circle may be seen a succession of stones cropping out of the leaves. These appear to be the remains of a circular stone wall, no doubt one of the last existing monuments of a long departed race.

Just outside of this circle of stones there stand today three sassafras trees with bodies more than sixteen inches in diameter. They have every mark of great age, yet are all sprouts from a single large parent trunk. The trunk is all that is left of a tree that long ago may have sheltered a quiet Indian wigwam.

In addition to being protected on three sides from hostile invasion, this town of the Rappahannocks was well located in other respects to comply with the needs of the race. It was on a good navigable creek a hundred or more feet in width with a good landing. Springs of healthful flowing water were nearby. North of the town was a large plateau of level land on which corn could be grown. The creek furnished excellent fishing. There was fine hunting along the banks of its headwaters. The early records refer to it as Great Hunting Creek, and the branch to the east, which we call Menokin Creek, was called Small Hunting Creek.

The bounds of the lands of the Rappahannocks extended down Rappahannock Creek to within a mile of its mouth, thence along the edge of the hills a mile from the river down to Totuskey Creek one mile from the river, thence up Totuskey main creek and its east branch three miles.[12]

Though the Rappahannocks and their allies were the most powerful Indians in the lower end of Rappahannock County, yet all the time of Bacon's Rebellion they were not as great trouble makers as the Indians of the up-river tribes. Sometimes there was a spirit of genuine friendship manifested by the Indians. In 1658, Indian John, wishing to express a feeling of friendship to Elizabeth Fantleroy, the daughter of Moore Fantleroy, brought her a sow pig as a present [D2, p. 135 (106)]. Tradition has it that she, in turn, gave him a lamb.

After the outbreak of Bacon's Rebellion, the Rappahannocks fled their towns on the north side of the river, and immediately, under an act of Bacon's Assembly, white men took up their lands. Thus prevented from returning to their homes, they finally settled and built a fort on the south side of the river, well back inland near Hoskins Creek swamp or Piscataway Creek swamp, where they stayed for some years under the partial protection of the county, usually befriended by some one of the justices or large planters. When the hostilities of Bacon's Rebellion were quieted, the Senecas and other tribes from without the colony continued to harass the Virginia tribes. This constant peril seems to have caused much anxiety to both races, and the white man assumed more and more a protectorate over the native Indians.

Evidence that the Rappahannocks built a fort and were for a time seated on the south side of the Rappahannock River is found in the fact that when they removed again to a place farther up-river all the men who helped them haul their corn and lumber to the river side for transportation by boat were inhabitants of the south side of the river. Further proof that they were for a time on the south side is the fact that the farm and landing of Robert Tomlin, who, according to order had a sloop and boat ready on January 5, 1684, "to transport the Rappahannock Indians thirty-five miles up-river," were on the south side above the great marsh that forms a point above Mr. Andrew Gilson's [Mount Landing].[13]

At *Blandfield*, the home of the Beverleys, there are several pieces of Indian pottery that are thought to have been left behind in the fort by this departing

---

[12] P.B. 3, pp. 73, 97; P.B. 4, p. 235; Will Bk. 2, p. 68.
[13] Essex Co. Land Trials, 1711-1716, p. 66, contains a plat of Tomlin's farm and location of his house in 1666.

tribe. They have been handed down in the family with this tradition. Another strong proof of the location of the Indians is that when the court of Rappahannock County was negotiating with them preparatory to their departure up the river, it was Henry Awberry who acted as interpreter. He seems to have been the one white man who knew them best and to have been intimate and friendly with them. He was a very large land-holder whose lands were well back inland on the south side of the river. It may be that the fort was actually on his lands; or since the Beverleys have the pottery that seems to have been left by them, it may have been on their land. It was not far from either, and was near Indian Neck.

The following quotation reveals the care and thought given by the colonists to the welfare and safety of this tribe, November 29, 1683:

> The board taking into their serious consideration ye great dangers our neighbouring Indians (whom by Articles of Peace wee are obliged to defend), are daily exposed to, by ye incursions of ye Seneca Indians, and endeavouring to find some expedient for ye future to defend them from their violence, doe conclude it absolutely necessary, for ye preservation of our Indians, that either Rappa: & Nanzattico Indians be united & incorporated (ye Nanzatticos being willing) or that ye Rappa: Indians remove to their new fort, and that this may be effected, It is ordered that both ye said Indian nations be made sensible to ye care of this board for their defence, and likewise friendly admonished, that an union will produce ye better effects and that ye Indians may be safe on their way (if they consent thereto) a party of horse is ordered to be in motion, and to conduct ye Rappa: to such place for security, as they make choice of, either to their new fort, or ye Nanzattico Town.[14]

Thus it was that this diminishing tribe of a proud race, driven to the shelter and protection of the English below the Rappahannock during Bacon's Rebellion, moved again across the river northwestward, and settled itself at the fort of the Nanzatticoes. Here they were near the Porttobagoes opposite them.

For their services in transporting the corn and lumber of these Indians, the men of the county were paid by the day. Robert Tomlin for "his sloop and boat himself and two men for services from January 5 to February 2, 1684," was paid 3000 pounds of tobacco by the General Assembly [O1, p. 20]. Recorded are the names of the men and the amounts ordered to be paid each of them.[15]

Portobago Town

The Portobago Indians were a rather peaceful tribe. They had two principal towns. One was located at Latitude 38° 8' and Longitude 77° 4' 5", on Green Bay. The other was located on the northeast side of Portobago Bay at Latitude 38° 9'

---

[14] *Executive Journals of the Council of Colonial Virginia*, Vol. 1, p. 54.
[15] *Journals of the House of Burgesses*, Vol. 1659-1693.

10" and Longitude 77° 6' 5". These villages were both near good hunting marshes. The lower town was located in a sandy field about fifteen feet above water level and east of the mouth of Meader Creek. This field even today abounds with bits of broken flint, rocks, imperfect arrows, and scraps of pottery. The writer himself, walking over the field, found a half-perfected tomahawk and many arrows.

This tribe is thought to have become amalgamated with the Nanzatticoes (also spelled Nansatticoes and Nanzatticons, etc.) who had their principal town almost directly opposite them on the north side of the river, at Latitude 38° 9' 35" and Longitude 77° 7', on a point projecting southerly into Portobago Bay. The Rappahannocks had joined the Nanzatticoes in 1684. A claim exhibited by Lt. Col⁰ᐧ Richard Covington for 1930 pounds of tobacco for transporting the Nanzattico Indians through Essex to King and Queen was proved and certified to the Assembly on June 6, 1706 [EO3, p. 245]. Doubtless the Rappahannocks and Portobagoes who had joined the Nanzatticoes were included in the movement. Just how far south these Indians were moved is not known, but they must have been united with the Mattaponies or the Pamunkeys.

Tacopacon Spring was an Indian name for a place, doubtless a spring, at which the patent of Edwin Conway began when he took up his lands, now called Port Conway [P.B. 7, p. 111]. The spring was across the river from Port Royal and somewhat down river.

Nancimum or Nanzimum Town was the seat of the largest Indian tribe in the upper part of the Rappahannock valley below the falls. This tribe seems to have had before 1652 a town on the north side of the river in the vicinity of what is now Leedstown. It is a fact that they moved their town up-river in the early days of English settlement. They were apparently in their new home on Nancimum Neck, also called Cleve Neck, by 1654. The exact spot of the new town has not been located; but according to many documentary references, it was probably on the lower side of the neck at a point convenient to the two great marshes above Port Conway, the one on the north side and the other on the south side of the river, near a creek and Cleve marsh, and near to or at Latitude 38° 14' and Longitude 77° 12'.

Other Indian Towns

Berkeley referred to the Doeges in 1675 as being northern enemy Indians. They had come to Virginia and were in the Rappahannock valley by 1655. With other wandering northern tribes, they gave the Rappahannock settlements much trouble. They finally settled below Nanzimum by Doeges Run, and fattened upon the wildlife of the marshes and creeks.

There are on this river traces of many pre-historic Indian towns. In fact, near practically every marsh of fair size, can be found traces of some deserted and unrecorded Indian village that had vanished before the first boat of the white man sailed up the river. In the lower part of the county there are many water front places where oyster shells may be found in quantities. Wherever they are found, one can also find broken flint, fragments of arrow heads, and perhaps a broken Indian axe or piece of pottery, for at such spots once stood villages. The Indians feasted on the delicious oysters, always to be had by merely diving or wading into the river for them. These shell fields may be found on both sides of the river scattered at intervals all the way to Chesapeake Bay.

An added attraction was a small creek where fish ways (traps) were built and fish stabbed or caught. A good spring or stream, sandy soil or a southern sloping hill, a small creek, and a marsh are the usual conditions near the larger Indian towns. Their food being largely caught from streams, marshes and swamps, such things as turtles, frogs, ducks, fish, and muskrats played an important part in their daily diet.

In 1654, every Indian tribe had its bounds marked off to it by the county justices. These bounds usually embraced several thousand acres, including all the lands within a three-mile radius around the town on the same side of the river. References are often made to these lands in deeds and patents; and when a place is described as being near or opposite to certain Indians, the reference indicates that it is near or adjoining the Indian reserve named; but when the word town is used, it is meant that the relationship to the town itself is described.

Occasionally white man patented land within the Indian bounds. Such patents had to be confirmed by treaties with the Indians affected, as was the case in the treaties involving the lands of Edward Lewis, of Francis Brown, and that part of the lands of Moore Fantleroy known as *Mangorite*.

CHAPTER 4

Od Rappahannock County
Indian Troubles and Military Activities

The history of the early Indians and of the Indian wars in northern Virginia, especially the wars of the Rappahannock River valley, is all closely associated with the territory embraced by old Rappahannock County. Though not all of the tribes camped regularly on her soil, yet most of them hunted upon it. As the county extended from the head of the Pianketank up the ridge between the Mattaponi and the Rappahannock rivers indefinitely westward as far as white men roamed and back again down the ridges between the Rappahannock and Potomac rivers for more than sixty miles of actual habitation, it was vitally affected by almost all Indian activities in northern Virginia. With the counties of Stafford and New Kent, it bore the brunt of the Indian wars, slaughters, and pillaging in those parts. They were the frontier counties and became the battle ground where the red race and the white race sought dominion. Hence there was no permanent peace of long duration without some minor clash of arms upon these lands.

In the early days, the Rappahannocks were one of the largest of these tribes. Here also were the Pastancies and the Potomacs, who dwelt on the isthmus-like neck of land in what is now King George County, and prowled over the valleys of both rivers. These tribes, with their friendly allies, the Mattaponies, the Totuskeys, the Portobagoes, and the Nanzatticoes, the Morraticoes, the Doeges, the Cickacoons, and the Machoix, were of themselves strong and powerful confederacy. They may be classified in general terms as the Rappahannock and the Potomac Indians.

Prior to 1642, the Indians of the Rappahannock valley held this section undisputed. The taking of patents of land in their valley that year, as cited in a former chapter, was as a sting of a serpent to them, for well they knew the anxiety of the struggles of the James and the York River tribes against the English. It led them to take part in the massacre of 1644. By this they hoped to regain all their lands. It appears, however, that no white men were living in the Rappahannock valley at the time of the massacre, and it is probable that none were killed here.

The fact that the Indian tribes had no united organization and that they had no adequate instruments of warfare made it impossible for them to keep back the English when they violated the treaty with Opecancanough to keep south of the York River. In a few years the English took possession of much of the Rappahannock valley.

At the time of the settlements in the Rappahannock, Indians were in the lower parts of the river valley. As white man came into these parts, he took up land nearer and nearer to the inhabitations of the Indians. This caused constant and growing friction between the races. The ox, the cow, the sheep, and the hog were absolutely necessary for the economic maintenance of the English. The right to grow corn and hogs and to hold abounding hunting grounds was absolutely necessary for the existence of the Indian. Since both races turned their stock loose in the woods without restriction of fences, there was no end to the number of cows and hogs of the English that strayed over the Indians' corn fields; and in like manner the hogs belonging to the Indians had no respect for the corn of the English and, at times, destroyed much of it.

This friction over stock, together with the constant taking up of land nearer and nearer the Indians, and the continual stealing of cattle by both sides, led to animosity that was followed by reprisal in kind, by murder, and by frequent clashes in arms. The outcome was that the Indian tribes were gradually depleted in numbers and finally moved westward. After the massacre of 1644, Francis Poythers, in March 1645/6, was sent with fifty men to arrange terms of peace with King Oppechankano; and Captain Henry Fleet, who settled a few years later in Lower Lancaster and who patented much land in Rappahannock County, was sent as chief advisor. Fleet was given fifteen thousand pounds of tobacco to defray the expense of this trip.[16]

As soon as peace was secured, the Grand Assembly passed many laws that were intended to keep white man from again exposing himself to the dangers of massacre. As many Indians had tried to murder the governor, he was given a guard of ten men to protect him.[17] Death was the penalty for any Englishman who should entertain or conceal an Indian.[18] There was a heavy penalty imposed for selling or lending an Indian a gun or gunpowder. None but Indian children under twelve years of age might live among the English.[19]

Peter Johnson, who later lived in what became Rappahannock County, is the only known soldier of the massacre of 1644 whose name survives to us. In 1652, in what was then part of Northumberland County, he was sick and was declared levy free [N1, p. 13].

In 1650, six men of old Northumberland crossed into Maryland and took from the King of Patuxom two Indian women and three beaver skins. For this offense they were required each to give the king a match-coat [NO, p. 42]. Another raid of a similar nature was made by six men against the King of Murkekotos. They also were required to pay a fine of a matchoat each [NO, p. 51].

Though the law prohibited the lending of a gun to an Indian, Mr. John Motram, Gent., did lend two guns to Indians. The guns were seized by Wm.

---

[16] Hening, Vol. 1, p. 318, March 1645/6, Act XVIII.
[17] Hening, Vol. 1, p. 354, October 1648, Act IV.
[18] Hening, Vol. 1, p. 324, October 1646, Act I.
[19] Hening, Vol. 1, p. 326, October 1646, Act I.

Cornish and Peter Preseley. Mr. Motram was required to give bond to appear in James City to answer to this complaint in 1651 [NO, p. 59]. William Harper was found guilty of the same offense, and was fined 1,000 pounds of tobacco in 1654 [L1, p. 164]. Andrew Taylor was found guilty for shooting and wounding an Indian, and was bound out for a short time to pay the fine [L1, p. 43].

Still the settlers continued to lend guns to Indians. Dominic Sherott violated this law, and Mr. Denby delivered it to the Indian and poured powder and shot to load it. They were discovered and were fined 1,300 pounds and 700 pounds of tobacco respectively. Record is made of an Indian who, not skilled in the use of this type of arms, accidentally killed himself in 1654 [L1, p. 163].

Nicholas Hale suffered the penalty for lending an Indian a gun [L1, p. 93]. This gun was found at the house of Margaret Grimes [L1, p. 163]. She was the wife of Edward Grimes and lived on land adjoining the Rappahannock Indians. This event was probably the cause of the trouble with the Rappahannock Indians which is recorded as follows in Hening:[20]

> In 1654, Capt. John Carter was instructed by the House of Burgesses to raise a company of 40 men from Northumberland, 30 from Westmoreland, and 100 from Lancaster County. The counties to furnish arms and ammunition.

They were to meet the first Wednesday in February at the house of Thomas Meader [also spelled Meador] and march to the Indian town of the Rappahannocks to receive such satisfaction as he should see fit, but to abstain from hostility except in case of attach. Capt. Henry Fleet and Wheatliff attending as interpreters. The location of this meeting is fairly definite, since the above Thomas Meador acquired the lower half of Mr. Underwood's patent of 1300 acres located between Melbeck and Bushwood creek on the north side of the Rappahannock River. His place later became the property of Benjamin Rust, from whom Rust's oyster rock, off Lowry's Point is named. The farm is now called *Islington*.

As Thomas Goodrich and other Englishmen were having trouble with the Mattaponi Indians, on January 1, 1657, at the county court the justices of Rappahannock County sat in conference with their king and great men and hunters. At this meeting were Tapoisen, the king, and four of his great men, Ownchowlue, Moineichrom, Ereopchese, and Pepounglis. This conference resulted in a treaty with the Mattaponies in which it was agreed that any Indian caught stealing a hog or committing any other offence on the cleared lands of the English should be surrendered to the English for trial, and any Englishman who fled and dwelt among the Indians was to be surrendered to the court of the English [O2, p. 28].

---

[20] Hening, Vol. 1, p. 389, November 1654, Orders of Assembly.

The Court Order Books of old Rappahannock County prior to 1683 have beenlost, so that until 1683 there is no record of events to be found from that source. A few facts may be gleaned from other records which give some light on the events of that interesting time.

The next event of note was the confirmation of the treaty by the Rappahannock Indians to Moore Fantleroy [O2, p. 39] as quoted in this volume. In 1658, Mr. Underwood and many other white men were much disturbed for fear the Indians would again claim the land they had sold to Moore Fantleroy. A similar fear was entertained by Francis Browne and others living near the Mattaponies for land bought from them. A knowledge of this fear existed among the Mattaponies for we find a protest they made against the charge of ill-faith. This is recorded in an ancient entry in the deed book, though much worn in places, except for the words indicated by ellipses. In the following copy it is entirely legible [D2, p. 142 (111)]:

Mattapony Indians Affirm Good Will

To all persons to whom these present ... greeting wee the King & great men of Mattapony do give to Certify that ... are certain ill Reports Issued among the English Inhabiting Rappahannock River that wee should lay claime to or desire the Land or plantation now Inhabited by ffrancis Browne nere adjacent unto us, wee do utterly deny the same & lay no claime thereto & also further Certify that during the time of his abode neer us he hath demeaned himself civily without doing us any manner of Injury. In witness whereof wee hereto sett our hand & at our [quinqinson] ... of September 1660.

In 1661, Col⁰· Moore Fantleroy, who was in charge of Indian affairs in this river valley, was having difficulties with the Rappahannock Indians. He was finally accused of arresting and binding the king. For this he was reprimanded by the new assembly under Berkeley in March 1661/2, as follows:[21]

Whereas collonel Moore ffantleroy before the committee appointed for the Indian [business] did falsely and scandelously declare that he bound the king and the great men of Rappahannock for denying tribute to the right honourable Sir William Berkeley, and endeavouring to excuse or to extenuate his own fault in his said unjust proceedings against the Indians, said that the Roanoke he received of them for ransome was in satisfaction of their said tribute, and paid by him to that noble person Sir William Berkeley the then honourable governor. *It is ordered by the assembly,* that for the same and his other illegal proceedings the said collonel ffantleroy be made wholly incapable of bearing any office or command civill or military in this country, and forthwith give bond with very good securitie for his good behaviour and civill carriage especially towards those Indians; and for prevention of the further damage the hogs of the said ffantleroy may do the Indians before the ffence be made according to act in that case provided, it is

---

[21] Hening, Vol. 2, p. 152. March 1661/2, At a Grand Assemblie.

ordered that collonel ffantleroy keep one hog-keeper, the Indians another for the present yeare.

This severe treatment of Col°. Fantleroy by the burgesses was largely prompted by the governor because of the fact that Fantleroy had sympathized with the Commonwealth in England, and had indeed been appointed to office of justice while Cromwell was in power. Berkeley, as soon as he returned to the governorship of Virginia, began to use the difficulties of the settlers with the Indians as a pretext for punishing those whom he regarded unfavorably. At this same Assembly:[22]

> IT is ordered by the assembly that lieutenant colonel [Thomas] Goodridge [Goodrich] be summoned to appear before the honourable governour and councill at next quarter court to answer complaint of the king of the Mattapony Indians concerning the burning of his English, and that the said Indian king have notice given him to be present.

Thus we we see another commoner is put out of office.

Other troubles grew out of a murder of an Indian in this county by Rice Powell and George Norman, servants unto Mr. Samuel Gilson. For this offence they were tried; and on March 29, 1661, Powell and Norman were sentenced to prison for a long term [O2, pp. 176-7]. This murder and other offences were not forgiven by the Indians, for on September 8, 1661, a band of Indians went to the home of Edward White while he was away from home and murdered his son, Thomas White, and pursued and murdered his two servants, Daniel Pignell and John [   ], and cut them in pieces. John Evans, servant, was the only one who escaped. In September, Edward White complained to the Assembly telling the legislators of his great loss and saying that, because of the Indians, he had lost the use of his estate all summer.

During this year a statute was drawn to the effect that Maryland Indians were prohibted from lurking or trading in Virginia.[23] These northern Indians were here to strip up trouble. Murders were committed, but it was difficult to prove which tribe was accountable. For this reason an act was passed making the Indian town nearest the spot where an Englishman was murdered answerable with its "lives or liberties to the use of the public."[24]

Berkeley decided to take vigorous action. He advised the killling of all Indians from without Virginia who invaded it. A copy of the letter of June 22, 1666, to the justices of Rappahannock County, is recorded as follows [D3, p. 57]:

---

[22] Hening, Vol. 2, p. 155, March 1661/2, At a Grand Assemblie.
[23] Hening, Vol. 2, p. 152, March 1661/2, At a Grand Assemblie.
[24] Hening, Vol. 2, p. 219, October 1665, Act VIII, An act concerning Indians.

41

Sir. I wrote my first Lett[r] to you in hast the minute after I read yours, but since I have collected my selfe, I thinke it is necessary to Distroy all these Northerne Indians—for they must needs be conscious of the coming of these other Indians twill be a great Terror and Exemple & Instruction to all other Indians. If ye Councell nere ye and the Councell of war be of this opinion it may be done w[th.] out Charge, for the women & children will Defray it, lett me heare from ye w[ht.] ye thinke of it and if the first impulse of [our] first resentm[ts.] doe not Deceive me and lead=too much. I thinke this Resolution to be of absolute necessity if yr. young men will not Undertake it alone there will be errors from hence will undertake it for their share of the Booty. Your Most Affectionate, Humble Servant. [signed] William Berkeley. June 22th 1666.

Immediately following the governor's letter is the following:

To My Most Honor'd Friend—Maj[r.] Genrll. Smyth. These Hast post hast for the service of his Ma[tie.] & the Country. Hon[ble.] Sir: Uppon Serious Consideracon of the Hon[ble.] Governor's Letters and yr. Hon: desire of our opinions of them wee are by Manny circumstances convinced and tis our joynt opinions that the [late] Excerable murders are & have bin committed by a Combination of our Notherne Indians p'ticularly the Doagge conjunct w[th.] our Neighbour Indians above all which with their Complices wee Doubt not with assistance of Almighty God by the strength of our Northern Parts utterly to Destroy & eradicate with out Further Incouragment then the spoyles of our Enemies. [signed] John Catlett, Tho: Goodrich, John Weire jr., Hum. Booth.

Not only were the Rappahannock settlers having trouble by land because of the invasion of northern Indians, but a new enemy appeared off the coast to give them trouble by water in the form of the Dutch fleet. It met the ship commanded by Col[o.] Robert Conway of this county. For more than two hours his crew fought four enemy ships. In this engagement Col[o.] Conway and all of his crew were either killed or wounded before his ship was captured by the Dutch.[25]

In addition to the Indians and the Dutch it seemed that the very elements turned against the colony. On November 8, there occurred the worst storm that visited Virginia during the seventeenth century. Hail stones larger than turkey eggs fell. A great hurricane swept the colony destroying more than ten thousand houses of various kinds.

To meet the danger of the Dutch invasion, the Assembly, in September 1667, ordered forts to be built on the great rivers. The counties of Lancaster and Rappahannock were formed into an association for the protection of the Rappahannock River. Delegated commissioners of these counties were ordered to meet at the house of Major Ball on October 28th:

---

[25] Winder, Vol. 1, pp. 235-240.

to consider the most expeditious ways of erecting the fort taking care that it have a court of guard and a convenient place to preserve the magazine and that it have 8 great guns at least; this ford to be erected in Rappahannock River at Corotoman and it to have proper and full charge of Rappahannock and Lancaster Counties.[26]

The county courts were asked to choose the commissioners. Any failure on the part of the court commissioners or the workmen was to be severely punished. The fort was to have a constant guard of a gunner and four men. The two counties were to lay levies to pay the expenses of the fort.

The fort was built. Its walls were of the logs of pine trees. On the side next to the river additional heavy, thick walls of dirt were erected. These logs cost six pence per tree. In time of danger ships lay under shelter behind the fort. In the war England was waging against the Dutch, the governor, in reporting the strength of the Virginia navy said that there were at that time five ships lying in the Rappahannock that might be called on to defend the country.[27] The fort was in Lancaster County near *Millenbeck*.

The Dutch ships came into Lynnhaven Bay on June 11, 1668, and later sailed up and into the Rappahannock River and lay off in front of the fort at the mouth of the Corotoman River for five days, but took no action.[28]

By September 1668, peace was restored, and ships were no longer required to ride at anchor under shelter of the forts already erected.[29]

These forts of pine logs and dirt did not long endure, but fast fell into decay. On September 20, 1671, the Assembly ordered that "no more work be done on the several forts now built until such funds are available to build with brick in quantity." The commissioners of forts of the Rappahannock River were ordered to meet on November 20 and elect a new treasurer. The court was ordered to appoint any commissioners that were needed in place of those who were dead by that date.[30] The commissioners were required to levy additional quantities of tobacco on their counties to defray and expense of permanent forts to replace those fallen into decay.[31] This fort continued in use until the outbreak of Bacon's Rebellion. A petition of Sittingbourne Parish refers to it as one of the heavy burdens from which they had gotten no good.

Though the Dutch war was concluded, the Indian troubles continued. Someone wrote, "An axe in the hands of an Indian is a dangerous weapon, for it seems that he hath not the power to descerne the difference between good and evil." Berkeley says that at this time the Indians had learned to use guns much better than they had in the massacre of 1644.

---

[26] Hening, Vol. 2, p. 256, September 1667, Act I, An act for fortes to bee built in each river.
[27] Winder, Vol. 1, p. 280.
[28] Winder, Vol. 1, p. 282.
[29] Hening, Vol. 2, p. 265, September 1668, Act II.
[30] Hening, Vol. 2, p. 291, September 20, 1671, At a Grand Assembly.
[31] Hening, Vol. 2, p. 294, September 1671, Act I, An act for the defence of the country.

At the January General Court, 1672/3, all county courts were ordered to receive a report from the captains and colonels as to the arms and ammunition needed by their respective companies and troops.[32]   Though the burden of taxation was great, the people were getting little or no actual protection from the governor against the petty crime perpetrated by the Indians. The Indians on the other hand could not rely on the governor to protect their interests. It was not surprising that events culminated in Bacon's Rebellion.

After Bacon's Rebellion, more seems to have been done than had formerly been Berkeley's custom to defend the frontiers against the Indians. Forts were again established in the heads of the four great rivers. In 1676, there were ordered to be built a storehouse 20 by 60 feet to keep supplies in and a small house to hold ammunition. Quarters for the soldiers were provided. A fort had been established on the upper Rappahannock in 1671 by Major Lawrence Smith, who owned the tract of land between Snow Creek and Massaponax Creek. The fort must have been near to or at the mouth of this latter creek for there a dam could have been built and a grist mill put in operation to grind the corn.

---

[32] Hening, Vol. 2, p. 304, October 1673, Act II, An act for providing for the supply of arms.

CHAPTER 5

Old Rappahannock County
Bacon's Rebellion

It is very difficult to say just what was the cause of Bacon's Rebellion unless it was Sir William Berkeley himself. As governor, he more and more exercised his power tyrannically. In 1642, he came to Virginia at the age of thirty-two. Educated at Oxford, handsome in appearance, polished by foreign travel, with exquisite taste in dress, he was one of the most accomplished cavaliers of his day. He proved to be a very popular governor during the first ten years he was in office. During the years of the Civil War in England he managed the affairs of the colony with discretion and toleration. In 1652, he was supplanted by Richard Bennett and William Claiborne, Commissioners, sent over by Oliver Cromwell, and he retired to his estate, *Green Springs*, not far from Jamestown.

During the period of the British Commonwealth, the Virginia burgesses elected three "Gouvernors and Captains Generall," Richard Bennett, 1652-1655; Edward Digges, 1655-1656; and Captain Samuel Mathews, 1656-1660. In 1660, Berkeley visited England and received from Charles II a royal commission as Governor of Virginia.

Though a demand for protection against the Indians was the immediate cause of the colonists springing to arms in 1676, there were other deep-rooted grievances that justified them in rising against Berkeley. It was these extra hardships that finally drove the colonists to arms.

Nathaniel Bacon always recognized the power of the Crown; and if the governor had taken reasonable precautions to protect the frontiers of the colony from Indian massacres, there would have been no rebellion. Berkeley chose rather to ignore the cry of the overwhelming mass of the people.

From the election of the first assembly in 1619, every free man had been allowed to vote in the election of assemblymen (burgesses); but in 1670, Berkeley succeeded in getting through an act which stipulated that only freeholders and house-keepers could vote for assemblymen. This curtailment of rights was a great blow to the poor free man who expected to, but had not, acquired land. He paid his county poll tax, and he could not see why a free white man should be taxed without representation in the General Assembly.

Again in 1673, Berkeley persuaded the Assembly to pass a bill that exempted members of the county courts, of the church vestries, and other important persons from the payment of the levies, thus relieving the rich and placing a heavier burden of taxation on the poor. Even at this early date such a policy was un-American. If the sheriff and the officers of the court only were exempted, it meant the exemption of about twenty-five free men with many of their tithables in this county. This probably increased the tax burden of the poor about ten percent. Many of those of the county who were rich and who were influential tools of the governor were made exempt from the tax.

Northern Virginia was especially tried, for in the same year, 1673, the crown granted to Lord Culpeper a thirty-one year lease of all the Northern Neck, it being that portion of Virginia lying between the Rappahannock and the Potomac rivers. This affected Rappahannock County, for it included that half of the county lying on the north side of the Rappahannock River.

In the Minutes of the Council[33] the following statement is recorded: "The king's grant of the 25th of ffeby. in the 25th year of his reign [1674] to Lord Arlington & [Lord] Culpeper is in the Gen'l. Ct. deed book No. 3, p. 28 to 34." In the same volume is: "Deed of the 10th of September 1681 from Lord Arlington to Lord Culpeper for rights under the king's grant to them of the 25th of ffebruary in the 25th year of his reign. This grant is p. 28 to 34." Before the above dates there had been considerable litigation over lands that had been patented before other earlier grants to Lord Culpeper.

These unjust tax exemptions along with the assigning of huge grants to favorites of the king finally kindled the Grand Assembly to action. It wrote the king asking him to revoke these patents, and recommended that a committee be sent to England to present this grievance to the king. It passed a resolution which reads in part:

> Whereas the Grand Assembly are duly sensible of the many and grievous pressures that are daily growing and still likely to grow and be imposed on the inhabitants—on a pretence of protecting the good of the colony and augmenting his mater's revenues and which tend to void old patents and impose new rents, etc.

In order to defray the expenses of the committee a special tax was imposed on all the counties affected. In 1672, Francis Morrison, Thomas Ludwell, and Major General Robert Smith were appointed the committee to go to England. They went and entered into several conferences. They tried to buy back from the Crown the Northern Neck, but failed. They were able, however, to get Lord Culpeper to recognize the rights of land holders in that section who already held title; but all free rents or untaken land and all escheated or delinquent lands were to be his.[34]

The committee came home disappointed. For two years the planters had paid fifty pounds of tobacco per year for each poll to fight these grants to Culpeper and Arlington, and their efforts had largely been defeated. Those who had land could not sell it; and those who temporarily were driven from their homes by Indian raids lost them. Returning to find their crops of corn and tobacco

---

[33] H.R. McIlwaine, *Minutes of the Council and General Court of Colonial Virginia, 1622-1632, 1670-1676* (Richmond, Va.: 1924), pp. 515, 523.
[34] Hening, Vol. 2, pp. 311, 531.

destroyed, they were without immediate means for payment of taxes, and their property automatically reverted to Culpeper. The very year of the Indian invasion many planters found themselves cheated out of house and home.

Not only was the feeling strong against Berkeley because of these large grants of land, but also because of the increasingly heavy tax burdens. In addition to the special tax for two years to raise funds to send the committee to England, the planters paid a levy of seventy pounds of tobacco per poll, and thirty to seventy pounds of tobacco individual tax for every trial in any court in the county. This entire tax was given to the Crown so that the colony received no benefit. There was also a tax on all trade with New England. There was a two pence hogshead tax against the merchants on every hogshead of tobacco shipped to England. This the planters, in the end, really paid. A tax was exacted on all lands held by patent from the governor, and a quit rent tax for all land rented from Culpeper to Arlington. There was a parish tax, a tax on all leather, wool, furs, hides; a tax, in fact, on practically everything sent to England.

To increase his hardships the planter was often required to pay his tax in money, despite the fact that his one great source of revenue was tobacco. At this period tobacco had become a drug on the market in England. The king and Parliament had passed laws prohibiting the shipping of tobacco into any country except England. Virginia and Maryland had become rivals for the supremacy of the tobacco market and raised more than the limited market could consume.

Efforts were made to get a program of cooperation with Maryland in controlling the size of the tobacco crop; but the agreement when finally secured was a severe blow to the small planter. It was ordered that no tobacco should be planted in the year 1667. The poor man who had already sold his crop without provision for the next year's taxes was left without resources. Many throughout the colony were driven to despair, lost their homes and all that they possessed. This was also the year of the great storm that caused so much suffering. In petitions to the king in which they listed their hardships, twenty-five groups refer to the suffering from this storm.

The Indian fur trade was another source of friction with the governor. Up to 1675, there had been considerable trading between the Indians of Virginia and the Indians of Maryland on the head of the Chesapeake Bay. These Maryland Indians made many trips to Virginia, buying furs, and then selling them to the "Merchants of Monodas" (New York). These merchants bought the furs at the head of the Bay. They did not come directly to Virginia and trade because of an excessive tax which they could evade by trading with Indians on the frontier.

Beverley says:

> These Maryland Indians excited great hatred in the Virginia Indians because they could not come peaceable to trade in Virginia inciting them to commit robberies and murders upon the people, and that the Indians in our own frontier were inspired with ill thoughts towards Berkeley's intended discoveries.

In 1675, Berkeley ordered all fur trade between the Indians and the planters to cease, and immediately appointed certain of his own friends to trade with the Indians to his own special benefit. These agents of Berkeley's gave the Indians powder, shot, and many guns in exchange for furs. This private trading of the governor with the Virginia Indians, supplying them with ammunition and guns at the time of the massacres, and much stealing and raping, aroused all the frontier to anger against him.

Even before this, when a band of Indians had crossed the Potomac into Virginia and murdered two white men, the local citizens had rushed to arms, and about thirty men had pursued the Indians into Maryland where they killed an Indian king and ten of his men.[35] Resentment for this deed and for the treacherous slaying of six Indian chiefs caused the large body of Susquehanna Indians on the north to go on the warpath. They swept secretly down out of Maryland, and on January 25, 1675/6, massacred thirty-six people in the upper end of Sittingbourne, north of and within a radius of about ten miles of Port Royal. They continued for several days slaying, pillaging and burning all in their path.[36] Their avowed purpose was to kill ten white men for every Indian chief that had been treacherously slain. They were joined by the upper river tribes, who had fled from their towns into the wilderness at the head of the Rappahannock River.

News of this massacre, which left Rappahannock County bleeding, was heralded to every corner of the colony. Men ran from plantation to plantation in small bands without a head, there being no one to lead them. They sent messages to the governor to send up men with commissions to lead them against the Indians. No commissioned officers were sent. The governor merely replied that nothing could be done until after the meeting of the Grand Assembly. His only order for the defense was that forts be built in the head of the river. To the settlers who knew the ways of the Indian this brought no solace.

To make matters worse the governor, in February, issued an order that the people should draw themselves together in groups of not more than ten men-at-arms. Knowledge of this restriction greatly encouraged the Indians. They raided and destroyed many of these small groups. Murder and fires continued almost daily until in late May the Grand Assembly sent a commissioned officer with troops of horse and orders that he fight only the northern Indians. This brought no great relief, for by this time most of the northern Indians had moved on to the head of the James River and into southern Virginia; and the massacring, burning, and pillaging was being done by certain native Indians, who, encouraged by the havoc wrought by their brethren from the north, were harassing the settlers in every way they could. For nearly four months, in small

---

[35] Winder, Vol. 2, p. 460.
[36] Winder, Vol. 2, p. 106.

groups, the people of northern Virginia defended themselves as best they could. They attempted to plant their crops under the protection of guards, constantly exposed to slaughter.

All this time the friends of the governor were trading with the native Indians and furnishing them with powder, shot and guns. The people of the Rappahannock valley were desperate. Berkeley would not give them protection. In allowing the sale of ammunition to the Indians he kindled the wrath of the colony against him.[37] Even before Bacon came on the scene as a leader, the people were preparing to organize an army to go against the Indians. This intent is clearly set forth in a will of May 4, 1676. It was written weeks before Berkeley sent the first commissioned officer into the Rappahannock valley and reveals utter disregard for Berkeley's orders. It reads in part: "I, Richard Barber, being in sound and perfect memory, and being intended to go in pursuit of the Indians, do by these presents make this my will and testament."[38] The will is a graphic commentary on the feeling of the people. Since it was probated less than a year later, it is to be feared that on this trip Barber came to a disastrous end at the hands of the Indians.

In the meantime the people on the James River were not idle. News of the massacre in Rappahannock County raised apprehensions for their own safety. Several formidable tribes of Indians had been seen in the head of the James. "The inhabitants began to beat the drums for volunteers and so continued for sundry days drawing into arms without interference by the Magistrates." This band, assembled from among the planters of the upper James and of New Kent, cried out for one head to lead them.[39]

Living among them was Nathaniel Bacon, Jr., who had been brought up at the court in England and had a moderate fortune. He had come to Virginia in 1670 and owned a large estate on the James below the falls and another near the falls. He was by nature a leader. In 1672, he was elected a member of the Council. The people came to his house and demanded that he lead them in defending their homes against the savages. At length he consented, and rushed to James City to obtain a commission from the governor.[40] The commission was at first denied, but a few hours later was granted; and with it, Bacon marched against the Indians. He had not reached the Roanoke River before Berkeley proclaimed him a rebel, and ordered his commission revoked and that his followers disperse. The greater part of them, however, continued with Bacon against the Indians; and the people of the lower counties arose in insurrection and demanded a dissolution of the so-called aristrocratic assembly and the election of true patriots. A new assembly was chosen, and to this Bacon was elected from Henrico County.

---

[37] Winder, Vol. 2, pp. 460-65.
[38] Sweeney, p. 69, dated May 4, 1676, proved March 6, 1676/7.
[39] Winder, Vol. 2, pp. 460-65, 480-85.
[40] Winder, Vol. 2, pp. 480-85.

In the meantime the Indians had moved into southern Virginia, and were a hundred and twenty-five miles southwest of Jamestown. Bacon pursued them. En route he was met by Persicles, the king of the southern Virginia Indians, who persuaded him that he would attack the northern Indians in Bacon's stead. It was agreed. The king did attack and capture many of them, among whom were six Manokin Indians who had come south with the Susquehannas. Bacon wanted them transferred to him as hostages; but during the conference on the matter, one of the prisoners bolted, grabbed a gun, and fired. He was not recognized as a Manokin, and a regular engagement ensued in which many Indians were slain.

Bacon returned, and received a severe rebuke from Berkeley. When the Assembly met in May, Bacon, knowing Berkeley's opposition to his being seated, dropped down the James on a sloop carrying forty men as a guard. He sent a message to the governor asking permission to come ashore and sit in the Assembly. The governor at once ordered the big guns of the fort to open fire on him. Bacon sailed up the river out of range of the guns. In the night, with a party of his own men, he landed and had a conference with his friends, Drummond and Richard Lawrence, and returned aboard ship.

Captain Thomas Gardner, the commander of the ship *Adam and Eve* lying at Jamestown, was ordered by the governor to capture Bacon and his men. He brought them back to Jamestown and delivered them to the governor, and was discharged of them. Bacon's sloop, left un-manned, was beset by a storm and destroyed.

Instead of being rewarded for this exploit, Gardner was fined forty pounds sterling by the Assembly, and was put in jail until he could give security;[41] and Bacon, finding the Assembly against him, fled into Gloucester. Bacon and his friends put through the Assembly a number of bills that revolutionized the colony's government.

An army of one thousand men from the eighteen counties was authorized. Each county was directed by the Assembly to raise its quota, Rappahannock County taking fifth place in regard to the number assigned. The quota of Gloucester which included the present county of Mathews, was 140 men; that of Rappahannock, 53; Northumberland, 49; Westmoreland, 45; Stafford, 45; Middlesex, 34; and Lancaster, 29. From this group of counties in northern Virginia, 397 men were raised.

The Assembly made Bacon a general. The governor would not sign the commission, and Bacon withdrew to Middle Plantation (Williamsburg), where five hundred followers proclaimed him commander-in-chief. With these men he appeared before the governor and demanded his commission. The governor, when his anger had cooled, not only gave it, but recommended Bacon to the king as a zealous, loyal, and patriotic citizen. This was done July 4, 1767, one hundred years before the signing of the Declaration of Independence.

---

[41] Winder, Vol. 2, pp. 470-3.

Bacon immediately marched northward against the Indians. When he reached the Pamunkey River he learned that Berkeley had called a convention of the citizens of Gloucester and asked them to proclaim Bacon a traitor. These refusing, he issued a proclamation on his own responsibility. Bacon, addressing his soldiers, said:

> It vexes me to the heart that while I am hunting the wolves and tigers that destroy our lands, I should myself be pursued as a savage. Shall persons wholly devoted to their King and country—men who hazard their lives against the public enemy—deserve the appelation of rebels and traitors? The whole country is witness to our behaviour. But those in authority, how have they obtained their estate? Have they not devoured the common treasury? What arts, what sciences, what learning have they promoted? I appeal to the King and Parliament where the cause of the people will be heard impartially.

He withdrew to Middle Plantation, and, with the best men in the colony, debated from noon till midnight the best course to be taken. They took an oath to support their leader in subduing the Indian and to prevent civil war. And Bacon went against the Indians. Fearing what might happen, Berkeley fled to the Eastern Shore.

For a time thereafter, there were two governments contending in arms for supremacy in the colony. Berkeley also sent men against the Indians. While the troops of the northern counties, raised by order of the Assembly, were gathering at Piscataway in Rappahannock County, Major Lawrence Smith had been sent by Berkeley into the head of the river to fight the northern Indians; and Major Thomas Hawkins had later come up with a commission to fight the neighboring Indians in the head of the river. These officers were returning with fifty men to report to the governor the good news of the departure of the hostile Indians, and to put down the insolence committed in Piscataway on the ten of July by Bacon's assembling troops, when they met unexpected numbers of Bacon's men, and after a minor skirmish were carried away prisoners by the Bacon forces.

This northern Virginia unit of the insurgents who gathered at Piscataway was put under the command of Colonel Brent of Stafford County. Bacon, after getting legislative affairs at Jamestown straightened out and his southern army of six hundred men organized, marched north toward the upper York; Col. Brent and his forces marched south along the old King's Highway and joined Bacon. They searched the headwaters of the Mattaponi and the Pamunkey, but found few Indians. Their expedition was of little avail.

Since the Indians had disappeared, and since it was difficult without camp equipment or wagon trains to feed these combined forces, which numbered a thousand men, Bacon sent the northern Virginia forces home, and turned south with his own men.

The expedition into the head of the York River had been wearisome and fruitless; and many men on the southern unit, feeling that they had served their purpose, dropped out of the ranks and returned to their respective homes. As Bacon moved south, tidings came to him that Berkeley had raised an army of six hundred men and was marching against Jamestown from Gloucester. When he reached Jamestown, he had only 136 men to face Berkeley's six hundred. Through stragegy, however, he captured the town and burnt it, retiring to Middle Plantation. Berkeley fled to the Eastern Shore.

On August 3, 1676, while these things were happening, the General Assembly of Virginia sent a petition of complaint to the king. It read in part:

> All persons in the head of the rivers have to work with guns at their sides in the fields, & all are filled with fear of the Indians.
> 1000 Englishmen in a whole winter could not overcome 100 Indians in a cow pen.
> Poor men go unprotected by soldiers while great ones keep soldiers for their defence.
> If more than 10 assemble to protect their homes they are proclaimed mutineers & thus we go like butcher's sheep in the pasture.

After the troops of northern Virginia returned to the Rappahannock, many were disbanded; but a good, active, and efficient force went into the head of the river under the leadership of Major Simon Miller of Rappahannock County, who lived near what is now Port Royal, on the south branch of Peumensen Run.

Nathaniel Bacon, Jr., went to Gloucester County with some of his men, and while there was taken with some malignant fever and died near Wood's Crossroads in that county. His men, fearing that Berkeley might seek his body, took it secretly, tradition says, in the night, and turning aside a stream, buried him beneath its bed where no man could find him. If this tradition be true, it is probable that he was buried beneath the flowing waters of Paropatank Swamp.

After Nathaniel Bacon's death, his followers were without leadership; and Berkeley with little, if any, opposition returned to his place, *Green Springs*, where he again established himself as governor.

While Bacon was sick, Indian troubles were still continuing in the Rappahannock section, for on October 20, 1676, when Edward Gunstacker, a friendly Indian, made his will, he stated it in that he was about to depart with an expedition of the English against his countrymen, the Indians [D6, p. 75]. There appears to have been fighting on this last expedition, for soon afterwards witnesses established the oral will of John Godfrey who had perished when he left his home and went into the freshes [fresh water section of the river] [W2, pp. 47-8].

There have come down to us the names of only a few of those who were killed or murdered by the Indians in this great and final struggle for supremacy.

Thomas Dart, of Rappahannonck, was killed by the Indians. Soon afterwards, Bowin was murdered by them [W2, p. 46]. Though the names of most of those who perished in this struggle cannot be conclusively proved, yet during this period a much larger number of wills than usual was probated. In the years preceding the rebellion only about twelve wills were probated annually; and, in the years following, about the same number. The greater number during the rebellion was doubtless due to the fact that many fell in the struggle, or perished because of the hardships incident thereto.

Among the wills probated in Rappahannock County at this time were those of: Thomas Page, Nathaniel Baxter, Lawrence Washington (brother to Col. John Washington who was the grandfather of George Washington), Richard Simms, John Penn, Robert Bishop, Peter Mills, Thomas Jenkins, Thomas Ellverd, Richard Clarke, Elizabeth Kirk, Hesekiah Turner, Robert Hopkins, William Ealles, Roger Williams, Enoch Doughty, James Toone, James Dempster, Edward Rouzee, William Kenny, George Nicholls, Thomas Hawkins, John Killman, John Prosser, William Browne, George Nangle, Thomas Blissed, Nathaniel Frith, John Godfrey, Thomas Dart, Thomas Pannell, Henry Creighton, Timothy Pells, Samuel Scott, John Curtis, and John Mott. Practically all of these wills were recorded in the summer and fall of 1677 after the re-establishment of law and order in the county. Some were recorded earlier in Lancaster County where the county court continued to function regularly, and whither the wives and families of the deceased had fled and were dwelling safe from Indian slaughter.

Though the overwhelming majority of the people in northern Virginia were in sympathy with Bacon, yet some of the more prominent citizens and justices did not forsake the governor. Col. Richard Lee was imprisoned by Bacon's followers for seven weeks.[42] Sir Henry Chicheley of Middlesex County was imprisoned for months. Col. Augustine Warner, speaker of the House of Burgesses, who owned a vast estate in the upper Rappahannock and in New Kent, had his place pillaged. Col. William Cole and Col. James Bridger's plantations shared a like fate, as did those of Major John Page, Mr. James Bray, and others whose names are not known.[43]

Not all of the pillaging was done by Bacon's men. Col. Hill of the James River and Col. Robert Beverley of Middlesex were active in burning and pillaging the estates of those who sympathized with or supported Bacon. Major Thomas Powell of Rappahannock County was wounded by the rebels in the taking of Jamestown.[44]

---

[42] Winder, Vol. 2, p. 441.
[43] Winder, Vol. 2, p. 444.
[44] Winder, Vol. 2, p. 444.

Charles II Orders Investigation of Grievances of the People

By January 16, 1676/7, the fort at West Point had surrendered, and the whole colony had submitted to the governor.[45] On February 3, 1676/7, a general order was sent out by the authority of King Charles II to all the counties of the colony to make a report of their various complaints to a committee appointed by the crown composed of the following commissioners: Hon. Herbert Jeffreys, Esq., Sir John Berry, Knt., and Col. Francis Morrison, Esq., who were appointed to make inquiry and to administer to every man.[46]

In answer to the government's request for statements of grievances, scores of them came in from every part of the colony. Two from Rappahannock are here given as most representative of conditions in this county. One is the petition of Sittingbourne Parish located in the upper end of the county, signed by Cadwallader Jones and John Rouzee. The other petition is signed by the justices of the court of Rappahannock County. Signers of both were Berkeley adherents, yet they set forth the hardships of the colony.

Cadwallader Jones was a man of noble English heritage who had held his equity in his English manor and had come to Virginia to live. He was also a captain in command of troops in the head of the river for about ten years under Berkeley. He was a large landholder and a leader in this section. John Rouzee was an active and prominent citizen in the parish. Their testimony as witnesses of the disasters of their section should be considered conclusive.

Grievances of Rappahannock County

The grievances of the court of Rappahannock County are from the *Journals of the House of Burgesses of Virginia, 1659/90-1693*, taken from Winder Transcripts II, page 228, and following:[47]

A duplicate of grievances of the County of Rappahannock taken at a court held the 13th of March 1676/7 by virtue of a warrant (to that purpose) from the Right Honble. Governor, whereof the one part to be humbly presented to the Right Honorable his Majesties Commissioners, and the other part unto the honorable, the present Grand Assembly, as followeth, vizt.

1st. The first thing that we complain of to your honors is the great want of honest able sober pious and orthodox Ministers the want whereof and of the due administration of the Divine ordinances have been the original cause of the severe Judgments that have fallen upon this Land, wherefore it is desired that your honors would be pleased to move his Majesty to send us an annual supply thereof.

2nd. That an honorable peace may be concluded with the Indians if possible or (our) necessities being such as render us uncapable to maintain a Warr we not

---

[45] Winder, Vol. 2, Bacon's Rebellion, p. 509.

[46] Winder, Vol. 2, Bacon's Rebellion, p. 225.

[47] Among the manuscript material that Winder found in England and brought to America were many old colonial Virginia documents from the British records there still extant. See Winder Manuscript, Vol. 2, pp. 216-221.

having wherewith to subsist but must of necessity perish if we make not corn this present year, the Indians having already robbed most of us of whatever may render life comfortable.

3rd. That if your honors see convenient to continue a Warr with the heathen that it may be prosecuted effectually, and managed in such sort that some Counties may not be totally ruined while others live in their full bloom height and happiness, flourishing in the profits of their labourswhich they enjoy in peace and quietness whilest poore RAPPAHANNOCK lies bleeding whose number of people murthered and estates destroyed can find no parallel in Virginia, yet some of our neighboring counties are so narrow hearted and close fisted as to think it none of their duty to assist us in destroying the blood thirsty Indians, but would willingly leave us to fight the battle of the Republique or else not to enjoy either freedom or profit, of both which we have bin debarred a long time.

4th. That if the War be continued with the Indians that Rappahannock County may be exempted from paying any charge thereof by reason the Indians daily entrenching on us hath rendered us incapable to Contribute anything thereunto being at present left in so low an estate that it would be a hard matter for us to maintain life if we escape an Indian slaughter, which will undoubtedly befall us unless your honors send men to our assistance, for while we are tending corn to feed our wives and children the Indians (if we have no guard over us) would butcher us in our fields, they being so frequent about us, that we dare not stir from our plantations, other Counties making crops have induced our free men to leave us, who are gone to more safe receptives, where they may profit of their labors and if the burden be so great to individuals who have no charge, we leave it to your honors serious consideration how great it must of necessity be to those who have great Charges, and nothing wherewith to maintain them in a Word our great fear continuall Danger and Known wants are such that we want words to express them—therefore leave the redress thereof to your honors wisdomes.

5th. That your honors would be pleased how the 60 per poll which was collected from every tythable two years late past hath been disposed of the Comonallity of this County being altogether in the dark and still ignorant what advantage accrue to them by that great Assessment, and if the said tax be found by your honors to lie dormant in the hands of some particular persons, that they be forced to reimburse the County.

6th. That an account be rendered to your honors of the 2 shillings per hogshead and how disposed of, and if it should be found his sacred Majesty hath not disposed thereof, it is humbly desired your honors would move his Majesty in our behalf that he would graciously please to condescend that the said Imposition may for the future go to defray the publique taxes of this poor Country and that an annual account thereof may be rendered by the collectors of that duty to the Assembly.

7th. That all persons whatsoever pay levie except the aged and Impotent and that every person that shall informe against any delinquent in this case and afterwards comply for less than the law allows that he or they who can prove the same may have the like judgment against the first Informer, as he had against the delinquent to avoid future fraud.

8th. That no man hold more land than what he paid quit-rent for and that whoever shall conceal any land by him holden and not paying the King's due the first person who petitions for the same may have a grant thereof proving the fraud.

9th. That none who have freely and voluntarily assisted Bacon in his damnable conspiracy may be admitted to sit as Judges in any court.

10th That all officers of public trust may be conferred upon none but discrete and knowing gentlemen, and that none may be admitted to sit in the seat of Justice whose years and slender education speak him uncapable to act in so high a sphere.

11th. That all ships arriving in this country do for the future pay their castle and fort duties according to an act of Assembly made to that purpose, viz. in powder and bullett and that a publique magazine be raised for our defense.

12th. That a convenient place may be appointed in the center of the country for the future meeting of the Assembly and that all General Courts may be there kept which will be a great ease to the people of this country, and that care may be had for the erecting towns in every county in the Colony with all convenient speed.

13th. That if reparations cannot be had in our great losses from the other parts of the country (by reason) of the poverty thereof occasioned through the late unnatural commotion (to whom we have been a bulwark of defense) regard may be to our great sufferings and loyalty in the ease in the public levies or from his sacred Majestie.

14th. That as often as there shall be occasion for any new election of Burgesses that the free men of the country who pay their proportionable parts of all rates of assessments may be admitted with house-keepers to give their votes for such election.

15th. That your honors would be pleased to examine and know by what authority Colonel George Mason and Major George Brent went over into Maryland and killed several of the Indians there which we suppose was the original cause of the murders committed in our County. God Save the King.

[signed] Warwick Cammack, Alex. Donyephann,
Henry Awbrey, Thomas Goldman

Two members of the Vestry of Sittingbourne Parish sent grievances. Many of them are similar to those sent by the County Court and here-in-before given. The second grievance they recite ended thus:

We had trouble in these upper parts until at last our firebrand (Bacon), who had taken our good Major that had by God's assistance so well defended us, sent to our assistance one Captain Simon Miller a liver amongst us, and since his time we have had no men killed, nor great damage to our stocks, though since this war began we have lost over 600 pounds sterling. Now since by an evil hand we his Majesties always liege people have in a manner had our lives defended by the said Miller, in gratitude we desire he may be looked upon with an eye of favor.

They complain that because of the tax on all tobacco sold to New England, "... they therefore would not take our tobacco, yet if we had not had their corn in 1674 we would have perished." "We need better protection." They pray that a proportionable part of the arms sent over be assigned to this County's use. [signed] Cadwallader Jones, John Rouzie. Feb. 14, 1676/7.

A few new and interesting facts are found in the grievances of the citizens of Gloucester County, who reported that more than three hundred were slain by the Indians in Virginia. At some time during this struggle and a short time thereafter nearly every county and many parishes submitted grievances. They were all decrying the heavy taxation, the corrupt and wretched management of the affairs of the colony, and, in the frontier counties, the losses at the hands of the savages with no succor from the governor.

Berkeley, on February 10, 1676/7, writing to two of the commissioners of the Crown appointed to hear these grievances, said that out of 15,000 men there were not 500 untainted subject left, and that they were not actual sufferers.[48]

Two of the commissioners appointed by the Crown to consider the grievances of colonists were in America. They did not dare act upon their findings until after the arrival of the third commissioner, Hon. Col. Herbert Jefferys, who had to come from England.

During this interim Berkeley was active, devoting his time to trying, executing, or levying heavy fines on the last of his personal enemies. He charged the men of Bacon's army with treason, and quickly brought to trial as many of the leaders as he could capture after the death of Bacon. Very heavy penalties were inflicted on these men for protecting their homes and their country. Nathaniel Bacon, Jr., Edward Chessman, William Hunt, and many other had perished in the struggle.

This is the long list of those who were hanged:

    Thomas Hall, on January 11, 1676/7

    Thomas Young, of Rappahannock County, on January 11, 1676/7

    Henry Page, on January 11, 1676/7

    Wm. Drummond, formerly governor of North Carolina, on January 20, 1676/7

    John Baptista, on January 20, 1676/7

At *Green Springs*, on January 24, 1676, the following were hanged:

    William Cockeson

    John Digby

    William Rookings (died in prison before execution)

    Thomas Hansford

    Thomas Wilford

    William Carver

    John Johnson, of Rappahannock County

    George Farloe

    James Wilson

On March 9, 1676/7, the following men were hanged:

---

[48] Winder, Vol. 2, pp. 76-82.

Giles Bland
Anthony Arnold
Robert Stoakes
John Isles
Richard Ponfrey
William Scarborough
John Whittson

William West and John Turner broke prison and escaped after they were sentenced. Robert Jones, probably of Rappahannock County, broke jail and escaped.

Those banished from the country were:

John Taylor, of Rappahannock County, who was foreman of Col. Thomas Goodrich's quarter at Hobbs His Hole [Tappahannock]

John Richens, who had land in Rappahannock County

Henry West, banished for seven years and stripped of his estates

Captain Josiah Pickus, of Rappahannock County

Sands Knowles, pardoned after all his property was confiscated

George Seaton, pardoned after all his property was confiscated

Those heavily fined and stipped of the rights of citizenship were:

Thomas Goodrich, of Rappahannock County, fined 50,000 pounds tobacco

Benj. Goodrich, of Rappahannock County, fined 50,000 pounds tobacco

Robert Holden

Thos. Gordon, preacher of Rappahannock County, pastor of Farnham Parish, lived back of Hobbs Hole [Tappahannock]

Stephen Manning

John Taylor, of Rappahannock County

Anthony Hamilton

Richard Barton

James Hardridge and all those who were in arms in the garrison against the King's majesty and governor and government here with the said Barton and Hardridge and did not willingly and readily surrender themselves when they were summoned thereto by Capt. Thomas Powell.

Those who were described as "notorious actors" and were condemned to undergo punishment not extending to life were:

Richard Thomson, of Northumberland County

Dominick Rice, of Rappahannock County

James Bagwell, of Rappahannock County

William Potts, of Rappahannock County

Arthur Long, of Rappahannock County

Thomas Lushington

Robert Weeks

Charles Death

John Lawson

John Browne, of Rappahannock County

Matthew Sadler

John Sadler, was fined 2,000 pounds tobacco

Capt. Charles Scarborough, was fined 70 pounds sterling, and William
    Kendall was fined 70 pounds sterling.

The act of pardon did not extend to those in command when West Point surrendered, and they were forever barred from filling any public office whatsoever. They were:

John Ingram, of Rappahannock County

George Wachlett

John Lawson

Those tried but not fined were:

Thomas Yewell, of Westmoreland County

Richard Thomson, of Northumberland County

Dominick Rice, of Northumberland, formerly of Rappahannock County

William Potts, of Rappahannock County, who owned 200 acres at the
    mouth of Occupacia Creek along the church lot. He bought it from
    Robert Synock in 1673.

[   ] Long, of Surry County

Three citizens of Rappahannock County fled from the country. They were:

Thomas Whaley

Capt. Josias Pickus

John Ferth, rebel [D7, p. 363]

Richard Lawrence, who in earlier years designated himself as a citizen of Rappahannock County, was outlawed and fled.

In February 1676/7, it was enacted:

that Thomas Goodrich do with a rope about his neck on his knees beg for life of the Governor and Council and in like posture acknowledge his crimes of rebellion and treason in Rappahannock County Court and that he be fined 50,000 pounds of merchantable tobacco in cask to be paid before the 20th of January next.

Col. Thomas Goodrich, of Hobbs His Hole, did finally appear in Rappahannock Court with a Manchester cord about his neck to fulfill Berkeley's order. The use of this Manchester cord, a mere shoe-string in strength, by the sheriff did comply with the governor's order, but in a manner that showed that the people of the county, even the officers of the court, had little respect for the governor and his orders. This act of contempt was reported by some person, and Robert Beverley was instructed by the Assembly to look into the matter, but nothing was done.

Thomas Gordon, clerk of Farnham Parish at this time, must have been rather active in denouncing the governor in his pulpit as he was singled out to be punished. The governor ordered that with a rope about his neck, on bended knee, he appear before the governor and council to plead for his life, and in like manner in Rappahannock Court, and "that the said Thomas Gordon is forever made impossible of officiating in ministerial office."

Judging by the number of Rappahannock County people punished by Berkeley, it would seem that the second around what is now Tappahannock was one of the greatest centers of opposition to him. This was probably due to the fact that the county of Rappahannock was one of the greatest sufferers at the hand of the red man.

At least one Indian continued his friendship with the English, for in the will of Edward Gunstacker, an Indian, called "Friendley Ned" by white men, dated 1767, but not recorded until 1686, he says, "I am about to go on an expedition against my brothers, the Indians." That he had befriended the white man from time to time over a period of years is proved by the following order [D3, p. 258]:

At a General Court held at James City, March 25, 1665, it is ordered:
Whereas this Collony of Virg$^{a.}$ have Receid. divers Emminent Services from Ned an Indian of the Nanzatocons of Rappa: w$^{ch.}$ have mightily Conduced to the peace and quiett of the Country, Whereas the Court understud that the said Indian is like to run into Great Dangers from other Indians for his services don[e] to the Country, The Court have thought fitt to Comand all officers belonging to this Collony to be Continually Assistant to the sd. Ned the Indian, and Doe him all Right ag$^{st.}$ any Indian that shall goe aboute to doe him Injury, and it is Further ordered by the Court that the said officers give Notice to all Indians that if the said Ned come to any Hurt that then his blood shall be required at their Hands. Test. Fra: Kirkman, Cl. Court.

Edward Gunstacker was the only Indian to patent and to hold land among the white men. On October 28, 1682, he leased his farm for ten years to John Easter and William Geere for the cheap but luscious rent of two capons on each 25th of December yearly [D7, p. 28]. Without doubt he was a Christian.

During the summer and fall of 1676, Major Simon Miller, who was in command of Bacon's forces in the upper Rappahannock, and who lived very near Friendly Ned, devoted his efforts to fighting the Indians and keeping them under control. His lands lay on the south branch of Pneumendson Run, sometimes called Mill Creek; and later on he lived on Golden Vale Creek above Port Royal. His wife had been the widow of John Prosser, who had patented more than seven thousand acres near Port Royal. Miller's lands adjoined those of Cadwallader Jones and were within the area of the massacre of January 25, 1675/6.

So great was the service of Major Miller in protecting the settlers when their homes and lives were imperiled by the red men that even his nominal enemies joined with his friends in petitioning the governor to look upon him with an eye of favor "because of the good he hath done to protect this section from the Indians keeping them under control."

Berkeley was finally recalled to England in 1677. The people lighted a bonfire and fired guns in celebration of his departure. He was severely criticized in England, and is said to have died soon after of wounded pride. Charles II is credited with having said, "The old fool has taken more lives in that naked country than I have taken for the murder of my father."

The frontier counties were the ones that suffered the greatest loss at the hands of the Indians. It was in the upper part of this old county, on January 25, 1675/6, during a cold and bleak winter season, that thirty-six white citizens were massacred by the red men, that hundreds were driven from their homes, and the toil and labor of the home building of more than two decades wiped out by the fiery torch of the Indian. Practically every house within a radius of ten miles was burnt on that frightful day. The Indians swept eastward down the river valley, slaying settlers, driving away cattle and burning houses and granaries. Many of the native Indians joined the marauders, and for a time the whole country north of Totuskey and Piscataway was invaded. Wherever opportunity offered, the Indian slew and burned and destroyed the white man and his possessions.

In the spring of 1676 the country lay desolate. The county government was disrupted. The county courthouse, which had stood for many years near Bushwood Creek, across from and about a mile below Tappahannock, vanished. The order books prior to this period have been destroyed. The re-filing of the wills of Thomas Pettit and of Epaphroditus Lawson reveal that the will book in which they had been recorded had been destroyed by fire about this time. These facts point to the conclusion that the courthouse and certain of the county records were destroyed during these dark days in the history of the old county.

Nearly three centuries have passed, and practically all records or knowledge of those awful days has slipped away from the transient memory of man. Most of the acts and deeds of those pioneers in defending their homes in the spring of 1676 and of going in pursuit of the Indians during the summer are lost. Not a comment is to be found anywhere to commemorate any act or courage or to mark the section in which thirty-six men, women and children perished in a day at the hands of the ruthless northern Indiana. Not even a slab marks the grave of any man who stood courageously against the savage, and with his life helped to save Virginia for the white man.

Time has obliterated nearly every trace of the struggle. Even the children of the heroes have forgotten them. These were men to whom much honor should be given; but for the most part they are unknown. Their actions were not countenanced by Berkeley and his friends who were restored to power, and their names, except for a few, have not been perpetuated in history. Murdered by savages, executed by Berkeley, driven into the western wilderness, deprived of their lands, their children condemned to poverty, their deeds have been obliterated from the history of the people that they saved. And though they were the saviors of the colony, unjustly they have come down in political history as rebels instead of patriots.

CHAPTER 6

Old Rappahannock County
Ships

Ships and sloops were the life-blood of the colony, and rivers and streams the arteries. The passengers and their merchandise created the colony, and without them no planter could have pushed another rod into the wilderness, cleared another acre, or built another house. The gun and the ammunition with which he drove back the Indian, the axe with which he felled trees, the nails in his house, the clothes he wore, the copper and pewter vessels for his food were all brought in ships. And once he was settled it was the boats that brought him his supplies, that brought reinforcements against Indian attack and massacre. The ships brought to the colony the maids that became the mothers of the nation.

The sea captains who commanded the ships were men of broad experience on many seas. The sailors who manned them were sometimes rough men, but undoubtedly ready and fearless. That they were well paid is evident from the fact that when a sailor sued in the court of old Rappahannock for his back pay, his petition named five pounds sterling per month as his due recompense. Sometimes the ship was the sole property of the master. More often, however, he owned a share in it along with several English merchants or Virginia planters. Occasionally a ship was the property of one man or a group of men with the master hired to sail it.

Berkeley reported to the Crown that there were "about eighty ships sailing to and from the colony annually." Of this fleet the American ships were scarcely more than coastwise vessels, and there were hardly more than two of twenty tons each. The English ships were larger. In 1612, Argall's carried about forty tons including a cargo of fourteen hundred bushels of corn. In the old records a sea-going boat is called a ship; and a vessel or sloop is a smaller craft sailing the Chesapeake and its tributaries, picking up cargoes at James City, Point Comfort, or other settlements, constantly collecting and distributing passengers and merchandise, transferring troops, taking delegates to James City, or moving Indians, grain, or lumber. Historians have made little mention of them, but without them the economic, social and political life of the colony could not have developed. And it was by means of these small craft that the colony was cemented into a unit.

The sloops are rarely named. We are merely told that John Paine's boat carried the burgesses to James City, or that Robert Tomlin's sloop transferred the Rappahannock Indians up the river. In April 1683, Capt. George Taylor was given 1,200 pounds of tobacco a year by the Assembly for keeping a big boat in the Rappahannock River for use in transporting troops back and forth across the river.[49]

During the time of the Commonwealth an act was passed that all vessels owned solely by inhabitants of the colony should be exempted from all castle duties (Hening). This doubtless stimulated for a short time the ownership of boats in the colony. Under the Commonwealth, Col. John Carter was collector from ships for Lancaster County in 1655. In March 1659/60, an act of Assembly was passed giving the Dutch and all other Christian nations the privilege of free trade, but requiring ships trading here to give bond not to molest or disturb any other ship trading in these waters.

Beverley tells us that prior to 1660 all ships had to report in at James City, but after that date the Assembly passed n act permitting ships to report to the collector of the river in which cargo was to be broken.

Boats not designated as ships or sloops were variously known as long boats, ferries, and shallops. These plied the Rappahannock to its head and every creek and stream along its course. Every planter and settler found a boat one of his first and more essential possessions. It served him as horse and wagon and buggy. He went to church on Sunday by boat, to court, to mill, to the neighbors, to see his girl, and to the nearby ordinary to take a social drink and get the news. Far removed from civilization, with no roads, he dared not penetrate far into the forest for fear of encountering some wandering savage who might seek his life. This dependence on the water prevailed generally until after the departure of the Indians from the immediate vicinity, and to a considerable degree until the close of the history of old Rappahannock County.

There were also public ferries. In December 1653, Lancaster County court, after a long debate, ordered a ferry to be kept to transport all passengers from Grimes' land or the Island Poynt or thereabouts as the Commissioners might agree and appoint; Lancaster to pay 2,500 pounds; Northumberland, 1,000 pounds of tobacco annually, and "other counties to be notified that it would not cost their citizens if our citizens are allowed to cross their ferries free" [L1, p. 101]. This ferry was to be chiefly for the public, and probably was the first ferry up the Rappahannock River. It was in the vicinity of what is now known as Port Royal. The next recorded reference to a ferry is in Lancaster County records [L1, p. 135], in June 1654, when Mr. Thomas Carter sold to John Carter his residence and ferry. This was probably a ferry over Corotoman River.

Since all the early court orders for Rappahannock County are lost, we find no further reference to county ferries until October 1, 1684, when Jacob Debello was ordered to continue plying the several ferries for the ensuing year. These were the ferries that George Southing had formerly run. On February 5, 1684/5, his salary for maintaining the upper ferry, "commonly called Southing's ferry," was ordered by the court to be paid from the county levy [O1, pp. 29, 88].

---

[49] Hening, Vol. 3, p. 21, April 1684, Act VII, An Act for the better defence of the Country.

The next year the court instructed David Sterns to keep Southing Ferry "for men and horse to go to and from church" [O1, p. 96]. The church was near to what became Leedstown. On January 16, 1686/7, the court contracted with John Ford to provide and keep a sufficient boat for the transporting of footmen from the mouth of Rappahannock Creek to Mr. John Daingerfield's landing on the Rappahannock River and over the said Rappahannock Creek on the day before court, the day of court, and the day after court [O2, p. 14]. This ferry was doubtless the lower ferry for the county near what became Tappahannock.

At the court of October 5, 1687, Maximillian Robinson contracted to keep Southing Ferry to transport people to church and back again—he to be paid from the county levy. Two months later, on November 16, 1687, the court ordered the discontinuing of free ferries [O2, pp. 57-8]. However, on January 2, 1688/9, John Ford was ordered to keep a ferry for horse and man over Rappahannock Creek from his own landing to Henry Austing's on the day before court, the day of court, and the day after court [O2, p. 141].

In 1689, we find the first reference to a ferry at Totuskey Creek [D8, p. 103]. This was probably a private ferry. On September 3, 1690, the court ordered the "Every person that hath tithables here, even though he do not reside here, have free passage on every ferry paid by the county [O2, p. 253].

In 1655, Ann Kirkman was ordered to be paid "ten pounds of tobacco yearly for every freeman she carried over the ferry to the creek by her house [N1, pp. 31-2]. This item does not properly belong listed with ferries in old Rappahannock County, but is inserted that we have a better understanding of how some ferries were financed in that day and time.

From the very beginning the public ferries were considered very important institutions of public welfare. In 1653, after burgess charges and four thousand pounds of tobacco for a minister were allowed from the levy, all but a few pounds of tobacco went to pay the ferryman's salary. While there were years in the history of the county when no daily ferries were maintained, yet church and court ferries were maintained fairly regularly by the counties. In 1683, when the existing court orders for Rappahannock first appear, the upper ferry was a well established public carrier.

CHAPTER 7

Old Rappahannock County
The Colonists

There has been much confusion regarding the social status of the English colonists who came to Virginia. These may be divided into three groups: first, the free man who paid his own passage; second, the man who had to work out his passage; and third, the political prisoner. When John Doe got fifty acres of land for bringing over William Roe, it does not follow that Roe is the indentured servant of Doe. It may mean only that Roe sold his headright to Doe. There are three out of four cases that Roe, a free man, paid his own passage to the commander of the ship, and upon his arrival here went out and looked for a place or a job as a might do today; or Doe may have loaned roe money for the trip, and been paid with his headright. A headright entitled a man to fifty acres of land.

After emigration into Virginia had become popular, the commanders of ships found no difficulty in persuading people to come to Virginia. Whether passengers paid for themselves or came indentured to some Virginia planter, the captain received pay for bringing them over. If he brought them over at his own expense, he received credit for it and was entitled to rights for land. He, in turn, frequently sold the rights thus acquired, as did Captain Sheapherd to William Moseley.

Large numbers of royalists, as formerly stated, came to Virginia in the days of the Commonwealth. Some of these were men who had succeeded in preserving their fortunes in England and were able to establish themselves at once as planters in Virginia. Many, however, fled from England with little in the way of tangible possessions. They pitted their gallantry and courage against the hardships of pioneer life. Those who came without funds indentured themselves as servants till they could work out their passage and establish themselves. They constituted the second group. Later, under the favor of the government of Charles II, they acquired wide influence and large tracts of land. These men, from indentured service, rose to the posts of burgesses, justices, and military commanders. Many young men considered it wise to work as indentured servants until they became acclimated and learned to make a living in Virginia.

About 1655, Cromwell sent over a large number of Irish prisoners whom he caused to be sold as slaves. These were among a very few white men ever held as slaves in Virginia, and they were ordered set free after serving, usually, six years. Charles II, in like manner, sent to Virginia many political prisoners who were sold into servitude. Soon their term of service expired; they became free, and in nearly all cases acquired land, thus becoming freeholders and voters. They were, for the most part, a sturdy, middle-class English stock of the type that was willing to fight and to die for an abstract principle, for religious freedom, and for the rights of the Saxon English. Their descendants married the descendants of the Cavaliers and produced a type which combined the dash of gallantry of the latter with the unswerving devotion to right of the former; and men who, clinging to their rights and freedom as Englishmen, fought the American Revolution and established a free country, the ideals of whose institutions they have since defended and preserved with their lives.

The colonists who came to Virginia in the seventeenth century were, to a large degree, the very best stock of the nation from whence they came. They were men of vision who faced probable death and certain suffering and hardship to establish themselves in the new land. They crossed the sea in small wooden ships, hazarding their lives in making the venturesome journey. They wanted freedom and the plenty that would be theirs if they had the strength to wrest it from the soil. They exchanged the cramped living and war-trodden soil of England and the continent for the free spaces of Virginia. If they could survive disease and encounters with the savages their future was their own. They had within them those qualities that go to make a strong and virile nation. They planted the seed of real Americanism that was to blossom in spite of tyranny and oppression.

Into Tidewater Virginia came a peculiarly high type of settler. Into the valley of the Rappahannock came the cavaliers in usually large numbers. A remarkably large proportion of the country's leaders have been descended from the early settlers of this river valley. Rappahannock County included parts of Westmoreland, King George, Caroline, Spotsylvania and Stafford, and all of Essex and Richmond counties.

In 1766, the famous pledge known as the Richard Henry Lee Bill of Rights was signed at Leedstown, Westmoreland County, in that part that had once been included in old Rappahannock County, and most of the signers lived within the bounds of the old county. George Washington was born only five miles from the line of old Rappahannock. His grandfather, Col. John Washington, had extensive lands in this county. James Williamson, a justice of the old Rappahannock court, who resided at *Cobham Park* near Warsaw, had a daughter, Margaret, who married William Ball of Lancaster County, an ancestor of George Washington. At the age of twelve, Washington himself moved into the area that had been part of Rappahannock County, and received much of his childhood training there.

James Madison was born near the center of the bounds of Rappahannock County, his ancestors being among the first settlers here. It was he who won the freedom of the seas for Americans. He became America's greatest Constitutional statesman, and in his writings blazed the trail that made possible the application of the Constitution as law.

In old Rappahannock were the Zacharys and the Taylors, ancestors of a fourth president, descended from the early settlers of this county. Through Zachary Taylor as president the addition of Texas to the United States was possible. Nancy Hanks, mother of Abraham Lincoln, is thought to have been

66

descended from the Hanks Family of Rappahannock County. Robert Edward Lee was born but five miles from the bounds of the old county. His early American ancestors had landed here. Here lived the ancestors of at least these five who are among the best loved of all Virginians. Here today live their kinsmen. It is impossible to estimate, much less to name, all the great men of America who could trace their ancestry back to the pioneer settlers of old Rappahannock County.

It is here that lived the ancestors of Francis Scott Key, author of our national anthem, "The Star Spangled Banner." The families of many state governors lived here in the seventeenth century. John Clarke, great-grandfather of General George Rogers Clarke who took the great northwest territory, and his brothers, Jonathan Clarke and Gen. William Clarke, of the Lewis and Clarke Expedition, who conquered the far northwest, lived here.

The following are the names of just a few of the men of international fame whose ancestors lived in old Rappahannock:

> General Henry Young and General Woodford, of the Revolutionary War
>
> General Winfield Scott, of the Mexican War, and General Robert Selden Garnett who was with him. In the Civil War, Gen. J.N. Crittenden was under Gen. Scott.
>
> Robert M.T. Hunter was Secretary of State of the Confederate States of America

Some Early Colonists
Recorded in Lancaster County Records (Deeds Etc. Book 1)

In 1651, Lancaster County was formed from Northumberland with the portion south of the Rappahannock River taken from York County. About four years later, in 1656, Lancaster was divided, and about half of the first settlers were living in Rappahannock County. The following list contains names taken from Deed Etc. Book 1, 1652-57, of Lancaster County.

Oct. 1652	Mary Peirce, Richard Smith, Thos. Naylor, Hugh Jones [p. 15]
1652	Teage Floid brought over his wife Elizabeth [p. 15]
1652	Clement Thrush brought over John Flood, Joane Flood, Arth. Elliott, Joane Broadribb, Alice Spencer and Ellen Steale [p. 15].[50]
1652	Thomas Paine brought over Henry Odum, Penelope Paine and Joane Staples [p. 15]
1652	Toby Smith brought over Robert Springe, Geo. Morell [or Marall], Ralph Broadhurst, Ben. Forby, Elinor Andry, Ann Burgess, Hen. Foster [p. 16]
1652	Land is granted Domonick Cheriott for bringing over Wm. Sparow and Richard Franklin and Frances [p. 16]

---

[50] *Cavaliers and Pioneers*, Vol. 1, p. 268, in Patent Book 3, p. 143, in the original manuscript, the last name is written Alice Spencer.

1653	John Edgecomb brought himself into this country [p. 43]
1653	Wm. Tigner brought over James Markmun, Tho: Smith, Elizabeth Harwood, Wm. Cookman, Hugh Jones and Mary Rowles [p. 43]
1653	Edwin Conway brought over Wm. Collins and Edward Bennett [p. 62]
Aug. 1653	Daniel Welsh brought over Tho: Courtman, John Owen, Edm.ᵈ Yeomans, Garret Woldman, Sarah Foxall, Mary Doldin, Edwd: Wmson. and James Wilson [p. 62]
1653	Certificates of land were granted to Oliver Segar, John Edwards and Daniel Johnson, for bringing over themselves [p. 62]
Oct. 1653	Richard Perrott brought over Sarah Keys, Da: Simpson, Wm. Dunston and Hen: Sharpe [p. 77]
Oct. 1653	Abraham Weeks brought over himself, John Barnes and Tho: Chatton [p. 77]
1653	John Cable brought over Rawleigh Travers [p. 79]
1653	Capt. Henry Fleet brought over twenty persons: Henry Roote, Mary Williams, Mary Fry, Jas. Haling, Rob: Thomas, Eliza. Collings, Jno. Brathard, Fra: Bland, Tho: Land, Jere: Hoge, Hennsit Carter, Darby Hanrauly, Thack Cullaine, Willm. Ball, Daniel Morill, Jno. Brent, Tho. [Hind], Jere: Lodwell, Tho: Harris, Joan Wood and Tho: Beard [p. 89]
1653	Fra. Gower brought over Wm. James, Ann Bartlett, Antho: Peeters, Ann [Taylor] [p. 89]
1653	Certificate of land was issued to Da: Folys for transporting himself twice, and bringing over John Humphreys, Eliz. Colonies, Tho: Smyth Sen., John Cox & wife, and John Sharp [p. 139]
1654	Wm. Clapham Jr. brought over Jno: Cooke, Fran: Sewell, Marga: Malle, Eliza Cornish, Jno: Cornish, Sara Cornish, and Xpher Harford [p. 145]
Aug. 1654	Toby Smyth brought over Abig: Ridge, Thos: Crowder, Seath Edwards, Tho: Bumbridge, Wm. Swan, Wm. Talbot, Jno: Warner, Jno: Clowen, Kath. Moraughan [p. 151]
1654	Certificate of land was granted Ja. Vaun for his own transportation [p. 151]
1654	Alexander Porteus brought over himself and Eliza: Browne [p. 151]
Aug. 1654	Abra: Moone transported his wife An, Jno: Brerton, Wm. Allawaye, Ja: Allison, Eliza. Paine, Jno. Craford [p. 153]
1654	Certificate of land is granted Geo. Taylor for bringing over Geo. Adams, Eliza: Shaw, Columbus Cloyd and August Cloyd [p. 162]
1654	Andrew Gilson brought over Anth: North, Jno. Smyth, John Stainingbrow, Hen: Carter and Eliza: Mynshem [p. 162]
1654	John Gillett is given a certificate of land for bringing over Fra: Thrush, Jane Woulman, Susan Han, Thos. Powell, Elnor Peeterson, Fra: Sargan, Geo. Keale and Tho: Tramer [p. 162]
1654	John Weir is granted a certificate of land for bringing over Robert Chambers twice, Rich. Wms., Ann Collins, Magda. Steephens, Mary Steephens, Wm. Hardinge, Daniell Elsmore, Jno. Marke and Margra. Allen [p. 162]
Feb. 1654	Hugh Brent brought over himself and Jno. Noble, Robert Warner, Jno. Girton and Mary Osterson [p. 171]

1654	Thomas Carter is granted a certificate of land for bringing over Susana Carter, Wm. Shirt, An[n] Hughes, Mary Smyth, Jos. Maxy, Mark Smyth, Edw. Lunoe [p. 172]
1654	Row. Lawson is given a certificate of land for bringing over Henry Berrey, Patrick Clearke, Sarah Turner, Eliz. Sachell, Rolas Richering, Wm. Wilkinson, Geo. Goodall, Jno. Marshesell, Daniell Cooper and Katherine English. The last two were added in June 1655 [p. 172]
1655	Capt. Henry Fleet is given a certificate of land for bringing over Bridget Lee, Cornelia Hargan, Hen. Shuldren, Wm. Murren, Daniell Woolka, Mary Battle, Eliza Symon, Jno. Yeates and Thos. Allison [p. 198]
1655	John Eyers brought over John Taylor, Joan Eyers, Elnor Gill, and Henry Peeters [p. 208]
1655	Ja: Bagnall brought over David Rode, Alice Longworth, Baro. Harris, Wm. Ratclif, Johnnathan Williams, Rice Powell, Ed. Foster, Cha: Peksbury, Thos. Follo, Mart. Cooke and Maria Sladen [p. 208]
1655	Tho. Hawkins brought over John Humphreys, Peter Hamlin, Ral: Parray, Richard Cooper, Eliza Warner, Francis Atkins, John Corneshel, Wm. Crisp [p. 208]
1655	John Harker brought over Robert Reines, Jno. Stevenson, John Aikens [p. 208]
1655	Sill. Thacker brought Wm. Bullock, Rollin Clark, Ann Miles, Roger Thomas Jr. [p. 208]
1655	Thos. Griffith brought in Reginald Johnson, Eliza. Roberts, John Paine, Anne Garrett, Peter Ellis, George Minfrey [p. 246]
Feb. 1655	Walter Dickerson brought John Williams, Jane Bradman, Richard Thyreld and Mary Snell [p. 254]
Mar. 1655	David Phelps brought over himself, Hugh Maydox, Edward Porter and Willm. Smith [p. 257]
1656	Edwyn Connaway brought Richard Cartreeke and Susan Warren [p. 263]
1656	Vincent Stanford brought over Peter a Negro, Mary Stanford, Edward Stevens, John Rygens, David Gaspie, John Wells, Barbary Thasheley, Ann Tompson, Tho. Bond and Robert Thompson [p. 263]
1656	John Sherlock brought over Sam Salesbury and Ann Cartwright [p. 266]
1656	Humphrey Booth brought over himself twice, Mathew Goare, Anne Reddinge, Edward ap Lewis, Abraham Stevens, John Suckett, Thomas Freshwater, Gowyn Younge and Mary Fisher, and Aarob a Negro [p. 267]
1656	Lt. Col. Moore Fantleroy brought over Abraham Collice, John Lathbury, Dorothy Dansar, Thomas Newman, Joseph Webster and a Negro [p. 267]
1656	James Williamson brought over Maudline Thomas, John Roberts, Robert Smith, Francis Settle, Daniell Hunter, John Stray, Mathew Whaite, Henry Carpenter, Thomas Stevenson, Alice a maid servant, John Hull, Robert Hull, Tho. Chittwood three times, Xtopher Browninge, Mr. Ja: Williamson, Ann Lonton, Wm. Hastell, Nich. Redferne, Richard Walker, Stephen Gostell, Zach. Effate, Mich. Filliott, Henry Robert, Jo: Gostell [p. 268]

1656	David Fox brought over Glenham Drury, John Handerson, Francis Hugan, Michaell Bayly, Jo: Kinge, Roger Gibson, Valentine Painter, Jo: Waight, Mary Taylor and Margery Axon, six Negroes [p. 285]
1656	Sir Henry Chicheley brought over Abraham Appleton and wife Elizabeth, Gabriell Littleton, Tho: Bruerton, Dennys Downinge, Tho: Tomlyn, Tho: July, James Cadwallader, Robt. [blank], Tho: Billby, Geo. Gudloe, Wm. Croshaw, Jo: Reyley, Tho: Loe, John Harrys, Philip Kirby, Margaret Gudlow, Margarett Arnoll, Mary Lamory, Joan Burley, Tho: Walgrand, Roger Smith, Tho: Hubbett, two Negroes [p. 286]
1656	Cuthbert Potter brought over Richard Colt, Robert Newby, Richard Robinson, Anth. Barley, Willm. King, Tho: Knowles, Jo: Allen, Constant Minshaw and Giles Robinson [p. 286]
1656	Jo: Millessent brought over himself, Robert Millessent, John Braddie and Alexr. Faxon [p. 287]
1656	John Paine brought over Mary Smith, Lawrence Thompson, Willm. Walker and Thomas Folly [p. 289]
1656	Andrew Gellson brought over Sarah Smart, Eliza Minshaw, Anne Thornton, Anne Miles, Katherine Goldinge, Anthony Edwards, Willm. Bruce, John Sherrine, Tho: Pool, Edward Paggett, Charles Blurteene [p. 290]
1656	Wm. Underwood brought over Peter Leonard, Mary Hawkes, Willm. Carter and Paull Wood [p. 290]
1656	George Marsh brought over himself twice, Cornelius Coreshore, Edmond Munro, Robert Canderloe, Leonell Canston [p. 295]
1656	Maj. Tho: Goodriche brought over Capt. John Goldinge, Edmond Keney, Anne Blanton, Anne Caston, Mary Miller and Mary Bunston [p. 318]

Northumberland County Orders, 1652-1665

1652	Andrew Monroe brought over John Wright, Andrew Edenborough [p. 4]
Mar. 10, 1652	Mary Keene brought over herself, Tho: Keene, William Keene, herself and Susanna Keene [p. 22]
1653/4	Anne Moore brought over herself and daughter Anne Moore [p. 43]
1653/4	Wm. Nash and wife Anne brought over Thos. Pearce and others [p. 43]

CHAPTER 8

Old Rappahannock County
Indentured Servants

In considering the so-called indentured servant, usually called Christian servant in the old records, six points should be kept in mind: economic conditions in England, requirements of the youth of the time, the nature of the indenture, most important of all the age of the indentured, the influences that moulded his life, and the law that regulated it.

Youth is always eager for adventure, and to youth the green pastures are on the far hills. England's great new empire forming across the seas called for her young men. Colonists who went home on business told flowing tales of Virginia. Thousands were fixed with the desire to come hither, to conquer the wilderness, and to make their fortunes. The young man who was twenty-one years of age and had a bit of money had no difficulty in finding his way to Bristol or some other port and obtaining passage. Even without money, he could probably find some sea captain or some returning planter who would partly or wholly pay his passage because of the fifty acres of land that would be gained thereby. For the young man of twenty-one without money there was also a way. Since there was no place in Virginia for the homeless and penniless freeman, many a youth, filled with tales of hawkings and fowlings, of the conquest of the Indians by the English, of great tracts of land to be had as a reward of adventure, was eager to sign a contract to work for a Virginia planter in return for his keep, for the experience he would gain, and for the supplies his master would give him at the end of his service. Such a contract was called an indenture.

Larger even than the group above was the number of the young men under the age of twenty-one who came to Virginia. Being under the age of accountability, these had to be with their parents or to present papers of indenture before they were admitted to the colony—for such was the law. The conditions were such that it was no happy refuge for free vagrants. For this reason and because of the law, a boy usually pledged in writing with his parent's consent that he would go to Virginia as a servant.

Prior to 1642 the terms of indenture were not fixed by law, and such servants were sometimes sold to unduly long service; but during that year the Assembly passed a law that henceforth servants above twenty years of age were to serve but four years; if one were twelve years of age but under twenty, he would serve five years; if he were under twelve he should serve seven years. In 1659 it was enacted:

> ... that all persons brought into this country from what Christian nation soever should serve no longer than those of our own nation which is five years if above sixteen years of age, if under until they are 21, that being the time limited by the laws of England.

The indentured was a Christian servant, not a slave.

In 1666 the law was adjusted so that all should serve five years from the time of indenture, and that everyone intending to claim the benefit of this act:

> ... is hereby required within two courts at furthest after he hath bought him or them or imported a servant as aforesaid to carry him to the court who by a present inspection at that time will be best enabled to pass judgment on the matter.

In compliance with this act many children were brought to the court by their masters and their ages adjudged by the court. The names of these from 1682 to 1692 and even later are preserved in the court order books. Unexpected as it may seem, close examination of these court orders shows that the children examined by the court were in a large degree the orphan children of the deceased planters of the county.

By the Assembly of 1672 it was enacted that:

> the justices of the peace in every county to put the laws of England against vagrant idle persons in strict execution and the respective County Courts shall hereby and are impowered and authorized to place out all children, whose parents are not able to bring them up, apprentices to tradesmen, the males till one and twenty years of age, and the females to other necessary employment until eighteen years of age and no longer and the church wardens of every parish shall be strictly enjoyned by the courts to give them an account at their orphans court annually of all such children within their parish as they judge to be within the said capacity.

It was in conformity with these last two acts, limiting terms of service and outlawing vagrancy, that most of the indentures were made after those dates in Rappahannock County.

The cruelty of masters was prohibited as early as 1661. There are several instances in the old Rappahannock County records of masters of complaining servants being dealt with by the court. Complaining servants were sometimes freed by the court. A recorded statute:[51]

> Whereas the barbarous usage of some servants by cruell masters bring soe much scandall and infamy to the country in general, that people who would willingly adventure themselves hither, are through fear thereof diverted, and by that means the supplies of particular men and the well seating of his majesties country very much obstructed. Be it therefore enacted that every master shall provide for his servants competent dyett, clothing and lodging, and that he shall not exceed the bounds of moderation in correcting them beyond the merit of their offences; and that it shall be lawful for any servant giving notice to their masters (having just cause of complaint against them) for harsh and bad usage, or else for want of dyett or convenient necessaries to require to the next commissioner to make his

---

[51] Hening, Vol. 2, p. 117, March 1661/2, Act CIII, Cruelty of masters prohibited.

complaint, and if the said commissioner shall find by just proofs that the said servants cause of complaint is just the said commissioner is hereby required to give order warning of such master to the next county court where the matter in difference shall be determined, and the servant have remedy for his grievances.

The indentured servants of Virginia have been pointed out as the cause and origin of many social conditions. They have been said to have formed the basis of the so-called "lower caste," of the "tenant caste," of the "poor white trash." There is no justification for such statements in the records. In the first place the author has not found evidence that there were definite caste lines in the early colony; nor does he believe that separate castes existed. In the early days society did not crystallize into distinct groups. No man has the right today to look down upon an ancestor just because he was at one time during his life a servant to some other man. The indentured servant in the seventeenth century held practically the same relative position as that of the thousands of young men in this day and age who enter into an agreement with a contractor to serve as an apprentice for a given number of years that he may be taught a trade and qualify as a master mechanic. This practice was very common in America in the nineteenth century.

The indenture of the seventeenth century was also similar to the general program entered into by thousands of our finest young men and women who go to our state universities, colleges, and normal schools, and contract to teach in the public schools, to serve the state as engineers, or to serve in the militia for two years at the end of their college training. These contracts are an indenture to serve the state, and in no wise can be construed to reflect against the moral character or the social standing of the young people of this generation.

The seventeenth century was an age of specialization, and every boy was expected to learn some trade. This was the fundamental cause of much indenturing. Since tobacco was an American crop, the proper culture of which was not well known in England, thousands of young men and boys who wished to come to Virginia to make a living as planters indentured themselves to learn the art of growing tobacco, the one crop in this country that paid money. To know how to grow it was to know how to make money. Every farm was a mint where money grew as leaves. Young men came, worked and learned. After serving the usual four to eight years of apprenticeship, they were well trained, ready to take up land for themselves, and to start their own crops.

When at liberty to make a beginning for themselves, they were not turned loose without substance, for a master was compelled by law to give each man a good gun with powder and shot, two complete new suits of clothes, one for Sunday and one for work, two full suits of underwear and linen, two new shirts, and for food two bushels of corn. Thus equipped a man was well supplied to go out and take care of himself until he could produce his own crop, whether by working some other man's farm on shares, seating by agreement another man's patent for a part of the land, or by taking up his own patent and clearing away the forest for his own house and tobacco crop.

There are several important reasons why it was unwise for a man to come direct from England to patent land the year he came over. Berkeley said that that in the early years of his administration not one free man out of five who came over endured the first year. Malaria, typhoid fever, and other disease played havoc with the newcomers before they became "seasoned" to the climatic conditions and the new mode of living. For a man to thrust himself into the forest digging stumps and clearing a house site with little or no shelter while doing it and with food of a new kind, often poorly prepared, was most unwise. Not until he had become accustomed to pioneer living, to an inequitable climate, and to the Indian corn and native gods, could he successfully meet the new world conditions. He must master the mode of growing tobacco, the art of building log houses and rail fences; he must plan and build his house on the frontier; and he must know something of the wild life of the country and of the ways of the savage. The indenture years of training proved a practical method of meeting these needs.

The indenture of orphan children appears often to have been little more than a guardianship. One by, whose father was dead and whose mother had married again, appeared in court and testified that he did not know that he had ever been indentured to his step-father. The boy's father, a prominent planter and burgess, had been a man of considerable means, and the boy was to heir his estate when he arrived at the age of twenty-one. The mother had indentured him with the understanding he should be given a liberal education. This mother would never have freely indentured her son to her second husband if, thereby, any stigma or disgrace had been placed upon her son.

The indenture papers of an orphan child usually specified that he should be given food, shelter, religious training, and that he should be taught to read and to write; and those of a girl that she should be taught to sew. These indentures were usually made with other men of the family, such as uncles or step-fathers, or with close friends who were prominent citizens, the child being so placed that he would be properly cared for and cherished by those to whose care he was committed, much as adopted children of the twentieth century.

In Northumberland, on October 28, 1651, John Kelly agreed to pay Hugh Lee 2,000 pounds of tobacco and two barrels of corn on March 20, 1652, and to serve Lee for one full year as an indenture on the condition that he would have Susan Watson, Lee's servant, to wed, and they to be free in one year. This contract was made and signed.

Some servants had it written into their contracts that they should be given fifty acres of land at the end of their period of service. It was a frequent thing for an indentured maid to stipulate in her indenture papers that she was to receive a cow with a calf at her side at the expiration of her term of service. As she was also entitled to her corn and clothes, she became, when married, a substantial partner with her husband in their home.

The conditions of regulating marriage in those days were about the same as these of the twentieth century. There is no tract of any special caste lines between the large and the small land holders, nor between those who had been indentured servants, and those who had not.

The following affidavit is an instance of the good standing of the indentured servant in the social and religious life of the colony. It shows that Nathaniel Pendleton preached in the parish church while serving his term of indenture to Edmond Crask, the clerk of the county court [D13, p. 118]:

George Ward, aged 57 or thereabouts, of South Farnham Parish in the county of Essex in Virginia, Planter, having examined and sworn at the request of Philip Pendleton, deposeth and saith: *That on or about the year of our Lord 1676 there Came Consigned to Captain Edmond Crask then living in the said parish two reputed brothers called and known by the name of Nathaniel Pendleton and Philip Pendleton sent as this deponent heard by their mother in a ship whereof the master was John Plover. And this Deponent sayeth that the said Nathaniel was reputed a minister and preached a sermon in the above said parish Church soon after his arrival and immediately thereupon sickened and dyed, and this Depont. further saith that he was a servant in the house where the said Nathaniel Pendleton died and did see the said Nathaniel interred in the earth and never heard that the said Nathaniel ever had wife or child, and this Deponent further sayeth that the said Phillip Pendleton went for England at the end of five years or servitude and came to Virginia the same year and since married and had several children all now resident in King and Queen County in Virginia aforesaid and further this depot. sayeth not.* [signed] George Ward. Recorded August 10, 1708 upon the motion of Phillip Pendleton.

This Nathaniel Pendleton was a graduate of Cambridge University. Phillip Pendleton's name often occurs as a witness to legal documents recorded about this time. He spent much of his time at the office of the clerk of court performing many of the duties of the deputy clerk under Edmond Crask.

All things considered the indentured man did not come out far behind the man who was able to pay his passage, but who had no extra money when he arrived in the colony. The indentured system was encouraged as an economic expedient by the government. It stabilized labor and largely eliminated spasmodic and mushroom growth in the colony. This system of stabilizing labor, however, was gradually supplanted by the system of Negro slavery even in the latter part of the seventeenth century, was providing itself to be more economical to the large planters. Out of the new system, slavery, developed a new interpretation of the words servant and master.

That no social stigma was attached to the status of indentured servant is proved by the facts herewith given concerning the male servants whose names have been preserved in the records of old Rappahannock County:

Thomas Alger, aged 18 in 1686, married Alitia, a daughter of John Kennedy, a large land holder. His wife's sister married Alexander Fleming, one of the largest planters in the Rappahannock valley [O1, p. 215; RD3, p. 65].

John Benger was ordered set free in 1689. He died in 1725, leaving lands and a large estate [O2, p. 171].

In the early days, an orphan under twenty-one years of age was considered a vagrant or vagabond, and was required by law to be indentured, usually to learn some trade, and to have someone to train and teach him.

Thomas Butler, servant, was freed in 1691. His master was John Smith, whose lands joined John Butler Jr. Thos. Butler was doubtless of this family, and a nephew to Rev. Wm. Butler of Westmoreland County [O2, pp. 305, 322; D13, pp. 334, 411; D15, p. 94].

Robert Carden, 17 years old in 1684/5, was the son of Robert Carden, a landholder. In 1690, the year he became 21, the son bought 200 acres of land [O1, p. 107; D6, p. 139; D8, p. 66].

Henry Clark, servant, was freed in 1658. He was sub-sheriff of Rappahannock County in 1670. He became a substantial land holder [LO3, p. 225; D4, p. 227; W2, p. 108].

Thomas Gaines, son of Thomas Games, was indentured in 1670. His father, Thomas Gaines, a landholder, was about to marry the widow of Thomas Pettit, deceased. With this family were connected many prominent families: Major George Morris, Capt. Richard Long, Capt. Thomas Pettit, all of whom were large land owners and outstanding men [D4, p. 344].

John Evans, orphan, who was 14 years old in 1686, was the son of John Evans, a large landholder. He was grandson-in-law of Martin Johnson, and with him are connected the Lee and Slaughter families. His father married Elizabeth Beale before 1681, and William Beale gave them 100 acres of his lands. This land was inherited by John Evans, the younger, who still owned it in 1708 [O1, p. 224; W1, p. 172; EO1, p. 132; D6, pp. 127, 163; D13, p. 91].

John Green, orphan of John Green, merchant and land owner, was bound by the court to Andrew Gilson in 1655. His father owned *Greenfield*, the rich farm just north of Tappahannock. His son inherited 200 acres of this land upon his arrival at the age of 21. He married well. He bought and patented other tracts of land in his later years [L2, p. 6; D2, p. 328; P.B. 6, p. 10; North Farnham Parish Register].

Thomas Green, servant to Thomas Bowler in 1662, had 50 acres of land by 1668, and other lands by 1675 [O1, p. 59; D2, p. 280 (217); D4, p. 15; D5, p. 456].

Thomas Goose in 1653, had one and a half years to serve. He died in 1682 leaving large landed possessions [L2, p. 6; W2, p. 172].

John Hawkins had 4 months to serve in 1684. He was the son of Major Thomas Hawkins, burgess from this county in 1676. John was an orphan at this time. His mother had bound him to his step-father on condition that the boy be given a liberal education. This boy did not know what he was bound out. Neither the boy's mother nor the court would have bound him out had there been any disgrace attached thereto. The boy was by inheritance a large land holder. Thomas Hawkins died about 1676 [O2, p. 277; D6, p. 19; Hening, Vol. 2, p. 406].

William Harding, servant to Andrew Gilson in 1663, was a land owner in 1670 [D2, p. 277 (215); D4, p. 471].

Isaac Hudson, in 1687, willed all his possessions to his master, Alexander Newman, provided he take his child and put him to school later. Newman was ordered by the court to take under his care and charge Isaac Hudson, orphan of Isaac Hudson, deceased, and gave bond for 10,000 pounds of tobacco to secure delivery to the child of the estate when he should arrive at the age of 21 years [O2, p. 28; D.W.B.].

In 1653, Peter Johnson had four years to serve. In 1658, he and a friend bought 100 acres of land. In 1671, he bought 200 acres alone. This land he re-sold a few years later for 100,000 pounds of tobacco. This was very rich land and lay around the Sittingbourne parish church, the center of the social life of the community. A place of such value as his decidedly took him out of the poor farmer group. His daughter married John Martin, a servant later discussed herein. Peter Johnson seems to have been the orphan of John Johnson, deceased in 1653, and the brother of John Johnson, orphan, servant who had three and a half years to serve in 1653. Peter Johnson's lands were at the mouth of Occupacia Creek. His brother, John Johnson, patented 737 acres in 1663 [D2, p. 32; D5, p. 11; L1, p. 296; L2, p. 6; P.B. 5, p. 290].

Samuel Johnson, orphan of Samuel Johnson, deceased, was given by his mother to Xpher Blackbourne after the mother had married Edward George. The boy's father was a land holder. He himself bought 100 acres of land and died in 1718 leaving a small personal estate [O2, p. 112; D5, pp. 76-8; D6, p. 267; D14, p. 438].

George Jones, aged 17, was bound out in 1685. His mother died when he was young, and his father married Mrs. Honoria Weir, widow of Major John Weir, a former burgess. George Jones Sr. was a large land holder even before his second marriage. He had more than 2,000 acres of land. Col. John Washington, ancestor of Gen. George Washington, designated the boy's father to be his attorney and called him "My loving friend Geo. Jones," even while his first wife was living. This George Jones, orphan and servant, in later years became a large land owner. His father's social position was of the best. As the father died about 1684, the son was bound out, doubtless by the county, to learn a trade according to law; but upon his arrive at 21 years of age he inherited his father's large estate [O1, p. 197; D5, pp. 15, 233; D15, p. 120].

John Martin, servant in 1683, was given his freedom by his father-in-law, Peter Johnson. The said Peter Johnson directed that he should have the tuition of his son, Peter Johnson Jr., until he was 20 years of age, and that the boy was to have a convenient education. Here is an instance where master and servant were of the same social class, and where the master bound out his son to his own servant. John Martin himself was the son of John Martin who had 360 acres of land [D2, p. 297 (234); D6, p. 17; L3, pp. 170-1].

John Penn, servant in 1661, died in 1676/7, a wealthy planter of Rappahannock County, with property in Virginia, Maryland and England [L3, pp. 170-1; D1, pp. 206-8].

Thomas Powell, orphan, servant, about 15 years old in 1687/8, was the son of Thomas Powell, deceased, a man who had owned about 1000 acres of land [O2, p. 59; D2, p. 37; Patents].

John Parker, orphan, aged 11, was bound out in 1691. He was the son of Robert Parker, who died leaving a 1600-acre farm and a mill, both of which he bequeathed to his wife, who married again. The boy was bound out according to law to learn a trade [O2, p. 335; D3, p. 425; D6, p. 89; P.B. 6, p. 424].

John Russell, orphan, servant, served five years to learn the cooper's trade, but was not adequately taught. In 1689, he sued his master and got 1500 pounds of tobacco, or the equivalent of a year and a half of service. He was the son of John Russell, deceased, chirurgeon (doctor) and wife Alice Bullington, and the grandson of Luke and Barbery Bullington, deceased. His father patented 1100 acres of land in 1673, and his grandfather was an even larger planter. This boy was raised on his father's large farm called *Ireland* [O1, p. 113; O2, p. 193; D5, p. 246; D6, p. 69; W1, p. 177].

Robert Slaughter, aged 15 in 1686, was the grandson of Capt. Francis Slaughter, and the son of Francis Slaughter, deceased. According to law he was bound out by the court. He died in 1726 leaving more than 2000 acres of land, many slaves, and a large family. He was the highest social standing [D2, p. 35; O1, p. 214; WB4, p. 179].

John Story, orphan in 1687, was the son of Joshua Story and his first wife. About this time, this boy's father married the widow of Major George Morris of New Kent. Story held considerable land. George Morris had owned many thousands of acres of land and was one of the leading men of the colony [O2, pp. 58; 202-7].

Thomas Wright ran away from his master in 1686. He was doubtless one of the orphans of John Wright, deceased in 1684. John Wright owned 1700 acres of land in 1667 [O1, p. 245; D3, pp. 41, 289; D4, p. 41; L2, p. 171].

Peter Price did in 1686 in open court voluntarily and of his own free will consent, covenant to serve Mr. Arthur Spicer for 7 years, not as a laborer but as a writing servant [O2, p. 218].

In 1661, Edward Carter servant to Col. John Carter (doubtless a kinsman) coming into this country without indenture did at this court petition for his freedom pretending that he was sold for but four years. The said Col. Carter did make oath that when he bought the said Edward Carter there was not any mention made of what time he was to serve whereupon it is so ordered that the said Edward Carter to serve five years according to the act of Assembly in such cases [LO3, p. 308].

Edward Carter of Lancaster County and Audrey Carter sold land in Rappahannock County to Henry Harley. Edward Carter sold 661 acres of land in 1683. He had 300 acres given him by the will of Thomas Wright [D7, p. 105; W1, p. 120].

In 1659, Bartholomew Clark entered a four-year apprenticeship to learn the art of farming. He indentured himself to Edward Rowzee who was to give him fifty acres of land at the end of his period of indenture [W1, p. 43].

On March 23, 1651, Mathew Welbeloved agreed to be assigned to Anthony Doney by Mr. Edward Conoway. Conoway had promised his mother that he would not assign him without his, her son's, consent. He was still the servant of Doney in 1653. He was later killed in an Indian massacre [L1, p. 63; L2, p. 90].

Thomas Ingram was, for reasons of good will, given his freedom two months before his time was up by Humphrey Booth [D2, p. 402 (330)]. By July 20, 1673, he was son-in-law to William Gray [O2, p. 338]. William Gray was a large land owner in 1657

[D2, p. 27 (16)] and the ancestor of a family that has held a prominent place in the life of Essex County. James Bowler married one of Gray's daughters, and it was a daughter by this marriage that married Richard Cocke of *Malvern Hill* on the James River and became the ancestress of the well-inown Bowler Cocke Family of Henrico County [W1, p. 145].

Thomas Powell, servant to Thomas Watkins, was 15 years old in 1687. He was son of Thomas Powell who had 300 acres of land in 1654 and 646 acres in 1668 [D3, p. 317].

Elinor Smith gave her son, Benjamin Smith, to Mr. John Rolt and wife, to be raised as their own child, "they promising further to teach him to read and write" [D5, p. 193]. Elinor Smith was the widow of Thomas Smith [D5, p. 267]. There were several Thomas Smiths of this period. All seem to have been landholders or children of landholders.

In 1687, Andrew Boyer, sick and weak, promised Mary Caper to relieve her from all manner of service after the decease of him and his wife Sarah. He gave Mary and her son for life "so much land as she and Thomas her son can tend in Indian corn and tobacco and to give them shelter for themselves and their crops" [D8, p. 8].

In 1684, Robert Vincent, the man of William Freath, was given the use of land and house for seven years. By 1687, he had acquired 200 acres of other land [D7, p. 351].

William Yates, twenty years old in 1684, entered a term of apprenticeship to serve John Alloway [O1, p. 65]. This John Alloway was his mother's brother. Their father, John Alloway, was a large land holder. John Yates Sr., who is thought to have been the boy's father, bought 100 acres of land from John Alloway in 1668, and later acquired other lands [D4, p. 41]. This John Yates Sr. died by 1683, shortly before the boy was indentured out.

John Stannos, servant to Thomas Wright, was given his freedom. He was Wright's son-in-law. Thomas Wright was a prominent planter of Morattico Creek, and was connected with the Madison, Carter, Bryant, Ryly, Pool and Scott families, all of whom were land owners in the county, their descendants later rising to the highest positions [W1, p. 120].

In England in 1670, one of the twenty-three inquiries directed to Governor Berkeley by the lords commissioners of foreign plantations was, "What number of planters, servants, slaves; and how many parishes are there in your plantation?" Berkeley replied:

> We suppose, and I am sure we do not much miscount, that there is in Virginia above forty thousand persons, men, women and children, and of which there are two thousand black slaves, six thousand Christian servants for a short time, the rest are born in the country or have come in to settle and seat, in bettering their condition in a growing country.

There is no way to ascertain just what proportion of these six thousand Christian servants was in old Rappahannock County. The two extant Order Books contain the records of about seventy-five. Above are given the pertinent facts concerning many of them. Some were not of age when the county was divided in 1692, and so were not checked; some died; some left the county; and a few may have been overlooked. Several bore the same names as landholders, and lacked sufficient identification.

An indenture, as the word is herein used, was a contract to work. In colonial Virginia such a contract had to be kept. It is true that among the indentured servants, as among the freemen of that time, here and in every other part of the world, there were criminals and some vagrants; but the great majority were honest men, seeking through the indenture system to gain a foothold in the new rich land of Virginia. In old Rappahannock County their position was like that of the apprenticed boys of New England. They learned "the art of raising tobacco," "the mysteries of the planter," and the various handicraft trades. Nearly every indenture of a youth carried with it the provision that he should be taught to read and to write. Girls were taught to sew. A short time after the close of old Rappahannock County, a man indentured himself out to acquire the necessary training to be a clerk of court.

The examples here-in-before given are sufficient to show the birth and breeding, the social position, and the wealth of the indentured servant. These instances establish the fact that they were not a class or caste distinct from the land holding class, and that a youth's manhood was not hampered by the fact that during his minority he had been bound out to another man to learn how to fight the battles of life, and how to make a good living. There was no stigma attached to being an indentured servant.

CHAPTER 9

Old Rappahannock County
Economic Development

Planters of Rappahannock County brought about its economic development by their almost superhuman efforts and untold sacrifices in overcoming the difficulties that beset them. At first the section was a great forest country where dwelt the subtle and treacherous savage. There were no roads, only foot-paths over which the Indians journeyed. These were scarce, there being one main path along the hills on each side of the river. White men could not travel them except under the ever present menace of attack by northern Indians. There were practically no cleared fields except around Indian towns. These were cultivated by the Indians until forsaken by them and appropriated by white men.

The settler had to cut the great trees of the forest to clear away the space where he wished to build his cabin and to plant his crop. There were few trees small enough to be easy to handle, and it was necessary that he glean from the forest at great physical effort such as were of fit size for the building of his log cabin. At first he fashioned this in much the same style as the Negro cabins of ante-bellum days—small but warm. His first chimney was of mud and sticks, unless, perchance, he located his home near the hills where nature furnished a small out-cropping of stone. Perchance also, he or a neighbor knew how to make brick. In that event he fashioned his chimney and his floor of bricks. Nails were scarce and at a premium. Wooden pegs were usually shaped and used for heavy construction. The few nails available were usually made by local blacksmiths.

After a dwelling for himself, came the need of housing for his stock, as he acquired it, and finally barns for his harvest. As tobacco enlarged its place in the program of the farmer, the tobacco warehouse became one of the most important out-buildings of the large farms. John Rice built a 20 by 60 foot one in 1684 [O1, p. 76]. Henry Corbin's was 60 feet long. These were among the largest planters. Most farms had tobacco warehouses smaller than these; but since the buildings were expensive, and it was difficult to get the tobacco to the wharf when the vessels were loading, the county, in 1680, built a public warehouse where the tobacco could be brought and stored until shipped. This, very suitably, was built at the new "town of trade," Hobbs His Hole, now Tappahannock.

In 1683, the county purchased stilliards (steelyards) to be kept at the warehouse for the use of the planters in weighing their tobacco, and a book in which to record all such weights before the tobacco was deposited or shipped [O1, p. 43]. At this time there was ordered out of England sealed measures, yard & ell, &c. &c., also small weights and small stilliards, scaled measures of bushel, peck, gallon and quart [O1, p. 43]. On February 3, 1683, the sheriff was ordered to take into his possession all weights and seals that were in the possession of Col.

Thomas Goodrich while living [O2, p. 69]. Goodrich had been in charge of the warehouse at Hobbs Hole, which had been built on his property.

After the decline in the price of tobacco, there came a popular demand for standardization in the grading of tobacco. In 1666, the good grade of tobacco is specified in the words, "Good, sound, bright and large Oranoco Tobacco" [O4, p. 192]. This same brand of Oranoco Tobacco is often referred to, as it is in 1682.

It became unlawful for anyone to tend or house seconds or slips. This law was enforced in Rappahannock County in 1683 [O1, p. 60]. In 1684 a reward was offered for the arrest of any violator of this law.

In the absence of a stable gold currency, tobacco, the principal export of the colony, became the monetary commodity of the colony, and all things here were sold in terms of tobacco value. Unfortunately it was a very unstable currency as its value was dependent upon a fluctuating English marked. When times were hard in England, the price of tobacco went down and the Virginia planter suffered.

England was often embroiled in war either at home or abroad. Often her enemies' fleets were formidable on the high seas, and played havoc with English merchant ships along the shipping lanes of trade with Virginia. This vitally affected the value of tobacco. In 1652, the first Navigation Act brought on war with the Dutch, whose ships were the chief carriers of Europe. the result was that the tobacco market became yet more demoralized, and in some years, there was practically no market. Mr. Thomas Griffin wrote a letter from London on November 22, 1655, to Mr. Samuel Tinsey, commander of the ship *Henry and David*, in which he said that tobacco was so low that four pence per pound was rarely given. Griffin referred to goods he left in the hands of Rose in Virginia, and asked that the letter be shown to "my boy."

As early as 1665, over-production became a contributing cause to the decline in price. By 1663, with the colony spread out into the Rappahannock valley, the Potomac valley, and over to the Eastern Shore, the production of tobacco had so increased that its supply far exceeded its demand.

Before 1663, attempts had been made to get Maryland to agree to some program of regulating tobacco production, but all efforts had failed. However, by June 1666, Virginia and Maryland agreed, and it was ordered by act of Assembly that there should be no tobacco planted between February 1666/7 and the first of February 1667/8. To keep the colonist working substitute crops of flax and hemp were urged. In spite of such drastic procedure, times did not greatly improve. In the following years greater efforts were made to grade tobacco.

By 1672, Charles II had begun strongly to favor the Catholics. Internal financial troubles developed in England. The king closed the exchequer and took out £200,000. This brought about a financial panic in England. To distract attention from the home government, the king declared war against Holland. This combination of panic and war again ruined the tobacco market, and greatly increased the tax burdens of the colony. The poor price of tobacco continued and was added to the grievances of the people at the time of the Indian massacres in Rappahannock County in 1675.

The value of tobacco was so fluctuating that the use of English sterling as the medium of exchange increased. Prices so declined that in July 1689 a hogshead of tobacco containing 100 pounds was declared to be worth only thirty shillings or one and a half pounds sterling [O2, p. 157]. However, when the war clouds rolled away, prices shot up again. By October 4, 1690, 10,000 pounds of good tobacco were worth fifty pounds sterling [O8, p. 256].

In considering land values of Rappahannock County, there must be taken into account a few factors that tended to stabilize the price of land, and a number of factors that tended to cause fluctuating prices. First of all there were always frontier lands and delinquent lands that could be gotten in fifty-acre units for the pains of transporting an immigrant into the colony. This exchange had a decided influence in regulating and holding down the price. However, the texture of the soil and the location of the land had a considerable influence on the value. The higher priced land was quite naturally the best adapted to tobacco growing. The highest priced was that best suited to tobacco and located on or near a navigable river or creek.

Land next in value to tobacco land was river valley land, which, though not adapted to tobacco, yet produced good corn and other crops. Rough and rugged inland territory remote from navigable streams seems to have been third in value. Least valuable of all were the marshes and pocosons along the streams and rivers. Before Bacon's Rebellion the distance from Indians was a factor what somewhat influenced the value of land. In 1662, there were sold 365 acres of land located on the Dragon Swamp for nineteen pounds current money of England [D2, p. 290].

Of the many conveyances recorded, the greater number fail to stipulate what the consideration in tobacco actually was. A few do give the price. Between 1660 and 1665, the average price of land in this county located near water was twenty pounds of tobacco per acre, the highest price paid being twenty-six pounds per acre. Rarely did land sell under twenty pounds. This, it will be remembered, was at a time when the price of tobacco was very low. The low price at which land could be purchased was partly due to the fact that not a great deal of land had been patented at that time, and it could easily be gotten by patent.

In 1673, the great Northern Neck peninsula was given to Lord Culpeper in spite of bitter protest by pioneers owning land within this area, and land values there were thrown into a chaotic condition. The entire foundation of the economic structure was disrupted. A vast difference existed between the escheating of land to the crown and the escheating of land to Culpeper. Laws and regulations governed its being reclaimed from the government; but in the Northern Neck if taxes were not paid on date due the land reverted to an individual who could do without hinderance what he chose with it. The owner of a valuable piece of land must be especially on guard to pay his taxes promptly, or he had but a meagre chance of getting it back once it became escheat.

From 1672 to 1690 there were scarce a score of patents recorded for the north side of the Rappahannock River. These were mostly where the vested title of the land had first passed by deed and not by assignment. Newcomers were slow to buy land there. Not until 1690, when the proprietor of the Northern Neck began to give patents and to escheat lands under regulations similar to those used by the governor for other parts of the colony, did land values improve in the Northern Neck.

Quite early the first water grist mills appear in the county. Which mill was the first one built is not known, but the first reference to a mill that we find is to Col. Moore Fantleroy's, which was completed by March 20, 1659. Andrew Gilson's mill may have been built sooner. There were at least twelve such mills in the county before 1692.

Many creeks and streams provided sites suitable for this type of mill. It was important that the mill be accessible by boat as well as by horse, since in the early years of the country's development most of the planters had their homes near the river or creek sides and could carry to mill much heavier loads by boat than was possible on the undeveloped paths over land.

For many generations the water grist mill was the most economical power unit available in rural sections. Only in the last generations did the patent roller mill begin supplanting the old stone mill, and the gas engine in any appreciable degree supplement or replace the power of falling water over the old wooden water wheel.

The mills gorund two types of meal. One was known as Indian meal and the other as English meal [O5, p. 64]. The former was the grist from Indian corn, and the latter, no doubt, the grist from wheat crushed in the same mill.

Prior to 1646 millers were allowed to take one-sixth part of the grain for toll.[52] Later this was thought to be too large a toll, and an act was passed by the Grand Assembly stating that millers were allowed to take only one-eigth of the grain for the grinding thereof.[53] This was not adequate in the eyes of many millers, and they, no doubt, refused to grind. It became necessary to pass an act requiring millers of public mills to grind grain whenever brought to the mill. Any offender was held liable to a fine of 1,000 pounds of tobacco for every offence.[54] This one-eights toll is taken to this day.

Col. Moore Fantleroy's mill was built by Richard Waddelle, who took the contract "to bring sufficient workmen to complete the building of a water grist mill by March 20, 1659, and agreed to employ all workmen needed for the job." This contract was signed in January 1658. The mill seems to have been built on

---

[52] Hening, Vol. 1, p. 301, November 1645, Act IV.
[53] Hening, Vol. 2, p. 242, October 1666, Act XIV, An act for Millers.
[54] Ibid.

Fantleroy's lower plantation on the Rappahannock River, and to have been located at the head of Farnham Creek.

The next mill mentioned was owned by Mr. Andrew Gilson prior to 1663. He finally sold it to John Weir with all water rights thereunto obtaining. It was on what is now called Mount Landing Creek, and a few yards above the spot where the present county road crosses Warings Mill Hill swamp on the road from Mount Landing to Caret.[55] The widow of John Weir married George Jones, and in 1677 they sold their equity in the mill to Thomas Bowler [D6, p. 153]. Robert Parker owned a part of this mill before his death [D6, p. 164]. Richard Gardner and wife Elizabeth sold her right and claim to it to Elizabeth Parker, the relict of Robert Parker [D7, p. 347].

There was a mill and a dam on Morattico swamp before March 25, 1663 [P.B. 5, p. 130]. It was called Morattico Mill on March 2, 1687 [O2, p. 20].

Old Piscataway Mill was located on the main west branch of Piscataway Creek swamp. On the southeast branch of Piscataway, known both as King's swamp and as Green swamp, and later named after various mill owners, was Beeby's Mill, which is still in ooperation, and is now known as Essex Mill. It is the property of Judge Deane Hundley of Dunnsville. Even in the last century this swamp has been navigable for good sized boats up to the mill. In later years there have been as many as three mills operating on this swamp.

On July 4, 1670, John Foxall of Pope's Creek bought from William Underwood Sr. a grist mill that was formerly in the possession of Archibald Combs, and later of John Payne [D4, p. 157; D7, pp. 121-2]. This mill was in Sittingbourne Parish in the vicinity of Pepetick Creek.

Robert Tomlin sold his mill on Totuskey to Mat. Wilcox, George Nichols, and Stephen Ryland in 1670 [D4, p. 327].

On September 7, 1687, Mathew Wilcox gave to Zachariah Nicholls a mill [O2, p. 47]. This mill formerly belonged to the said Nicholls's father [O2, p. 15]. It seems to have been located on the north side of Farnham Creek. The cost of the produce of this mill from 1678 to 1686 was 74,364 pounds of tobacco, and imbursements on the mill for the same time amounted to 87,651 pounds of tobacco; 8,760 pounds of this were allowed William Barber and John Alloway, administrators of the estate of Thomas Whitlock, for looking after the mill through those years [D.W.B. 1686]. The mill is referred to as William Barber's mill on July 6, 1687 [O2, p. 39].

Thomas Gunston bought a mill from Col. John Stone, commonly called Chestoon or Cheduxon Mill. This mill was conveyed to Col. John Stone on November 3, 1687 [D7, p. 273]. It was in Rappahannock Creek valley and was either on Mt. Airy pond or was on Menokin Run [O1, p. 257].

---

[55] Hening, Vol. 1, p. 99; D3, p. 460; D4, p. 102.

Henry Tandy built a mill on Occupacia Run by June 28, 1675, when he took Edward Moseley as a partner [D5, p. 424]. On February 12, 1683, Edward Moseley sold his part of Occupace Mill to Col. George Taylor [D7, p. 225].

There were also early mills near the mouth of Coleman's Creek, on Peumensen Creek, and on Golden Vale Creek. Taliaferro's Mill occupied the present mill site on what is now called Mill Creek, just below Port Royal.

Corn ground in these old mills varied in value from time to time somewhat as tobacco varied in price. In 1686, in the court of Rappahannock County, eight barrels of corn was declared by the court to be worth 1,000 pounds of tobacco [O1, p. 151]. In 1689, ten barrels of corn was declared to be worth 954 pounds of tobacco.[56]

There may have been a glass factory in old Rappahannock County, for in 1688, three cases of glass were shipped from here to New England.

Fish and oysters were among the principal sources of good in the colony, Beverley relates. Along the shores of the Rappahannock in 1661, this must have been true. Indians were allowed to secure licenses to oyster in the rivers provided two of the justices of the county saw fit to allow them to come among the English unarmed. This must have been a general practice here, for Rust Rock, one of the upper oyster rocks of the Rappahannock River, is very near sea level, and the Indians could actually have waded and picked up as many oysters as they wanted in the shallow waters. In many cases the sites of the old Indian towns on the Rappahannock River may today easily be located by the scattering of oyster shells that may still be seen on the high land close by.

An Ordinary

William Moss was issued a license to keep an ordinary (tavern) in 1685/6. Each license cost him two pounds sterling [O1, p. 212].

The names of several blacksmiths and wheelwrights have survived. Among them are John Chambers [O5, p. 232]; William Morgan, 1688; John English [D6, p. 1]; Charles Dodson, who used peach trees to make cart axles [D6, p. 112]. Edward James was a bricklayer [O2, pp. 55-6], and John Payne was a joiner in 1670 [D4, p. 467].

The following men are mentioned as carpenters: Walter Pavey [D6, p. 179; D7, p. 103]; Henry Tandy in 1670 [D4, pp. 184, 388]; Robert Bedwell [D2, p. 401 (327); D3, p. 434; D4, p. 182]; George Glascock [D.W.B.]; John Williams in 1660 [D2, p. 160 (88); D4, p. 113]; John Alloway in 1670 [D4, p. 371]; Valentine Allen [D4, p. 157]; David Hawsman [D4, p. 19]; and Thomas Maddison [D4, p. 48].

Sometimes a carpenter did the work of a cooper; but this was not usual, for there was a distinct group of coopers. Among them are found the names of: William Tignor in 1656 [L2, p. 122]; Michael Pattersley in 1653 [L1, p. 66]; Richard Holt in 1667 [D3, p. 276]; James Yates in 1667 [D3, p. 321]; and in 1689,

---

[56] Hening, Vol. 2, p. 222, October 1665, Act X, An act preparatory to a stint or cessation.

John Deane, a young man, indentured himself to serve five years to learn the cooper's trade [O2, p. 193].

In 1685, Frederick Grimshaw and Angel Jacobus failed to make sufficient casks to hold corn and tobacco according to their contract. They were fined for not making delivery of said casks by October 1, 1685 [O1, p. 128]. In 1688, James Tarpley [Trapley] won a suit with William Brockenbrough, who failed to deliver the following goods as per contract: 1000 staves of w. oak 5'6" by ¾", 500 w. oak heading of 36" long and 1" thick, 100 w. oak heading of 36" lond and 1" thick to be delivered at a convenient landing on Farnham Creek [O2, p. 171]. This material was to be used in making hogsheads.

The following is a list of equipment left by a carpenter and woodworker, December 28, 1683 [D6B, p. 23]: Part of a turning lave, one maindrill, four turning tools, 2 old fore plaines, one smoothing plaine, one old Joynter, one plow and two irons, 14 mounding plaines, 2 augers, one piercer, 3 mortis chisells, 2 pieces of plank. Mr. John Payne and John Sanders, according to their judgement have appraised them at 350 lbs. of tobacco. [signed] John Payne, John Sanders. Filed at Court Jan. 3, 1683/4. The most significant fact of the above inventory is that this man of modest equipment had fourteen moulding planes. This would strongly suggest that mouldings were extensively used in building the better homes of this area. Gregory Glascock owned both carpenter and "kooper" tools in 1689.

Ship builders seem to have done a lively business along the Rappahannock. Among them are found the names of: Seth Tinsley [D4, p. 159]; Simon Miller [D4, p. 266; D5, p. 165; D6, p. 82]; William Gray, Henry Peters [D2, p. 27]; and John Griffing. Thomas Sadler was a shoemaker in 1668 [D3, p. 507].

The following tailors are named: Anthony Williams in 1688 [O2, p. 166]; John Spicer in 1666 [D3, p. 276]; and John Soper [D3, p. 276]. Daniel Sansbury was indentured to serve as a tailor in 1689 [O2, p. 155]. Peter Byrom was a gunsmith. His name is variously spelled Byram, Byrum, Byrom and Byron.

Merchants

There were numerous merchants in the county. Thomas Bowler, of *Thomas Bowler & Co.*, came to Rappahannock County from Lancaster County [D3, p. 102; D2, pp. 279-80]. He was here prior to 1662.

Malachy Peale, a merchant, moved to Rappahannock from Stafford [D7, p. 486]. William Welsted had a son Samuel Welsted, who contracted to serve time as an apprentice to John Saffin, a merchant, to be taught the mystery and accomplishments of a merchant [D2, p. 276 (213)], in 1662. He further contracted not to marry until his time was up.

John Sampson, a merchant, died in 1685 [W2, p. 81]. Gerard Lowther, merchant, sued for payment of 8 pair of French shoes in 1690 [O2, p. 248]. Robert Coleman, Thomas Payne, William Hodgson, and others are among those named as merchants.

The following were merchants of England to whom tobacco was sent: Thomas Wise of London; Thomas Hardis of London, Peter Wadding of Bristol, Mr. Farnham of Liverpool. These were named as trustworthy merchants in 1675 [W2, p. 61].

Fences and Livestock

The planters early built rail fences about their fields and orchards; and outside of the fences cattle of all kinds were turned loose in the woods. Young horses and cattle would be left out all summer. Every planter was supposed to have a mark for his loose running cattle and his hogs. This marking of cattle was neglected somewhat in early days; but, about 1665, there was recorded a large number of marks of cattle.

Many pigs were born in the forest and went unmarked. The number was so great that, in some sections, they became a pest to the community. Beverley says that "hogs swarmed like vermin in the woods, lived on acorns, and were not fed." Often they were not even listed in the inventory of an estate. The General Court in James City, on March 21, 1658, gave Col. Moore Fantleroy, the first settler in those parts where he lived, permission to kill all hogs running at large and not branded for his own use and benefit [D2, p. 146 (113)]. It was unlawful to toll any marked animal, but one could capture unmarked stock at large [O2, pp. 168, 236].

Lack of proper shelter in winter was one of the serious problems confronting the stock raiser. Another was the fact that the forest was infested by wolves. These seemed to become even more numerous in the latter years of the county. Very early the General Court offered a reward of one hundred pounds of tobacco for every wolf head brought in. This reward was changed to one hundred pounds for a shot wolf head and one hundred and fifty pounds for a trapped wolf head. Sometimes, during a single county court, as many as a dozen wolf heads were brought for the reward.

Negro slaves were scarce during the period of old Rappahannock County, but their number was rapidly increasing. The number of indentured servants was apparently diminishing. In 1686, a Negro man was worth twenty-five pounds sterling [D.W.B.]. In the same record a Negro girl and an Indian boy were worth twenty pounds sterling; an old Negro woman was worth ten pounds sterling.

On November 14, 1679, John Rice was about to marry Mrs. Rebecca Travers, widow. She has reserved from her estate nine of her Negro slaves, including four colored men and their accepted wives, and one child [D6, p. 119].

Livestock was very valuable and contributed greatly to the development of the county. The following are some of the appraised values gleaned from inventories and sales recorded in the old records [D&B2, to p. 19]:

An old horse was valued at £1.11.00 in 1686.
Another horse was valued at £1.10.00.
A mare was valued at   1200   pounds of tobacco in 1682

A mare and colt were valued at	2000	do.
A guiding horse was valued at	1100	do.
A horse was valued at	1500	do.
A horse was valued at	1100	do.
A horse was valued at	1000	do.
An old horse was valued at	600	do.

The scarcity of horses listed in inventories is noticeable. They were little used except for riding.

A steer sold for 600 pounds of tobacco in August 1654 [L1, p. 164]

A cow for 600 pounds of tobacco in 1655 [L1, p. 212]

5 cows and calves were valued at 450 pounds of tobacco each in 1661

2 cows were valued at 400 pounds of tobacco each [D2, p. 200 (152)]

2 heifers were valued at 300 pounds of tobacco each

4 yearlings were valued at 125 pounds of tobacco each [D2, p. 200 (152)]

In September 1663, in the appraisal of the estate of James Williamson, the following values are given [D2, p. 294 (231)]:

6 cows total value	£15.00.00
3 heifers, do.	6.00.00
4 yearlings, do.	4.00.00
4 steers, do.	12.00.00
3 steers, do.	5.50.00
1 bull, do.	11.15.00
4 steers, do.	5.00.00
7 calves, do.	3.00.00
1 heifer, do.	2.00.00

In 1682, are recorded the following items [W2, pp. 2-19]:

4 oxen	value 700	pounds of tobacco each
1 steer	560	do.
6 steers, young & old	400	do.
2 steers, 7 years old	400	do.
4 steers, 2½ years old	250	do.
4 cows with calves	450	do.
9 cows with calves	500	do.
1 do.	600	do.
2 do.	500	do.
2 do.	450	do.
10 do.	400	do.
2 do.	510	do.
9 cows, young and old	360	do.
6 do.	400	do.
4 do. 2 years old	150	do.
1 do., do.	300	do.
9 do., do.	200	do.

2 heifers	300	do.
12 yearlings	200	do.
1 bull 3 years old	300	do.
1 bull 3 do.	200	do.

The above items are taken from a number of inventories occurring within the page designated.

The following items are listed in the inventory of the estate of Major Henry Smith in 1685 [W2, p. 38]:

7 cows with calves by their sides total value	3500	pounds of tobacco
5 do. more	2000	do.
4 steers, 2 of them 5 years old, and }		
2 about 13 years old }	1400	do.
8 yearling cattle & 1 other not yet found	800	do.
1 bull	200	do.
2 heifers	600	do.
1 lame stone horse named Sampson	600	do.
Major Smith riding nagg	1000	do.
Old horse and colt	1000	do.
A dark bay stone horse	800	do.
23 ewe & ram sheep at 90 a sheep	2250	do.
16 lambs at 45 a lamb	720	do.
8 cows	400	do.
2 cows & 2 calves	500	do.
2 cows & 1 calf	950	do.
2 cows 2 years old	300	do.
1 cow 3 years old & calf	400	do.
1 cow 4 years old, do.	450	do.
1 steer 5 years old	500	do.
2 steers 4 years old	400	do.
5 do., 2 do.	225	do.
4 yearling steers	125	do.
1 year old heifer	200	do.
1 bull 3 years old	250	do.

In the old manuscripts in the Essex County courthouse, there is record, dated March 1686/7, of 20 sheep valued at nine pounds sterling. In 1658, 33 hogs had been valued at 50 pounds of tobacco each [D2, p. 88 (68)].

The following is a list of some other items whose value is recorded:

- A small boat was valued at 11 pounds sterling in 1656 [D2, p. 79 (62)]
- A small boat was valued at 600 pounds tobacco in 1688 [D.W.B.]
- 750 six penny nails were worth 15 pounds of tobacco in 1657 [D2, p. 81 (63)]
- Several sorts of nails to the quantity of 6 or 7 thousand were valued at 200 pounds tobacco in 1682 [D2, p. 88 (69)]
- 2 used farm plows and irons were worth 500 pounds tobacco in 1683 [W2, p. 8]
- A used cart and wheels were worth 300 pounds tobacco in 1683 [W2, p. 8]

- Plow gear were valued at 15 shillings in 1658 [D2, p. 79 (62)]
- Bricks were about 10 for one pound tobacco in 1682 [W2, p. 5]
- A new bridle and saddle were worth 150 pounds tobacco in 1683 [W2, p. 8]
- 670 pounds of port were worth 1005 pounds tobacco in 1679 [D.W.B.]
- 9 pounds of shot were worth 13 pounds tobacco in 1658 [D2, p. 86]
- 2 deer skins were worth 20 pounds of tobacco in 1688 [D.W.B.]
- 1 old gun was worth 150 pounds tobacco in 1688 [D.W.B.]
- 6 canvas bags were worth 10 shillings in 1656 [D2, p. 79]
- A pocket Bible was worth 30 pounds tobacco in 1683 [W2, p. 8]
- A set of used carpenter and cooper tools was worth 600 pounds tobacco in 1689 [D.W.B.]
- The funeral charges of Robert Bayliss Jr., a man of more than ordinary means, were 1700 pounds tobacco in 1689 [D.W.B.]
- The funeral charges of William Gray, deceased, in 1683 were 1125 pounds tobacco [W2, p. 2]
- 8 barrels of Indian corn were worth £2.04.00 in 1656 [D2, p. 79]
- 1 barrel of Indian corn was worth 708 pounds tobacco in June 1657 [D2, p. 88]
- 4 barrels of Indian corn were worth 540 pounds tobacco in 1682 [W2, p. 1]
- 12 barrels of Indian corn were worth 1200 pounds tobacco in November 1682 [W2, p. 12]
- 7 barrels of Indian corn were worth 70 pounds tobacco each in 1686 [D.W.B.]
- Neighbors gathered a deceased man's corn crop and were allowed one bushel of corn for each day each man worked in 1682 [W2, p. 12]
- 6 bushels of salt were worth 12 shillings in 1656 [D2, p. 79]
- 3 bushels of sale were worth 100 pounds tobacco in 1683 [W2, p. 8]
- 2 bushels of beans were worth 100 pounds tobacco in 1682 [W2, p. 12]
- 3 bushels of peas were worth 30 pounds tobacco per bushel in 1686 [D.W.B.]
- 4 ells of canvas was worth 40 pounds tobacco in 1658 [D2, p. 88]
- 2 pair of stockings were worth 120 pounds tobacco in 1682 [W2, p. 1]
- 7 yards of red cotton cloth were worth 84 pounds tobacco in 1683 [W2, p. 8]
- 3 ells of flaxon cloth were worth 60 pounds tobacco in 1683 [W2, p. 8]
- 2 yards of calico cloth were worth 20 pounds tobacco in 1683 [W2, p. 8]
- 7½ yards of fine serge were worth 230 pounds tobacco in 1683 [W2, p. 8]
- 3½ yards of flannel were worth 65 pounds tobacco in 1683 [W2, p. 8]
- A buckskin coat and breaches were exchanged for a horse in 1690 [O2, p. 223]

The following values of used items are among those recorded:
- 3 table cloths and 12 napkins were worth 1 pound sterling in 1658 [D2, p. 76]
- A brass pestle and mortar was worth 5 shillings in 1658 [D2, p. 79]
- 3 white dishes were worth 1 shilling 6 pence in 1658 [D2, p. 76]
- 1 pewter flagon was worth 4 shillings 6 pence in 1658 [D2, p. 78]
- 10 of Sherlock's old earthen pans were worth 70 pounds tobacco in 1683 [W2, p. 8]
- 6 pewter plates were worth 60 pounds tobacco in 1683 [W2, p. 7]
- 1 small ceilskin [sealskin] trunk was worth 50 pounds tobacco in 1683 [W2, p. 7]

After the failure of tobacco prices in 1673, an order was issued by the Grand Assembly at James City that the county courts purchase one quart of hemp seed and one quart of flax seed for every tithable in the county, and that the court distribute the seed among the planters. A heavy fine should be imposed for their failure to do so. Each tithable was required to raise 1 pound of hemp seed and of flax seed each or 2 pounds of either, or to be fined 50 pounds tobacco for each pound not produced.[57] This flax was to be worked into linen cloth and the hemp worked into ropes and bags. This law was repealed in 1685, and re-enacted about the time of the close of Rappahannock County.

In 1684, before the act was repealed, several of the larger planters had their production certified to the General Assembly at James City by the court of Rappahannock County. James Bowler presented to court 35¾ ells of linen of his own growth and manufacture. This good was ¾ ell wide.[58] He presented 47 yards of linsey-woolsey of the same width and three pecks of flax seed. Robert Parker presented and had certified ten pecks of flax seed. Samuel Bloomfield had certified 4 bushels of hemp seed, and ½ bushel of flax seed, and 28 yards of wollen cloth one yard wide. Henry Williamson reported 5½ pecks of flax seed of his own growth. Henry Awbery reported eight pecks of hemp seed and fifty six ells of cloth ¾ ell wide and made by him [O1, pp. 23-4].

One of the planters reported the making of three pair of sheets of canvas 36 ells long and 10 ells wide valued by court at 600 pounds tobacco [O1, p. 146]. Robert Paine owned a large loom, and one of his men, named Taylor, operated it in 1690 [O2, p. 217]. Major Henry Smith had a spinning wheel.

These instances show the general trend of the age to produce at home the cloth necessary for making the clothes of the family and the dependents of the planter. In 1690 there had been no compulsory law for production of this kind. However, since the policy had proved beneficial, it was deemed good and wise that all should be required to produce the cloth consumed in daily life, and the law was re-enacted.

No Minerals

In the writing of deeds, there is practically no mention of mineral rights. In only one deed for land does the owner stipulate the conveyance of mineral rights. In the assumption that there were no valuable minerals, this seems to have proved the first settlers to have been right, as ten generations have passed and as yet no rich deposit of minerals has been found.

Wood

Wood was here in abundance, and was destroyed in great quantities. Beverley records that "all fuel was free for the hauling and that much timber was

---

[57] Hening, Vol. 2, p. 306, October 1673, Act IV, An act for the advancement of the manufactory
[58] An ell was about 45 inches.

burned for the clearing of land." Some was used in the making of boats, in building houses, and fences, and for many other needs of the planters.

In 1681, John Mills took a contract to saw a bill of 2,000 feet of one-inch boards of lumber for a house, and in exchange Thomas Harwar gave him a place on Morattico Creek [*D6, p. 144*]. In 1662, William Barber sold 250 acres of land back from the water for the right to cut timber for 1,000 years from the 1400-acre tract of John Ingram on Totuskey Creek, to build houses and boats, but not to sell [D2, p. 269 (206)].

Trapping

Trapping fur bearing animals as a source of income to the colony did not take as large a place as it might have. As before stated, it was a source of friction with the Indians and of hostility to Berkeley when it was felt that he controlled the industry to his own advantage. The general laws of the colony did not encourage the trapping of furs for income. It seems to have been the policy to encourage planters to trap wolves, but to discourage them from trapping with the idea of shipping furs to England. The local court as early as 1650 paid 150 pounds tobacco for each wolf head, but not until September 1671 was the extra duty tax on furs repealed, making it profitable to ship to England. There had been, however, a certain amount of smuggling of furs out of the country. John Saffin of Boston, New England, was accused in court here of purchasing and shipping hides out of the colony contrary to law, in the spring of 1671 [D4, p. 228]. There must have been many beavers caught, for early land surveys frequently refer to beaver swamps or dams.

Beverley tells how some animals were trapped. "For wolves," he wrote, "they make traps & set guns bated in the woods so that when he pulls the bate the trigger is tripped & the gun discharges upon him." They were caught in many ways:

> Stalking up to it by horses side or to cut down trees where deer could come & eat leaves, & setting sharpened stakes aback of fence where deer are in the habit of coming and jumping; the sharpened stakes penetrating the body of the deer as it lights in its favorite field of peas which they love extremely.

And again he wrote, "that destroying vermin was done by small dogs at night and that raccoons, possums, & foxes were in abundance around the plantation."

Many of these animals were used for food and their skins for coverings. Venison was considered choice food. Deer skins were used for coats and breeches. Fur trapping was for the most part carried on by the Indians, to whom it soon became an important source of income; but some of the white settlers were also able to make considerable profit from it. In January 1664, the catch of one English trapper was recorded in the inventory of a colonist's estate [D2, p. 402 (329)]:

3 otter skins were valued at 50 pounds of tobacco each	150 pounds
2 fox skins were valued at 10 pounds of tobacco each	20 pounds
2 fox skins were valued at 5 pounds of tobacco each	230 pounds
4 raccoon skins were valued at 10 pounds of tobacco each	40 pounds

Rum and Birth of of a King's Son

In 1652, in Book 1 of Lancaster County records, rum is called strong water. In 1683, in old Rappahannock County, a liberal feast was declared upon the birth of a son of King Charles II. A large quantity of rum was consumed in a single day. Occasionally a man was charged with selling drinks on Sunday or without a license. Most of the liquor seems not to have been distilled here, but to have been shipped in, for by 1689 the rum imports to the Rappahannock River had reached the figure of 6,760 gallons in one year. It was valued at £84.10.10.

The ships bringing that cargo of rum into the Rappahannock River that year were: *The Adventure* of London, *Haves Increase* of Virginia, *The Fast* of Bristol, *William and John* of Belfast, and *Port Royal* of Barbadoes.[59]

The next year the ships *Little Edward* of Virginia and *His Increase* brought in 5,505 gallons of rum valued at £66.16.03.[60]

Gun and Powder

A gun was worth 150 pounds of tobacco in 1683. Two pounds of powder were worth 450 pounds of tobacco in 1689 [O2, p. 174].

Postal System

During the history of old Rappahannock County there was no postal system; but, by 1693, one was established throughout the colony; and to a certain extent all ferries came under the control of the postmaster general [LO1, p. 135].

---

[59] Colonial Papers of 1690.
[60] Ibid.

CHAPTER 10

Old Rappahannock County
Courthouses

The earliest courts held in Rappahannock valley were those of Northumberland and Lancaster counties. These were conducted in the homes of different prominent planters or justices, and rarely were any two successive courts held at the same place.

So difficult was transportation that, in the first years of the settlement, no one place could be designated for a courthouse. It was necessary for the court to move from place to place to hear and judge the differences and complaints of the people.

This condition was not satisfactory; and, as soon as seemed practical, the justices began to consider the purchase of permanent quarters for the court. At the February court in 1654/5, the court ordered that the land at Corotoman lying between the lands of Grimes and Merriman be surveyed for a courthouse, and be patented and paid for [L1, p. 172].

According to Hening, the Lancaster County courthouse was on the north side of the Corotoman River against the place where ships ride, and by a creek that divided it from the land of Mr. Chewning. It was on this same creek that the Assembly ordered a town to be built in 1680.[61]

By June 6, 1655, "Major John Carter hath undertaken to provide for the building of a Court House on the land on Corotomon" [L1, p. 201]. The nails for the lower courthouse, furnished by Maior [Major] John Carter, cost 600 pounds of tobacco. Vincent Stanford was paid 1500 pounds of tobacco for several persons employed in building one of the houses.

The county levy of 1656 states that the cost of two courthouses was 10,000 pounds of tobacco. The lower courthouse was built by William Neasham, about October 25, 1655 [L1, p. 212]. On the first Wednesday in December 1656, the first court for the lower parts was ordered to be kept at the Court House [L1, p. 297].[62]

Mr. William Underwood was asked to provide for the building of a courthouse "on land near adjoining to his house and the charge thereof to be borne by the publique," at the same time that John Carter was asked to provide for the building of the lower courthouse, June 6, 1655 [L1, p. 201]. On this same day the court ordered men to buy housing (lumber) of Col. Moore Fantleroy for the upper court [L1, p. 199]. This courthouse was close to the line of Col. Fantleroy, whose land joined William Underwood's. Later deeds show that the courthouse actually stood on Underwood's land.

---

[61] Hening, Vol. 2, p. 473, June 1680, Act V, An act for cohabitation and encouragement of trade
[62] Previously courts were held in private homes, as stated above.

95

The furniture for the two courthouses cost 3,000 pounds of tobacco. A small clerk's table of this equipment is still in existence. In August 1656, John Paine was ordered to purchase for the service of the county one paire of stocks and a whipping post. For the wooden work thereof he was to receive of the county 400 pounds of tobacco, the iron work being otherwise provided [L1, p. 267].

It was ordered at the February court in 1655 that Edward Dale, "now clerk of the county," shall have the use of the courthouse to be built by Mr. Neasham (in Corotoman) with the use of the land so long as he shall remain clerk of the county [L1, p. 256].

The old courthouse for the upper parts of old Lancaster County became the first courthouse of old Rappahannock County. It was located on the north side of the Rappahannock River on an attractive elevation of rich level valley land fifteen feet above and nigh unto the river, but overlooking the mouth of a deep, smooth and placid creek but little more than 100 feet wide, first known as Bushwood Creek [P.B. 2, p. 231, May 22, 1650]. This creek was later called Mangorite; and is now called Little Carter's Creek. The great marsh above it is still called Mangorite.

Immediately in front of the courthouse lawn was a steep slope to a level space some two or three feet above high water. This piece of ground was about 100 feet wide and about two hundred feet long. It was a small part of the knob-like point formed through the ages by the accumulating shore sand. The south side of this point is constantly washed by the waves of the river. The northwest side is sheltered; and the creek waters in front of it afford an excellent harbor, being protected on the west by the extreme lower peninsula of Mangorite marsh, and on the north and east by this same great marsh and the upland of rich farm land which parallels the main course of the river.

The first shipping point of which we have any record in these parts was located on this point near the mouth of this sheltered creek. As early as 1651 this place was called Bushwood. The name Bushwood is used several times in reference to the place as a town or section; but the section, as well as the creek, soon took the name of Mangorite. This was the name of the farm above Underwood's, which belonged to Col. Moore Fantleroy, and embraced the greater part of the entire creek valley.

Just how long this courthouse continued to be at Bushwood cannot be determined. When William Underwood, justice, conveyed the upper half of his 1400-acre tract in 1659, he reserved the courthouse and did not then sell it. On July 1, 1662, Richard Loes and wife Elizabeth joined with Rice Jones and wife Margaret and sold this same tract of 700 acres, but explicitly stated that the courthouse was excepted and not a part of the conveyance [D2, pp. 70, 235-6 (179), 256 (194)].

About 1681, a town for trade was ordered established in every county. Rappahannock County being divided by a great river, it was natural that each side of the river should want the town on its side. In 1680, the Grand Assembly had ordered a town established at Hobbs His Hole, now Tappahannock. In September 1680, Benjamin Goodrich of Hobbs His Hole accordingly had 50 acres of land surveyed by Major George Morris. This land was on the south side of the river. He hoped to gain the support of friends and get the crown to purchase it as the port of trade.

This offering of this land by Goodrich and the act of Assembly designating Hobbs His Hole as the port must have met with great opposition from the former supporters of Berkeley because of the support given Bacon by Benjamin Goodrich and his father. Goodrich was trying to sell the land to help pay the fine of 100,000 pounds of tobacco that had been imposed on him and his father.

Berkeley's friends and a majority of the county court were against him, for most of the justices in office had been placed there by Berkeley. The court went so far as to purchase fifty acres, the prescribed acreage for the town, on the north side of the river. They doubtless offered this to the crown and made every effort to get it accepted.

Fortunately for Goodrich, the decision did not rest with the court, but with the Grand Assembly, whose members were elected by the people. The representatives from Rappahannock County were William Lloyd, who lived on Farnham Creek, and Thomas Goldman, who lived on the north[63] side of Mount Landing Creek at *Goldberry*. They spoke for the mass of the people as well as for themselves.

Lloyd's lands were far removed from the central part of the county, and he was not personally interested in either sale. He seems to have been of a smooth and placid nature, and showed no disposition to oppose the people who had elected him.

Thomas Goldman was a man of deeds, of action. He knew that the blame for Bacon's Rebellion rested not on Bacon and his friends, but on Berkeley and his supporters. His lands adjoined those of Goodrich. He knew the Goodrich Family at church and in their home. Col. Thomas Goodrich had maintained a boys' school to which his children had probably gone. They were friends and neighbors.

The people were kindly disposed toward Goodrich, who had aided them in defense of their homes in 1676, and had suffered for it.

Goldman, in defiance of the majority of the court and of the friends of Berkeley, threw his influence to Goodrich, and had the Assembly purchase Hobbs His Hole as the port. The land was purchased the 25th of March 1682, it being the first day of the New Year according to the Julian calendar. Only two lots in the new town were sold until October 9, 1691, at which date lots were purchased by twenty-seven persons at a cost of 125 pounds of tobacco each [O2, pp. 329-31].

---

[63] Corrected in a later copy to "south."

On the fifty acres purchased by the court of Rappahannock County on the north side of the river was erected the second courthouse for that section. This served the people on the north side for some years after the establishment of Richmond County. The exact location of this tract is not known. Later records reveal that it was in Sittingbourne Parish. This being so, it must have been above Rappahannock Creek, now called Cat Point Creek, which was the lower parish line at that time.

The following is a deed pertaining to this land [D6, pp. 145-a (323-4)]:

Know all men by these pr'sents that wee Will: Moss and of ye County of Rappa: with Bridgett my Wife for divers good Causes & considerations us thereunto moveing for us our heires Exors. admrs. & every of us have given granted bargained sould alliened confessed & Confirmed & delivered and by these pr'sents doe give grant bargain sell confess & Confirm & deliver unto John ffennell of ye same County & ffrances his wife their heires Exors. admins. assigns a certaine part or parcell of Land Contained specified & mentioned in my Patent for 1060 Acres of land & marsh in the County aforest. and thereinmentioned to begin at a gumm tree ye Corner tree of Mr. James Williamson's Land and Stower Creek, & from thence all ye land and marsh along ye line specified in the said Pattent on the eastermost side of ye sd. Creek soe farr as my land Extends the said Creek being the bound thereto. It being about fifty acres of land & marsh. To have & to hold all & and Every part & parcell of ye sd. land & marsh soe mentioned as before to them the sd. John & ffrances ffennell their & either of their heires Exors. admrs. & assigns from the day of the date of these pr'sents for evermore, etc.

In witness whereof we have hereunto sett our hands & seals this 20th day of October 1664. Sealed & delivered in ye p'sence of George Davis, Edmund Scott, Stephen Cater. [signed] the marke of William Moss (seal), the marke of Bridget Moss (seal).

Recorded in the County Court of Rappahannock County 3 9ber [November] 1681.   [signed] Edmond Craske, Clerk of Court

I ye within named John ffennell & ffrances my wife for & in Consideration of the sume of twelve thousand pounds of tobo. & cask to use in hand paid & ordered to be paid have given granted bargained sold assigned transferred & sett over to Coll. John Stone & Lt. Coll. William Loyd theire heires assignes & successors for ye use of ye County of Rappa. for Ever all ye within mentioned bargained land & premises with the appurtenances & every part thereof ... unto ye said Coll. John Stone & Lt. Coll. William Loyd their heires & successors, Justices of ye peace for ye County of Rappa. for ye use of ye said County forever free & Cleere of all Charges & incumbrances wt. soever (ye rent or rents to all Cheriff lord or lords of ye p'mises in respect to his or her seigniory or sinnioryes only Excepted). In witness whereof wee have hereunto sett our hands & seales ye third day of November Anno Domi 1681 ... Signum John [his mark] ffennell (seal), ffrances [her mark] ffennell (seal).

Sealed & delivered in the pr'sence of us
Edmund Craske

Benja. Goodrich
Jo: Almond
Edw: Adcock
Recognit in the County Court of Rappa. 3d day 9ber [November] 1681

The records show that the new county court property was a farm of some size with its own orchard, fields and woods. John Fenner [sic] resided in the courthouse. As keeper he was given free use of the house and place for the year 1684 [O1, p. 70]. The tenant who succeeded him was Peter Taylor, who was to live there and to have the use of the said house and plantation for keeping the said house and pasture fence in tenantable repair and for keeping fire sufficient during the sessions of every court [O1, p. 60]. A little later the court ordered Patrick Norton to clear the road from Rappahannock Bridge by Coll. Stone's mill to the courthouse, and particularly that part thereof which lay by Henry Bruce's plantation [O1, p. 75].

John Wariner was the next person to occupy the courthouse. In February 1687/8, he was given a contract similar to those previously issued with the additional phrase that he build a good fence about the orchard [O2, p. 58].

This courthouse was used by the county for the meetings of the court on the north side until the close of the county. After the formation of Richmond County, the court was moved to Warsaw where it is yet held. After the old courthouse and land had been paid for out of the county levy, the court saw fit to obligate itself to the additional expense of remodeling the old residence that it had bought so that it would be more suitable for court. The following order was entered by the court May 7, 1685, regarding the northside meeting place [O1, p. 131]:

Whereas it is agreed between this Court and Thomas Bradly that ye sd. Bradly do between this and the beginning of next July make and in Workmanlike manner set up Banisters Cross the roome where the Court is held on the North side the River of an usual highth & distance & incloseing them with a doore to pass to the Table convenient in some part of the sd. being, And that the sd. Bradley to make a form answerable to the said Table and a Bench of plank sufficient to sitt upon in the roome & place of the Bench that now is, also a Chaire for the President of the Court at the upper end of the Table next the Shed and lastly that he raise and enlarge both windows of the courthouse next the Orchard & make one more window on the same side foure feet in length & of a proportionable width and to fill up the back door of the sd. Roome if it shall hereafter seem necessary for wch: work to be done & performed in manner at the time aforesaid, this Court have ordered that the sd. Thomas Bradley be allowed at the next laying of the County Leavey eleven hundred pounds of Tobb: & cask convenient. It is also further ordered that the sd. Bradley during the time he shall be setting up & finishing the sd. work, have [his] dyett & lodging to wth: Peter Taylor who is also ordered a satisfaction for the same to be allowed at the next laying of the County Leavey."

County Prison

On this same day [May 7, 1685] the county prison on the north side of the river was ordered to be built [O1, pp. 130-1]. The lock for this prison door was ordered to be made, and was to cost 200 pounds of tobacco [O2, p. 38].

That this Court have covinanted & agreed to & with Capt. George Tayler of this County well and workmanlike to erect built & sett up in a place convenient on the County Land on the North side of the river whereon the Courthouse now stands, a good & sufficient Prison containing Fifteen foot in width Twenty foot in length seven & half foot in highth under a Stronge Doore providing Substantial hookes and hinges for the same, Also a stud round the sd. Building with strong studs in distance one from the other not exceeding six inches, Further that the sd. Capt. Tayler doth agree at this own proper cost & charge to find all materialls whatsoever fitt for setting up & finishing the sd. Building or Prison except a Lock for the Doore thereof as also to erect set up and finish the said Building (or cause the same to be don) well & in workmalike manner as aforesd. by the last of October next ensueing having Liberty to cut down & use about the sd. Building such Timber as he can find growing upon the sd. Land belonging to the County. In Consideration of wch: sd. Building or Prison to be done & finished in manner & at ye time aforesd. this Court do covinant & grant to pay unto the sd. Capt. Tayler Six thousand pounds of Tobb: & cask convenient in the County to be raised & paid out of the County Leavey this ensueing yeare.

Location of Courthouse

The grounds whereon stood the courthouse for the north side of old Rappahannock County were cut out of the patent of 1060 acres of land taken by William Moss. Moss had several tracts. At the time of his death he left considerable land in the vicinity of Doctor and Water View creeks. The latter might have been Storehouse Creek. The deed of 1662 stated that the lands were on Store House Creek. They adjoined the lands of James Williamson; but could hardly have adjoined the home plantation of Williamson, which was *Cobham Park*, east of what is now called Ball's Creek, as later records show that the courthouse was not far removed from landholders who dwelt on the north side of Rappahannock Creek.

On January 3, 1693/4, the court of Richmond County had already moved to the new location on what is now the court lot at Warsaw. On that date it was ordered that the deed for the old courthouse land, acknowledged by James Orchard to Captain Arthur Spicer, be recorded. This was the land on which the old courthouse stood [R O1, p. 157].

On July 4, 1722, Charles Barber and John Tayloe leased to William Fantleroy of Sittingbourne Parish, for five shillings, seventy acres in Sittingbourne Parish, commonly called the old court house tract, it being part of a tract formerly patented by William Moss [R D8, p. 136]. This places the old courthouse tract above Rappahannock Creek.

Location of Southside Courthouse

It is difficult to ascertain just where the first clerk's office for the south side of the river was located. The early court records being lost, there are extant few orders regarding it. When the orders begin in 1682, the southside courthouse was already in use. There are several known facts concerning this old courthouse, but they are confusing. Almost nothing is known regarding this courthouse or these courthouses prior to the establishment of the one at Hobbs His Hole.

After 1682, the ferry across the river on court days ran from the mouth of Rappahannock Creek to Mr. Daingerfield's landing. People going to court walked from the landing to the courthouse not far distant. This reference is to William Daingerfield's place, which was, in 1680 and later, southeast of Mount Landing Creek.[64]

Another item of information giving a hint of the location of the southside courthouse was that on a cold wintry day, December 6, 1688, because of the cold inclement weather, court adjourned at noon to meet later in the house of Robert Coleman [O2, p. 134]. Coleman was living in the town of New Plymouth, or Hobbs His Hole, now Tappahannock. It was at his home that the people met in 1682 for the auction of the lots of the new town of New Plymouth, when twenty-seven lots were sold.

It is apparent that the courthouse was not far from Hobbs His Hole, for on March 5, 1690/1 [O2, p. 289], the court ordered Mr. Robert Coleman to:

> forthwith take care of the courthouse of this county on the south side of the river, and to repair the benches thereof, and place others where they were wanting, erect new banisters in room of the old but more firm and substantial, and to do all other work that should be found wanting, and be necessary for the said Courthouse, and that he be paid for the same (if done) out of the next levy.

From this it is evident that the courthouse was in the same place for some years, and in or in the vicinity of Tappahannock.

Some Clerks of Court

The first clerk of Rappahannock County was Anthony Stephens. He shared a patent in the head of Farnham Creek in 1662, soon after ceasing to act as clerk. He was probably associated in earlier years with the same northside section. Walter Granger, the second county clerk, also lived on the north side of the river on his patent near Rappahannock Creek. The residence of Francis Kirkman, the third clerk, is not established.

Robert Davis, or Davies alias Pain, the fourth clerk, patented land toward the head of Piscataway Creek in 1662, before he became clerk of the county. While clerk, he owned a home in town. In 1665, he patented 2580 acres on Lucas Creek

---

[64] See [Essex Co.] Land Trials, 1711-1716, showing a map made in 1680.

and about a mile from the river on the south side, now *Kinloch*. Edmund Crask, the next clerk, and the one who served the greatest length of time, lived back of Tappahannock, on the road to Mount Landing.

There are many references to court on the south side of the river. On December 6, 1687, "It is ordered that the allowance given Mr. Richard Robinson of Hobbs His Hole for accommodations at Court-times on the south side of the River do from henceforth cease and determine" [O2, p. 58]. The residence of Richard Robinson stood just south of the present Riverside Hotel in Tappahannock. Thus this order shows that the court met at Hobbs His Hole prior to this date.

Courts were usually called to order at eight in the morning on the first day of session; but on the second day of court they frequently convened at seven o'clock in order that the business of the day might be completed as early as possible that the people might go to their respective homes which were often at a great distance. Court met once each month, the meetings on the north side alternating with those on the south side. In Essex Deed Book 15, pages 22-23, there is a list of old records, including those of old Rappahannock County, in 1716.

Prison at Hobbs His Hole

At court on November 5, 1691, it was ordered that Thomas Monday some time between that and the tenth day of May next following do build a sufficient prison on the Town Land at Hobbs His Hole, on the south side of the county, according to the dimensions and work of the north side prison and that the said Monday be allowed for the same six thousand pounds of tobacco in cask on the present levy [O2, p. 335]. On February 3, 1691/2, following this order, the court ordered John Morgan not to be paid for making a prison lock until he mend all faults being made in said lock [O2, p. 336]. In 1705, this building was used as a school house [O3, p. 147].

Plan for Division of County, 1677

In 1677, a proposition for re-dividing the counties on the north side of the river, between the Rappahannock and the Potomac, was made. Each county of the Northern Neck peninsula sent two representatives to a conference that met at the home of Captain Thomas Beale on May 3, 1677, just south of Farmers Fork in what is now Richmond County. This conference seems to have accomplished little as the waterways were still too important to travel to give way to overland paths. The proposal put before the conference was that the peninsula be divided into counties by lines running crosswise, each county extending from river to river. At that time the plan failed. Little has ever been done; but in 1742, King George and Westmoreland re-arranged their boundary lines in accordance with this plan.

CHAPTER 11

Old Rappahannock County
Parishes

In the pioneer days of Charles River Shire, no white men lived in the Rappahannock valley. As Englishmen moved northward along the west shore of Chesapeake Bay from Charles River (now York), the church followed. The section became known as Cheskyack or Chesapeakus, and is supposed to have reached north to the Rappahannock River.

In 1640, John Rosier, clerk, was the officiating cure of York and Cheskyack Parishes.[65] During the massacre of 1644, residents of Cheskyack were almost, if not entirely, driven out; and there was little, if any, parish work done north of the York until 1649 when the treaty with Opecancanough forbidding colonization beyond the York River was repealed, and white men came in numbers across the York into what is now Gloucester and into the Rappahannock River valley.

The date, therefore, of September 1, 1649, which marks the permanent settlement of the Rappahannock River valley, may also be considered as the date on which the religion of Jesus Christ was brought into this valley; and, though the principal instrument, the Church of England, by which it expressed itself was dulled by secular politics and its doctrines modified by the domination of the English government, yet it came and served and survived in the hearts of men.

John Rosier

The section north of the Rappahannock River, early called Chickacoon, became a part of Northumberland County about 1648, and was known as the Parish of Northumberland, with John Rosier, clerk, officiating here also as a minister in 1649.

John Rosier should be regarded as one of the great pioneer preachers of early colonial Virginia. A minister of the north side of the York River in 1640, he was pioneering with the church in Northampton County from 1641 to 1646 [P.B. 2, p. 69]. He was preaching in Northumberland from 1650 to 1653; and there in 1652 was a signer of the oath of allegiance to the Commonwealth. Though he was regarded as a non-conformist, he served under both governments of England; and the lessons of the gospel he preached found a place in the hears of the pioneers on the frontiers of Virginia [N D&O, pp. 41, 47; P.B. 2, pp. 69, 274; P.B. 3, pp. 37, 327].

Early Church Sites

The history of the parishes of old Rappahannock County is checkered. At times the church made real progress; and again outside influences forced

---

[65] H.R. Mcilwaine, *Minutes of the Council and General Court of Colonial Virginia*, p. 496.

themselves upon the people, hindering and casting down the work of the church, and sometimes causing it to be looked upon as a mere catspaw of a tyrannical king or governor.

The primeval forests, the entire lack of roads, and the ever present danger of ambush caused all of the first settlements of this section to be built along the rivers and large streams. On these every man could travel to church with considerable safety in his own boat with his gun by his side. In open water danger from lurking foes was minimized. In reality the river was the one great highway from one end to the county to the other with the creeks and their branches serving as feeders. For this reason all early churches and courthouses were located near the water.

On two of the larger creeks, not far from the river, Charles Grimes, the first preacher to settle in the upper Rappahannock River valley, patented land. He took out his second patent in the upper portion of the county on the river itself. On the river too was the first tract of land that we know to have been bought for the purpose of building a church thereon. It was purchased from John Barrow. The second tract of land bought was at the mouth of and on the south side of Occupacia Creek. It was bought for Sittingbourne Parish. The shores of many important creeks, as well as the shores of the river itself, were at some time the home of some preacher of Rappahannock County. As late as 1688, Dual Peade [Denel Prad] patented land at the mouth of and on the south side of Piscaticon [Piscataway] Creek. This patent was convenient by water to many settlements and to the churches; but by land was less accessible. Even to him, after departure of the Indians from the lower part of the county, the water appeared the simplest and best mode of transportation to his churches.

Church Vestries

The parishes were first organized in those early days with eight vestrymen chosen by the vote of the freeholders to serve for life. When anyone of their number died or moved away, the remaining members of the vestry chose his successor. For this reason the vestry soon ceased to be an organization representing the people. The vestrymen, from among themselves, chose the churchwardens in rotation to serve for two years each [Beverley, p. 212]. The churchwardens were amenable to the county courts, and could be called in question and punished or fined if their offences so warranted.[66]

Since the parishes were a part of a governing organization of the county, they shared in and were supported by a regular county or parish levy. They do not seem to have had any other source of income until April 6, 1691, when an act was passed by the Assembly at James City providing that "one third of all furs and skins shipped out of the county, and one-third of all fines levied for profanity be used for the maintenance and encouragement of a pious ministry & be equally

---

[66] Hening, Vol. 1, p. 291, February 1644/5, ACT VI.

distributed among the ministers of God's word incumbent in the several parishes of the county" [EO1, p. 227].

Burial Places

In 1661, all parishes were required [Hening, Vol. 2, p. 53]:

to set aside three or four burial places in their respective parishes to be used as public burial ground, each place to have a good fence kept about it, and no person slave or free to be buried in any other place than those appointed, unless during his lifetime he had signified his desire to be buried in some particular place elsewhere.

Most, if not all of these sites have perished. One is thought to be preserved at *Belleview Farm* on the Rappahanock River northeast of Dunnsville.

Some Parish Difficulties

Even as in the colony as a whole, the problem of the selection of acceptable clergy in this section was an almost continuous one. The blame for this trouble did not always lie in the character of the clergy as various petitions of the vestries might lead one to think. Sometimes the vestries themselves or certain members would try to dictate to their preachers in matters beyond their authority. In St. Stephens Parish, New Kent, now King and Queen, the vestry became so unpopular with the people that the latter met, drew up, and dispatched a signed petition protesting against the members of the vestry and asking the governor to allow them to choose by election a new vestry. The petition, about 1683, reads as follows:[67]

To the Rt. Honnobl. Sr. Henry Chicheley, Kt.
His Maties. Deputy Governor & Capt. Genrll. of Virginia
And to the Honnobl. Councill of State

Wee the Subscribers, inhabitants & House Keepers of St. Stephens parish in the County of New Kent, most humbly Sheweth:

That your Petitioners have beene for severall yeares past burthened with an Illegal Vestry Elected & made up for the most part without the Knowledge or Consent of the parish as the law Injoynes, and of such Illiterate & Ignorant men as are, and have been, Ever Ruled and Awed by one or two particulars persons, who are soe Insulting, and of such Ill disposed & turbulent spirits & dispositions, That noe Minister Cann or will stay with us or teach amongst us, by wch. meanes the Service of God is wholly neglected, our Church gon to Ruine, and Church Desipline & Government almost Clerely laid aside:

And for as much as our parish is not Destitute of such Able, discreet, and honest men as may fittly supply the places of severall week & Ignorant persons of the present vestry according to the good Lawes of this Country, Your Petrs. In all humility Supplicateth your honnrs. that wee may have Liberty to Elect & make Choice of good

---

[67] *Virginia Magazine of History and Biography*, Vol. 41 No. 3 (July 1933), pp. 196-203.

Persons (for a new Vestry) as in our Judgmt. may seeme meet & Convenient which will Indubitately tend to the Glory of God, and the peace & welfare of the whole Parish.

And your Petrs. as in all Humility and Duty bound for your Honors., shall Every pray&. [signed]

William Wyatt	Jos. Cockerhan	Daniel Scandon	James Didlock
Jacob Lumpkin	Richard Owen	Thomas White	Timothy Carter
John Davis	John Madison	Edward Shurly	John Derham
William Burch	Jonathan Grilles	George Weston	John Major
Benj. Arnold	Edward Pigg	David Cave	Simon Ramsey
James Taylor	Nath. Vies	Edward Hynon	Samuel Conaway
William Parker	James Cammell	Richard Pollard	Alexander Cammell
William Hanes	William [ ] (?)	James Gray	William Finny
Abraham Estes	Mathw. Yorke	William Semore	Ringing Gardner
Alexander Smith	Thomas Hoskins	Joseph Haile	William Blake
George Bredings	Henry Phillips	Robert Newis	Thom. Plunkett
Robert Spencer	Henry Pigg	Jerimiah Claiton	Nicholas Abbott
Anthony Richardson	Robert Coleman	E [ ]undin	John Brae
Richard Harman	Timothy Sovey	Will ----- (?)	John Dobbs
John Wood	John Lylly	Will: Sh-----y	William Harper
John Richards	John Cooke	William W. Nichols	Rich. Williams
John Middleton	Dennis Scandon	William Holcomb	

Influence of Nathaniel Bacon Jr., The Rebel

Several laws enacted by the Assembly during Bacon's Rebellion were intended to better the relationship between the church governing powers and the laity. One of these would have gone far toward furthering the work of the church. The followers of Bacon realized that there was too little cooperation between the vestry and the people of the pew. Too often the custom of the vestrymen choosing successors to deceased vestrymen led to the continuance of the same families in office for generations. The system left the people helpless to deal with arrogant and quarreling vestrymen chosen regardless of the people's desires. To ameliorate this hardship, Bacon's Assembly enacted the following statute: "Whereas the long continuation of vestries in severall parishes in the country is presented a grievance for remedy whereof for the future ... freeholders and freemen ... to elect and make choice of twelve ... once in every three years."[68]

The law hardly had time to function before Berkeley came back into power; and this act, along with all the acts of Bacon's Assembly, was made null and void; and the laws governing vestries reverted to the original statutes. The people, however, did not easily surrender the objective of which Bacon had given them in a glimpse; and they continued to voice protests against unpopular vestrymen. In the petition of the people of St. Stephens Parish, they sought the right to choose their vestry under the assumption that the law of Bacon's Assembly was still operative. Actually, at this time, in 1683, the vestry could choose its own new members.

---

[68] Hening, Vol. 2, p. 356, June 1676, Act VI.

Some Church Laws, Customs and Difficulties

As only the local vestry had the power to employ preachers, the latter sometimes came and went in rapid succession. To fill the demands for new preachers, the Council at Jamestown sometimes offered as much as twenty pounds sterling for the importation of any minister into the colony.

The duty of the minister, once he was employed, was to comply with a rather strict program. He was ordered by law to preach every Sunday in a church or chapel of his parish.[69] He must preach the doctrine of the Church of England or "depart the colony with all convenience."[70] He must read the Common Prayer of the Church or be deprived of the benefit of any part of the levy.[71] The minister must also keep the records of the Parish, the vestry book, and the register according all deaths, births and marriages. He must call meetings of the vestry from time to time as occasion necessitated. He must act as a judge and try most of the cases involving a breach of moral conduct. He was expected to see to it that all laws regulating the duties of the parishioners to the church, such as attending the services and having their children christened, refraining from swearing, etc. were carried out. The clerk (minister) was expected to decide matters of domestic relationship and to look after the well-being of all orphans. As minister of the parish, he was known as and called the "Clerk of the Parish," and was generally designated and referred to in that capacity as "Clerk." Many of the registers kept by these clerks are in existence today.

During the latter years of old Rappahannock County there was practically no religious freedom in the colony. Parents were compelled by law to take their children for baptism to the preacher of the parish in which they lived.[72] By an act of 1661, all Quakers and other non-conformists were required to pay a fine of two hundred pounds of tobacco whenever caught at their worship.[73] It was contrary to law for a non-conformist to try to seduce any person to accept his religious views. Captain Giles Brent, of Stafford, across the county line from the upper portion of Sittingbourne Parish, Rappahannock County, was on May 27, 1668, tried by the General Court at James City charged with seducing people to the Roman Catholic religion, but by the court was found not guilty.[74]

Marriage licenses, prior to 1660, had been by custom issued by the governor of the colony. At that time, owing to the scarcity of preachers, which often made the publication of banns impossible, and thereby necessitated the more frequent granting of licenses, and owing also the fact that the governor's knowledge of the people could not extend to the end of the ever enlarging country, the eldest magistrate in each county was given authority to sign marriage licenses. A

---

[69] Hening, Vol. 2, p. 47, March 1661/2, Act VI.
[70] Hening, Vol. 1, p. 277, March 1642/3, Act LXIV.
[71] Hening, Vol. 1, pp. 341-2, November 1647, Act III.
[72] Colonial Papers, 1657-1687.
[73] Hening, Vol. 2, p. 48, March 1661/2, Act IX.
[74] Minutes of the Council and General Court of Colonial Virginia, p. 511.

certified list of these marriages was required to be made annually to the governor by the clerk of the court.[75]

This plan does not appear to have worked long, for in 1661/2 marriage could be solemnized by a minister only after license was granted by the governor or his deputy, and after the curate of the several parishes had had time to announce the banns three times.[76] On October 25, 1669, at a General Court at James City, the Right Honorable the Governor in open court did constitute and appoint Henry Corbin, Esquire, to grant licenses for marriage in the Rappahannock River and no clerks of court to meddle in it [*D4, pp. 206-7*]. A fine of 100 pounds of tobacco was imposed on a parishioner for not informing the minister or reader of a birth, death or marriage. Fifty pounds of the fine went to the informer who exposed the neglectful person, and fifty pounds to the minister for making the records.[77]

Other fees allowed by law for ministerial functions were: forty shillings or four hundred pounds for preaching a funeral sermon; twenty shillings for marriage by license; five shillings or fifty pounds of tobacco were simply the banns for marriage were proclaimed.[78]

Establishment of the Parishes

In a study of the several parishes of this section, the writer will, for the benefit of the reader, first give a brief outline of their order of establishment.

The first parish of this section on the south side of the Rappahannock River was Cheskyack Parish extending from the York to the Rappahannock. It had practically no parishioners on the Rappahannock River. Organized later and co-existing with it was old Northumberland County Parish on the north side of the river before Lancaster County was cut off from Northumberland County. Most of its communicants were near the Potomac.

When Lancaster was formed in 1652, all that part of those two old parishes lying along the Rappahannonck River on both sides from its mouth to its head became the Parish of Lancaster. Sometime previous to 1656 when Rappahannock County was formed, the Parish of Lancaster was divided. The statute which directs the division of Lancaster County clearly indicates this fact, as the portion that remained in the new Lancaster County is declared to be the Parish of Lancaster. It is believed that the portion that fell in Rappahannock County was known as the Parish of Rappahannock. By 1662, there is evidence to indicate that the Parish of Rappahannock County had been divided and that the upport part of the county on both sides of the river was known as Sittingbourne Parish; and the lower part on both sides was known as Farnham

---

[75] Hening, Vol. 2, p. 28, March 1660/1, Act XXIX.
[76] Ibid.
[77] Hening, Vol. 2, p. 54, March 1661/2, Act XVI.
[78] Beverley, p. 211.

Parish. These two parishes continued to embrace all of Rappahannock County until some years after Bacon's Rebellion.

The Parish of Sittingbourne was divided about 1684, when the upper end of the extensive county, embracing what is now Caroline and King George counties, took the name of St. Mary's Parish. The lower end on the south side of the river took the name of St. Anne's Parish; and the lower end of the old Parish of Sittingbourne on the north side kept the name of Sittingbourne, the spelling of which soon became corrupted to Littingbourn.

Early Preachers
John Rosier

Some of the earliest evidence found of the existence of preachers and formation and activities of parishes is cited as follows:

John Rosier, here before mentioned as the first preacher in this section, had been in Virginia several years prior to 1650, but went back to England about that year and returned with his wife and several maids destined as brides for the colonists. For bringing these young women, he received rights for lands, and, no doubt, a little later marriage fees.

Mr. Clemovant

Apparently, before November Court, 1652, Mr. Clemovant served the parish, for at that court it was ordered that all those who were indebted to Mr. Clemovant, late minister of the county, "By subscriptions shall pay and satisfy the same to Col. Wm. Clayborn, Esq." [L1, p. 100].

Alexander Cook

Alexander Cook, minister, shortly after the formation of Lancaster County, wrote a letter dated September 26, 1652. He had visited the Lancaster section and wrote back stating the terms of the contract on which he wold serve as minister for the parish. His statement that four or five of the vestry might be chosen upon his arrival would indicate that there was but one parish in all Northumberland and Lancaster prior to that time. He was reasonable in his terms, and said that the church might pay him in corn and tobacco or in tobacco alone as they might choose. This letter was recorded February 9, 1652/3 [L1, p. 44]. At the April court, 1653, it was ordered that the people of Lancaster County should meet at the house of Mr. Thomas Brier to chose vestrymen and church wardens [L1, p. 44].

Charles Grimes

Charles Grimes, the next clerk, appears in the records on December 26, 1653. He patented 1,000 acres of land on Fleet's Creek just above and opposite Rappahannock Indian town [P.B. 3, p. 73]. He did not stay long on this land.

Rebuke for Slanderous Words

December 8, 1653, Mary Robinson was required by court to appear at church the next Lord's Day and before the minister and congregation apologize for slanderous words she had used. Also, Joane, the wife of William Thomas, for a similar offence was in "like manner and form required to appear and do likewise the next time the minister officiated up the river."

Two Parishes

A memorandum entry in Lancaster County records, dated August 7, 1653, states [L1, p. 152]:

> The County of Lancaster is divided into two parishes. The inhabitants being summoned thereto giving their votes therein. The said lower parish to begin on the east side of Morattico Creek, and the east branch downward to the bounds between the two parishes, the upper and the lower.

The bounds of the upper parish later became the bounds of Rappahannock County.

By the 1656 levy, the old County of Lancaster set aside 10,716 pounds of tobacco for entertaining ministers. Just how this was apportioned, when later the same year the county was divided, and the upper parish became Rappahannock County and the lower parish became Lancaster County, is not described; but on November 7, 1657, Samuel Cole, clerk, was engaged as minister for the lower parish of Lancaster. A church was ordered to be built on Boswelle Pointe, the first point above the present site of Urbanna, and another church on the Corotoman River; and the glebe on the Piankatank was ordered to be sold to buy a horse for the minister. A vestry was chosen, and it was agreed that the preacher should receive four thousand pounds of tobacco as long as he was in the parish of Lancaster [L2, p. 141].

There is no record of a parish or church in the upper parts of the river this early, but as the courthouse had been built as Bushwood by 1655, it is probable that services were sometimes held in it in the early days. Also services seem to have been held on the south side in the vicinity of Nanzamum Indian town, above the present town of Port Royal, where the Indians could be benefitted or won to the gospel. Certain of the preachers of the time were earnest and zealous in their efforts to Christianize the Indians, and the planters were ready to give special protection and consideration to Christian Indians.

Another reason why a church was placed at this point was that in 1653 the court had ordered a ferry established across the river in the civinnity of Charles Grimes Point. Almost immediately after the division of old Lancaster County, Charles Grimes, clerk, patented 1,000 acres on the south side of the river over against the Doeges land above Nansemum Town [P.B. 3, p. 297]. William White, clerk, witnessed a deed in February 1655/6 [L2, p. 25], and patented 1,000 acres on the south side of the river in the upper part of the county in the vicinity of Nansemum Town on January 5, 1657/8. William White and wife Martha were at Lancaster Court in 1658 administering an estate [LO&., p. 46].

Services were doubtless held in the lower part of what was soon to become Rappahannock County, and there may have been a chapel there, for, in 1656, Charles Grimes patented land on the north west side of Morattico Creek [P.B. 4, p. 49].

For some years, however, there is no other evidence of any church in the lower part of Rappahannock County. Nor did Grimes tarry long on his patent on Rappahannock Creek opposite the Rappahannock Indians, where he had hoped to serve the Indians and organize a church community. No doubt he found the site not a good selection. Here the Rappahannock River was wide, and, on many Sundays, rough and dangerous of crossing from the south side. The roads over land were mere Indian paths, at this time unsafe for settlers to travel to church. Only ten years had passed since the bloody massacre that had forced the English to evacuate nearly all the occupied territory north of the York. It must have seemed safer to withdraw to the Nansemum section where there was a free ferry and river was wide enough for worshippers to be safe from ambush by Indians, and yet not wide enough to be subject to great disturbance by storms.

Sittingbourne Parish

The first known church in Sittingbourne Parish was located just below the wide mouth of Occupacia Creek. The exactness of this location is sttested by the fact that on January 24, 1662/3, John Barrow sold one acre of land to the parish of Sittingbourne, "lying square about the church, provided the said acre of land be none more otherwise employed and made use of by the said parish than for a church and burying place about the same" [D2, p. 309 (245)].

This land of Barrow's was first the land of Richard Coleman, and was early known as Richard Coleman's. This Coleman patent lay back of a large marsh across the river from historic Leedstown, the upper end reaching the river above the marsh near the present *Otterburn* house, the lower end running easterly along the back of the marsh to a spot on Cabin Point, a point lying between Coleman's Creek and the before described great marsh. The creek just above Layton's Wharf was originally known as Coleman's Creek. North of this creek the town known as Richard Coleman's was planted; and here was built the first church of the section of which we have any record. Church Road is referred to as leading there.

Many lots, comprising two to three acres each, were sold in this town. A grist mill was built. Amory Butler, the preacher, had land here. There are references to a school-house path leading from it. Thus it is apparent that a school house was there. Very early Coleman had a trading post there. John Pain, merchant, succeeded him.

With the church located on a knoll back of the great marsh with the river bending in front of it, the people could easily come to it in boats. They could make fast their craft at the upper side of Coleman's patent, and walk over land to services. By this short cut more than two miles of water travel was eliminated.

Though the site was so accessible and safe, it was unfortunate in being near two swamps overabounding in mosquitoes and malaria. After some years it was necessary to abandon it and move to another location.

It was held as church property as late as 1677, for in that year John Barrow gave one hundred acres of land to Peter Foxsom, who was about to marry his eldest daughter Mary [D6, p. 127]. This deed of gift was for the most easterly portion of the original six-hundred acre patent of Richard Coleman, and was that part of the main land back of Coleman's Creek. The acre given to Sittingbourne Parish in 1662 was included in the survey, but was not given to Peter Foxsom in the deed. Thus it is evident that as late as that date, Sittingbourne Parish was in possession of the acre. We locate it exactly because the land north of the creek at Cabin Creek is very low, scarcely more than two or three feet above very high tide, and quite unsuited for church property. Since this acre was given to be used as a site for a church and a burial place, one must conclude that it was on the south side of Coleman's Creek near the river where the land is high and dry.

Thus is definitely placed the oldest known church site in all the Rappahannock River valley above the Corotoman. Here for years, with their guns by their sides, the pioneers assembled Lord's Day after Lord's Day for the worship of God. With the passing of time, they too perished; but there is left unto this day a little graveyard where they sleep. It is marked by a grove of beautiful trees, but marred by bushes, briers and vines, unkept and forgotten. To the passing mariner on the river, or the straying pedestrian, the presence of the green cedar trees has no meaning. Yet there they stand to mark the spot where a number of our earliest pioneer forefathers, who fought back the Indians and cleared away the wilderness, lie in peace. Longitude 76° 59' 55" and Latitude 38° 5' 40".

The lower or second church of Sittingbourne Parish referred to in the records of the county was at Latitude 38° 1' and Longitude 76° 55' 30", on the outer point of Occupacia Creek. The place is marked to this day by a heavy granite slab over the grave of Henricus Oswald, Chirurgus [surgeon], born at Kirkaldie in Scotland, son of Thomas Oswald, born 1694, died 1725/6. It carries a Latin verse. No doubt the cemetery was still in use when Oswald was buried. The best remaining monuments were recently moved to Vawters Churchyard. The old church stood on the crown of the bluff some thirty feet above the river.

The deed to this land was given by Peter Johnson, who sold four acres "with appurtenances" to the vestry of Sittingbourne Parish on October 10, 1664, for the consideration of five hundred pounds of tobacco. This land was described as "lying and being in the parish aforesaid on the south point that maketh the mouth of a creek called Occupacy, and to be laid as near as may be square on the said point the same to have and to hold, &c." [D&W1, pp. 33-4]. This was recorded in the court of Rappahannock County, "secundo die 9bris A.D. 1665 a^d. Superda."

This deed for the lower church lands, for which Francis Doughty was the preacher, was put to record only one day before Doughty was re-engaged for two years service. It is evident that there were plans to erect a church on this site at an early date.

Peter Johnson also sold one additional acre of land adjoining the four-acre tract, for in 1673/4, Robert Synock sold his place to John Bagwell, merchant, "except the five acres where the church is now standing, the same that Peter Johnson sold to the parish of Sittingbourne" [D5, pp. 192-3]. In Rappahanock County records, the location of the church lands is defined as at the fork between the two branches of Occupacia Creek. We find that later the location of the Glebe land was on the north side of Occupacia Creek. The old Glebe house still stands on the farm owned by W.F. Keck.

The names of the following ministers of the parish are found in the records in connection with their ownership of property:

John Phillips, preacher, on June 14, 1655, patented 1300 acres upon a creek proceeding out of Occupacia Creek and "beginneth upon the northernmost branch of the said creek called Wassamasson" [P.B. 3, p. 351]. This land had formerly been granted to Richard Coleman [P.B. 3, p. 142].

Justin Aylmer, clerk, owned 1400 acres of land on the east side of Pepitick Creek before 1673 [D5, p. 120; D7, p. 301].

Amory Butler, the next minister to follow, was brother to William Butler, minister of Washington Parish [D&W6, p. 113]. Amory Butler arrived in the parish sometime before May 1672, for on that date he was planning to be married to Mrs. Elizabeth Catlett, widow of Col. John Catlett [O5, pp. 20-1]. Butler served Sittingbourne Parish in 1674 [D5, p. 227]. He died testate in 1678, and his will named his brother William.

John Davis, appeared in court in 1688 and collected 3000 pounds of tobacco, the balance of his salary due him from the Parish of Sittingbourne for the year 1684 [O2, p. 82]. John Davis, clerk, is referred in court July 1, 1685 [O1, p. 140].

Thomas Perkins. There were 870 pounds of tobacco due Mr. Thomas Perkins, minister, late of Sittingbourne Parish, deceased, for the year 1683. The court ordered the amount paid to the executor of his estate [O1, p. 235].

Abraham Kenyan. In 1685, Abraham Kenyan, clerk, bought land in Sittingbourne Parish with Andrew Buckner [D7, p. 206].

Farnham Parish

Farnham Parish, at the lower end of old Rappahannock County, embraced all that part of the county lying on both sides of the Rappahannock River and extending easterly from what is now known as Mount Landing Creek on the south side and from Rappahannock (Cat Point) Creek on the north side to the present county lines of Middlesex and Lancaster. Separated by a river over a mile wide, it must have had two places of worship. The courthouse at Bushwood may have served for a few years as it was well located. There is no reference to any very early church on the north side of the river, only the fact that Charles Grimes patented a place near the head of Morattico Creek. It may be that Grimes settled and spent his last years there after the arrival of William Johnson, clerk, into the upper section of the parish.

The first reference to the existence of Farnham Parish is where John Walker and William Moss patented 238 acres of land described as lying in Farnham Parish and on the north side of Occupacia Creek [P.B. 5, p. 216]. This shows that in 1662 the parish bounds were not yet finally established. The patent was dated February 20, 1662. The second reference to it is found dated October 7, 1663 [D2, p. 312 (248)]. And though these are the only references to Farnham Parish that pre-date the swearing in of the vestry in 1665, they would indicate that the parish was completely organized as a unit. The fact that the parish was named for the plantation, *Farnham*, the place of Col. Moore Fantleroy, burgess of Rappahannock County, would strongly suggest that it was formed while Col. Moore Fantleroy was the leading citizen of the county, during the time of the Commonwealth of England, rather than after his disfranchisement by the burgesses when Berkeley returned to power in 1660.

In 1665, an act was passed that reads: "Whereas there is a law that binds us to the bounding of our lands, be in enacted by this Grand Assembly and the authority thereof that the same law be in force to the bounding of parishes and counties."[79] This act may have stimulated the people of the lower end of the county to revise the organization of their vestry, for there is recorded the following item [D&W2, p. 109]:

> The names of the Gent. of the vestry of Farnham in Rappa. County as they were sworn the third day of November 1665, viz:
>
> Mr. Francis Doughty, Minister
>
> | | |
> |---|---|
> | Lt. Col⁰· Thomas Goodrich | Thomas Button |
> | James Sampford | Robert Bayley |
> | Thomas North | Thomas Robinson |
> | John Grigory | John Williams |
>
> Recorded this 4 die 9bris 1665. Pr. Robert Davies, Cl. Cur.

In Deed & Will Book 1, pages 38-9, is found the following item:

> We whose names are hereunder written being vestry men for the parish of Sittingbourne & Farnham do here unanimously agree for the future maintenance of Mr. Francis Doughty Minister the two next Ensuing years & it is agreed upon as followeth: that Mr. Francis Doughty shall receive yearly of each Parish above sd. Sixty pounds Sterling to be paid in Tobacco according to act of Assembly ye said tobacco to be paid in Cask without Sallery or other charge to the sd. Mr. Doughty hereby revokeing & disannulling all former orders bargains & Contracts

---

[79] Hening, Vol. 2, p. 218.

whatsoever made by & between the said Mr. Francis Doughty & both or either the respective vestrys of the Parishes aforesaid to the true performance of which the said Mr. Francis Doughty & the vestry of both Parishes have hereunto set their hands this 3 day of November Ao. 1665.

[Farnham Parish]	[Sittingbourne Parish]
Fra: Doughty	Fra: Doughty
Thom: Goodrich	John Catlett
John Griggory	Alexr. Fleming
Tho: Button	John Weir
Robt. [his RB mark] Bayley	Tho: Hawkin
James Samford	Hum: Booth
Tho. [his TR mark] Robinson	W. Moseley
Ant. North	John Paine

Recognr in Cur Com Rappa., 3 die 9bris Ao. 1665
Rec. X Die of the said mensis a^{d.} Superda.
Test Robert Davies, Cl. Cur, Preda

Among the names of these vestrymen of Farnham Parish in 1665, the author can find no one who lived on the south side of Piscataway Creek. There was probably no place of worship in that section of the parish. At least three of the four vestrymen on the northh side of the river lived below Totuskey Creek.

An early record of the existence of a church on the south side of the river and in Farnham Parish is a reference in 1673 to a road known as Church Road running along the north side of Piscataway pocoson [D5, p. 255]. Thomas Cooper's will, dated September 1, 1675, reads in part: "My will is that my body may be decently buried by my wife in Piscataway Church Yard." Thus the churchyard in which his wife was buried must have been in use previous to that date. In 1677, a deed was given for one hundred acres of land extending from the Church Road to the Church swamp [D6, p. 127]. The location of these areas is fairly well defined. From these and other references it has been found that Church Road began at the headwaters of wide Piscataway Creek at Latitude north 37° 52' 55" and Longitude west 76° 52' 48", where the old Piscataway warehouse stood in the early eighteenth century, and ran from this landing in a northeasterly direction crossing the Church swamp about Longitude west 76° 54' 30". It appears that there was a church in Piscataway about 1660 located on a branch of the creek known as Church swamp. From time to time, as new churches are built or locations were changes, other swampy areas were called church swamps.

Charles Davis

Charles Davis, who resided on the north bank of the Rappahannock River almost opposite the mouth of Piscataway Creek, followed Doughty as minister or clerk. The river and the creek served him as a way of travel to and from his southside church.

Farmham

The great *Farnham* plantation extended from Morattico Creek northward along the river front to a point or mile or more above what is now Sharps Wharf and inland into the hills.

Early Northside Church

Little is known of the early northside church, but there are two records that clearly indicate that there actually was a church. One is a deed given by John Partridge when he sold land to Joseph Davis in 1690, stating that the land was near Farnham Church and at the head of Richard's Creek. The other, dated January 5, 1688, is the purchase by William Richardson of land defined as two miles from Totuskey Creek, adjoining the land of John Partridge and facing on Farnham Church Road [D8, p. 94]. The fact that the old name is employed in both cases, even though the parish had already been divided into north and south, implies that the building of the church pre-dated the division of the parish. The old church was southeasterly from the present town of Emmerton. The east branch of Richard's Creek was called Church spring branch.

Early Preachers

The history of the parishes in old Rappahannock County was largely moulded by the preachers who presided over them. From the coming of Charles Grimes into the river in 1653, the affairs of the first parish were for some years almost a family affair. Charles Grimes was succeeded as clerk of old Rappahannock County parish by William White, who almost immediately married Ann, a connection of Edward Grimes, who seems to have been a brother of Charles.

Francis Doughty

Francis Doughty, the next minister, was popular with a large part of his congregation, but stirred others to high indignation. He must have been a vital person, for in the five years that he was here he organized and revived the church work. In Sittingbourne Parish he planned, bought land for, and erected churches. The church apparently near Cabin Point below Coleman's Creek had been planned, and the one at the mouth of Occupacia Creek erected in 1665. He must also have built a church at Piscataway, and a church on the north side. In Farnham Parish, to which he gave half of his time, he organized the vestry. In 1672, when Charles Davis came as a minister for Farnham, he settled at the most convenient place to the two Farnham churches that he could choose.

While popular with the people, Doughty was repeatedly unseated, either because of the control of the church by the state, or because of the vagaries of his own personality. He was driven out of England, off Long Island, away from the Eastern Shore of Virginia, and finally out of Rappahannock County into Maryland. In 1669, "old and infirm," he put 200 acres in Charles County, Maryland in trust with Richard Boughton for the care of his wife.

He was accused of implacably censuring his parishioners conduct, and of refusing to administer the sacrament of communion on Easter Sunday. For this he was tried, his accusers being not only vestrymen, but also justices of the court. This charge made it very difficult for things to happen otherwise than for Doughty to be convicted, and we find him pathetically making provision for his wife and son to continue residence in Virginia while he departs to other fields. The trial of Doughty has aroused much interest. He was "put out" as minister of the parish. This trial largely grew out of the quarrel over whether he should be paid in sterling or in tobacco. It preceded by more than a hundred years the famous "Parson's case," which has been immortalized by the fiery eloquence of Patrick Henry.

North Farnham Parish

About 1684, North Farnham Parish was carved out of Farnham Parish. This date is cited because on November 22 of that year the county court ordered a free election of the vestry for the parish of North Farnham to be held at the church of the parish. "In the election of the said vestry the one half to be chosen of persons living in the upper parts of the said parish above Totuskey and the other half to be chosen from the lower parts of the parish" [O1, p. 76]. The next mention of the parish is in 1685, when the court ordered the vestry of North Farnham Parish to lay the levy for the year [O1, p. 190]. It embraced all that part of old Farnham Parish on the north side of the Rappahannock River and lying between the east branch of Morattico Creek and Rappahannock Creek. Some years after the creating of North Farnham Parish, Totuskey Creek became the upper boundary of that parish, and the lower church was then built at what is now Farnham, Virginia.

It is difficult to ascertain just who was the first minister.

It was not until May 5, 1732, many years after the passing of the name of old Rappahannock County, that North Farnham Parish was re-divided. The upper church and portion above Totuskey became known as Lunenburg Parish. The lower church and the portion below Totuskey Creek retained the old parish name.[80] The old Lunenburg Parish church, built of brick, stood just west of the present town of Warsaw. About this time also, the brick church at Farnham was probably built to allow for adjustment of parish bounds. Moreover, for many years after the formation of Richmond County, the court records refer to the stream just southeast of Emmerton (east of Beale Middleton's home) as the

---

80 Hening, Vol. 4, pp. 366-7.

Church spring branch. This branch flows into Richard's alias Richardson's Creek.

In North Farnham Parish, on June 7, 1693, John Davis, clerk (minister), sued for his salary due from the said parish. He appears to have been the last minister in that parish before Richmond County was formed, and the first minister of the parish under the new county [R O1, p. 84]. He was succeeded by James Booker, clerk, and Isaac Wright, reader, of the parish [R O1, p. 91]. James Booker soon left Virginia and returned to England.

South Farnham Parish

After Bacon's Rebellion, the parishes of the county were disorganized, for though Farnham Parish nominally extended on both sides of the fiver in the lower end of the county, yet John Lightfoot in a trust deed says "I, John Lightfoot, of the parish of Piscataway" [D&W6, p. 354]. This is the only reference to any such parish, and he probably meant that he lived near or attended Piscataway Church.

South Farnham Parish embraced that part of old Farnham Parish which lay on the south side of the river and extended from the Middlesex line to Andrew Gilson's Creek, now called Mount Landing Creek. The first direct reference to South Farnham Parish by name is found in Rappahannock County Orders [O1, p. 56], when John Waters and Anthony Smith, "late wardens of South Farnham Parish," were in court on October 1, 1684. Since they had already served their two years as churchwardens as prescribed by law, this would indicate that the parish had been organized at least two years previous to this date. The parish was again mentioned on November 4, 1685 [O1, p. 183].

Dewell Prad

The first known minister of this parish was Dewell Prad, who patented three hundred acres on the south side of the mouth of Piscataway Creek, April 13, 1688. On November 7, 1689, he reported to the court of Rappahannock County that he, Dewell Prad, minister, had solemnized the rites of matrimony between John Armstead and Mary Browne [O2, p. 187].

Charles Davis

Of another minister, Charles Davis, little is known except that he served as clerk of Farnham Parish.

Nathaniel Pendleton

Nathaniel Pendleton, preacher, is mentioned as coming to Virginia as an indentured servant, soon after his arrival, and while still an indentured servant preached at the Farnham Parish church, but died shortly afterwards.

Thomas Gordon

Thomas Gordon, clerk, first appeared in Rappahannock County in 1673/4. He must have been well thought of and highly respected, since soon after his arrival he married the widow of Thomas Button, who, during his life, had been a large land holder and prominent member of the vestry. After his marriage,

Gordon doubtless lived at the old place of Thomas Button. The house was located on the crown of the hill overlooking his large farm in the valley.[81]

Gordon was the preacher for this section during Bacon's Rebellion; and when the northern Indians were massacring the burning, he came out vigorously for defense against the savages, taking an active part in the rebellion against Berkeley. He was the only preacher in the colony signaled out for severe punishment. Throughout this time of turmoil and distress, he appears as an heroic and self-sacrificing figure, endeavoring to serve his people at the cost of his own living and position in the church.

This undoing of two of the last three ministers of the parish must have greatly incensed the people, who seem to have come to love and respect these pastors, who served not only their spiritual needs but also their physical needs.

Thomas Young, one of the members of the congregation at Piscataway, was executed by Berkeley; and Col. Thomas Goodrich and Benjamin Goodrich of Hobbs His Hole, who were severely rebuked and heavily fined by Berkeley, belonged to this church. John Waters and another person of the congregation living near Piscataway were arrested and finally pardoned after Berkeley was recalled to England. It is no wonder that the parish of Farnham became so disorganized that in 1681, John Lightfoot in a trust deed said that he was of the "Parish of Piscataway" [D&W6, pp. 354-5].

Out of the wrecked parish were formed the parishes of North and South Farnham; but the new parishes were not sufficiently organized to plan at once the erection of churches.

In 1693, two acres and fifty perches of land near the King's Highway and on the southside of Hoskins Creek were sold by James Taylor of King and Queen County to Edward Pagett and Capt. Edward Thomas, churchwardens of South Farnham Parish in Essex County [D8, pp. 229-30]. This church, built about 1693, was in later years often called and known as Upper Piscataway Church.

The lower church of South Farnham Parish, built of brick, was in existence before 1706. It was probably built soon after the upper church of South Farnham Parish. This lower church was sometimes called Lower Piscataway Church of South Farnham Parish. It passed out of use during the Revolution, and many of the bricks from it are said to have been used in building the nearby residence now the home of Waring Lewis [Marigold].

The crumbled ruins show that it was the same general design as Vawters Church. The main chapel was 60 by 33 feet, with a wing 40 by 20 feet. The building over all measured 53 by 60 feet, with a brick wall 90 by 120 feet built around it. At one of the corners of the east transcept is a granite tablet erected in recent years to mark the site of the old church located near what is now Ozeana, Virginia.

---

[81] See [Essex Co.] Land Trials, 1711, p. 145, for a plat showing his house.

Division of Sittingbourne Parish

In the days of reconstruction after Bacon's Rebellion, the old Parish of Sittingbourne was divided. For a few years the lower half of the parish retained the old name, but the up-river half became St. Mary's Parish. The latter is first mentioned on December 5, 1681 [D6, p. 146]; again on April 28, 1684 [D7, p. 136]; on May 6, 1685 [O1, p. 119; O2, p. 222]; and in 1686.

On February 2, 1688, Christopher Blackbourne was fined 1000 pounds of toacco for not collecting St. Mary's Parish taxes [O2, p. 65]. Evan Jones was made surveyor in the north side of St. Mary's Parish in 1688. We also find that St. Mary's Parish extended to the south side of the river [D8, p. 252].

Dr. Charles Dacres

The first preacher in the parish was Dr. Charles Dacres, "Parish Priest," who was tried in 1684 before Samuel Gore, Peter Knight, and Bartholomew Dameron and acquitted, they finding no fault in him.[82] There was apparently some question of his religious teaching. Dr. Dacres was also sued for debt in the county court in 1684 [O1, p. 75].

Thomas Viccars

The next known preacher was Thomas Viccars of Gloucester County, who patented two large tracts of land near the land of John Buckner in 1690 [P.B. 7, p. 700].[83]

After the Indian massacres that almost destroyed its people in 1675/6, the old Parish of Sittingbourne had a difficult struggle; and it seemed it could not survive having St. Mary's and Hanover parishes cut out of it.

On January 7, 1690/1, the court entered the following indictment: "The Grand Jury having presented the Parish of Sittenbourne for not enterteyning a Minister, or providing a Minister or a Reader, and for not keeping the Church in due repair," the sheriff was ordered to summon the churchwardens to answer [O2, p. 264].

This court action did not much improve matters, for the County of Rappahannock was soon divided and the upper side of the Parish of Sittingbourne was set off as a separate parish. On April 10, 1693, the court ordered the [EO1, p. 66]:

Inhabitants of Sittingbourne Parish do repair to their P'ish Church on ye first day of May next and then and there shew Elect & make Choice of a Vestry for ye said parish, and Capt. Wm. Moseley, Mr. Ben. Grimes and Robt. Brooke or any two of them are by this Court requested ... to administer ye oaths unto ye sd. Vestry.

---

[82] Colonial Papers, 1657-1687.
[83] See also Northern Neck Land Grants, Bk. 3, p. 1.

The south side of the parish of Sittingbourne finally appealed to the governor and their troubles are more fully explained by the governor's reply. It read as follows:

Upon the Peticon of the Inhabitants of the South side of Sittenborn Parish, setting forth, that wheras the said Parish of Sittenborn being of a large Extent, lying on both side of the River of Rappahannock in the County or Rappahannock, and upon the division of the said County of Rappahannock into two Counties (Viz) Essex and Richmond, the one halfe of the Parish on the North side of the River and in Richmond County divided from them and is become a Parish to themselves whereby the one halfe of the Vestry Men wch. live on that side of the River are parted from them, so that they have butt six of their Vestry Men remaining wth. them, whereby they are disabled to setle the Affaires of their Parish in repaireing their Church, Entertaining a Minister, and providing for the poor and Impotent, Therefore humbly prays his Excell^y. that he would be pleased to grant them an Order for the Election of meet and able men of their Precincts to fill up their Vestry, that so they may be Constituted a Parish may thereby be Capacitated to mentain a Minister, repair their Church and provide for their poore and Impotent. Ordered that some of the Vestry of Each side of the River Appear before the Govr. in Councill upon the 23d of Octo^r. next and bring an Account of the Number of their respective Tythables, and Ordred Accordingly. July 21, 1693.[84]

That part of Sittingbourne Parish which lay on the north side of the river had already been organized into a parish by July 21, 1693. Its church was built at Latitude 38° 5' 30" and Longitude 76° 59' 0", a short distance up Rappahannock River from Pedee Creek, not far from the river, and on the north side of it, near Leedstown. It was called Bray Church.

---

[84] *Executive Journals of the Council of Colonial Virginia*, Vol. 1, pp. 288-9.

CHAPTER 12

Old Rappahannock County
Education

The early settlement of the Rappahannock valley occurred when the colony of Virginia was under the control of the government of the Commonwealth in England. More freedom of thought was tolerated during that period than later.

About 1656, Mr. Lee appeared in the court of Lancaster County and asked permission to build a school near his place. He gave as a reason for this request the fact that many young people of the community were growing up in need of an education.

Berkeley, after his restoration to power, looked upon the education of the people as a crime against the state. The lords commissioners of foreign plantations, in 1670, asked him, "What course is taken about the instructing of the people within your government in the Christian religion; and what provision is made for the paying of your minstry?"[85]

He answered:

> The same course that is taken in England out of towns; every man according to his ability instructing his children. We have fforty eight parishes, and our ministers are well paid, and by my consent would be better *if they would pray oftener and preach less.* But of all other commodities, so of this, *the worst are sent us,* and we had few that we could boast of, since the persicution in *Cromwell's* tiranny drove divers worthy men hither. But, I thank God, *there are no free schools* nor *printing,* and I hope we shall not have these hundred years; for *learning* hath brought disobedience, and heresy, and sects into the world, and *printing* hath divulged them, and libels against the best government. God keep us from both!

Concerning this remark of Berkeley's, William Waller Hening wrote:

> Nothing can display in stronger colors the execrable policy of the British government, in relation to the colonies, than the sentiments uttered by Sir William Berkeley, in his answer to this interrogatory. These were, doubtless, his genuine sentiments, which recommended him so highly to the favor of the crown, that he continued governor of Virginia from 1641 to 1677, a period of *thirty-six* years, if we except the short interval of the commonwealth, and a few occasional times of absence from his government, on visits to England. The more profoundly ignorant the colonists could be kept, the better subjects they were for slavery. None but tyrants dread the diffusion of knowledge and the liberty of the press.

The same hostility of the introduction of *printing* which was manifested by Sir William Berkeley, was shewn by Lord Culpeper, who was governor of Virginia in

---

[85] Hening, Vol. 2, "Enquiries to the Governor of Virginia," 1660-1682, pp. 516-18.

1683, only *eleven years* after these principles were avowed by Sir William Berkeley. It will be seen from the following extract, which is from a MS. [manuscript] of unquestionable authority, that at the last mentioned date, a printer actually commenced his business in Virginia, but was prohibited by the governor and council from *printing any thing*, till the king's pleasure should be known; which, it may be presumed was very tardily communicated, as the first evidence of printing thereafter in Virginia was on the revised laws contained in the edition of 1733.

"February 21st, 1682, John Buckner [of Gloucester] called before Lord Culpepper and his council for printing the laws of 1680, without his excellency's license, and he and the printer ordered to enter into a bond in £100 *not to print anything* thereafter, until his majesty's pleasure should be known."[86]

Throughout the period of the government of Berkeley and of Culpeper no effort was made to educate the masses of the people. Our records bear evidence of this. In many cases where the immigrant father was a scholar and a beautiful penman, his son grew up with little or no culture, often being unable to write his name. In fact, it apparently came to be considered quite proper in the presence of officers of the law for a man not to exhibit his learning by signing his name when just to make his mark was more becoming as a private citizen. The justice or officer before whom he appeared would write his name.

The actual increase of ignorance and the pretense of ignorance may be regarded as one source from which rose the varied spellings of family names that often led to the ultimate change in the spelling during the latter part of the seventeenth century and the first part of the eighteenth.

This ear, when learning was discouraged partly explains why during this period offices of public trust were so often held by men but a few years from England, and why it was well into the eighteenth century before descendants of the early settlers again took the leadership in the politics of Virginia.

Under William and Mary, education under strict supervision was encouraged. Throughout the history of old Rappahannock County, however, the education of the youth was fostered by some planters. This is proved by their wills. In his will, dated 1656, Clement Thrush [Thresh], who had lands east of and back of the town of Tappahannock, and who is believed to have managed the plantation of Bartholomew Hoskins, left funds for this daughter-in-law [step-daughter], Ann Harris, that she might go to the school of Mrs. Peacock. To several other girls he bequeathed funds that they might go to Colo. Goodrich's school with his children. His young daughter, Frances, was his residuary legatee.

On May 8, 1678, Dr. Peter Hopegood requested in his will that his step-daughters be kept at Thomas Roberts' school, and after 1680 left to the tuition of their uncles, John Hopegood and Mr. Paul Allistree [D6, p. 126].

---

[86] Bland Manuscript, p. 498.

In 1687, Edward Keeling gave five pounds to be sent to England to buy books for the children of Sittingbourne and Farnham Parishes on the south side of the river. He gave a servant boy, William Jordan, his freedom and the charge of schooling. He gave the children of Elizabeth Brutness 500 pounds of tobacco each for their schooling when she should set them to school. He gave his God-son, Edward Goldman, a cow to be disposed of for his schooling.

Hezekiah Turner, in his will dated December 25, 1677, directed that his son, Hezekiah Turner, go to school to Mr. John Saffin for nine years [D6, p. 64].

Mr. Pearce had a school on his plantation.

Three instances bear evidence that men were concerned for the education of the children for whom they were responsible; and that they made an effort to provide them with an education in spite of the difficulties in the way.

During the closing years of Rappahannock County, there lived in the vicinity of Bestland on the road to Piscataway a school master by the name of Samuel Coates. He bought 300 acres of land and maintained a school on his plantation [D8, p. 263].

In the early days of Richmond County, a school-house path was referred to as on the south side of Cross Creek and very near where old Chicacoon path crossed. There is a reference to another school-house path back of the old place called "Richard Coleman's" above the present Layton's Wharf.

In 1702, when the county seat of Essex was moved from Hobbs Hole to Lloyds, the old public buildings were not needed, so at court, February 10, 1705/6, it was "considered by the court that the old prison standing at Hobbs Hole be appropriated to the use of a school and to no other use whatsoever." This school was actually operated, for later in that year Richard Cook was keeper of the school [EO3, pp. 147, 176-8].

The Port Royal community was a cultured one. Among preachers and clerks who resided there were Grimes, White, Doughty and Viccars.

Libraries

In his will, Amory Butler, clerk, of the parish of Sittingbourne and the county of Rappahannock, bequeathed all his "books, sermons, noats & papers" to his brother, William Butler, minister of Washington Parish. The inventory of his estate, made in 1687, lists "Wilson's Dixionery" valued at 150 pounds of tobacco, and 85 other books valued at 1226 pounds of tobacco.

The inventory of the estate of Dr. Henry Willoughby, made May 31, 1688, includes the following books [D6B, p. 101]:

		Value Pounds [of Tobacco]
It.	6 books of Phisick in folio	240
It.	14 Physick books in quarto	220
It.	8 Physick books in Octavo	75
It.	16 books of Physick in xyo	96
It.	6 History Books in folio	120

It.	12 History Books in quarto most old	120
It.	15 other small books of divers subjects	60
It.	a bible in large quarto	120
It.	2 Books of Divinity in folio	100
It.	20 Books of Divinity in quarto	340
It.	27 Books of Divinity in Octavo most old	270
It.	27 Books of Divinity in xvj	230
It.	13 old Books	30
It.	a Parcel of old imperfect Paper books	30
It.	2 Books of Law in folio	150
It.	4 Books of Law in quarto	80
It.	9 Books of Law in 8°	180
It.	23 Books of Law in xvj	230
It.	A Bible at John Batkin's	---

The inventory of the estate of Thomas Perkins, dated April 15, 1684, included [D6B, p. 27]:

	Value Pounds [of Tobacco]
A parcell of old parchmt. & paper covered books	50
Another parcel of books	258
3 books at	450
One bible & Common prayer book	124
Another parcel of books	200

The inventory of Paul Brewer, dated November 10, 1655, mentions together 2 books, 1 ax valued at 44 pounds of tobacco [L D2, p. 16].

Capt. William Brocas's inventory, dated May 24, 1655, lists a parcel of old bound [202] books, "most of them Spanish, Italyan & latin," valued at 200 pounds tobacco.

Mr. George Eaton left 1 old Bible, 1 small Divinity book, on October 8, 1653 [L D2, p. 7].

As early as January 1652/3, John Gillett appraised an estate that contained 2 sermon books valued at 30 pounds of tobacco, and 1 "bibel" at 50 pounds.

John Sampson's will dated September 7, 1680, and inventory dated November 10, 1685, lists [D6B, pp. 81-4]:

91 Law Books of this country (England)	The Heart kept from disinding
A Bible with silver clasps	Religio Medici
A book of Fran: Quarles intitled [Divine] Fancys	A Seamans Calendar of Friendship
A book of John Quarles Jr., Sans Lachrimar	A small trunk of writeings sealed wth: the sd. Sampson's owne seale
A folio written by Herue	Michll. Cope of the Prover[b]s
Heaven Opened by R.A.	A French Grammar
The life & death of Mr. John Janeway	poore man familie book
	Baxter Powell's Concordance

CHAPTER 13

Old Rappahannock County
Paths and Roads

Indians had comparatively straight paths. Since they had no horses, the traveled, in early days, entirely by water or on foot by land. In old Rappahannock County records, three paths are often referred to.

One of these, the Chickacoon path, was the trail up the Northern Neck peninsula. It led upward from Chickacoon, an Indian town on the Corotoman River, crossing the larger creeks at convenient fording places where wading was always possible. On this path, the largest stream that the Indians waded across was known as Cross Creek. This was the east branch of Totuskey in the head of the creek. This path should not be confused with the other Chicacoon Path over in Northumberland County. This ancient path in Rappahannock County passed near Farnham, crossing Cross Creek on a path about a mile northeast of Emmerton by old Moore's Mill, near Rappahannock Indian town, crossing Rappahannock Creek northwest of Farmers Fork at a place that, soon after the coming of white man, came to be known as Horse Bridge. It passed near Stone Hill, Horner, Robbins Fork, Shiloh, on to Passapatancy, on to the great north and south Indian trail that came to be known as the Port Tobago path.

There were several branches of this Cickacoon path. One led to North Point on the Potomac several miles northwest on Route 301. Also, from this path there was a fork in the vicinity of Horner, that ran to Nanzattico Town on the Rappahannock, where it crossed the river to Port Tobago Town and joined the King's Highway and the Port Tobago—Mattoponi upper path.

The King's Highway was first known as Rappahannock path. After it was developed, it was often called the cart road, though there were other cart roads. The King's Highway was ordered to be developed in 1662.[87] Port Tobago road crossed the county into the section now known as New Town in King and Queen County, and ran southerly, with branches running down the peninsulas between the several rivers.

The King's Highway crossed the Mattaponi about five miles below Walkerton, passed near Millers Tavern, east of Dunbrooke, then a mile or more west of Caret, thence just west of Loretto, and on up along the uplands toward the place where Vawters Church stands, and on up to the town of Port Tobago on Port Tobacco Bay as it is called today. Green Bay was near the town but a little below it. There were small trails that went a mile or more back of the Mattaponi and Rappahannock Rivers.

Over Mattaponi path, alias King's Highway, Captain John Smith was taken to the town of the Rappahannocks on the north side of the Rappahannock River.

---

[87] See D4, pp. 144, 246; D5, p. 3; D8, p. 230; Land Trials, Vol. 2, p. 15.

He was found not guilty of murdering their king, and was sent back south on this road.

It was south on this King's Highway that Bacon's army of 400 men marched and joined Bacon's forces in the upper Chickahominy River section, in what is near Hanover County today. It was along a part of this path that Governor Spotswood sent with his knights. After crossing the Mattaponi River, he must have turned northwest to the plantation of Robert Beverley, where he joined Richard Buckner and other Knights of the Horseshoe, and went on a trip to discover the frontier and encourage more pioneer settlements in the head of the river above what is now Fredericksburg. They went, we are told, to the summit of the Blue Ridge mountains. Robert Brooke Jr., also accompanied them.

Church Road was a short road only a few miles long. The location of it is definite for only about a half mile. Route 659 today runs southwest of Tappahannock toward Desha. Just southeast of Desha, on this Route 659, about 1693, was built a church that came to be known as the church of South Farnham Parish. There today, just to the north of the old church lot, stands, perhaps fifty feet distant, a good church known as St. Johns (colored).

Running from the old church, there was a road, now running southerly and used mostly for hauling lumber. Down it about a half mile, at the top of the hill on the west side of the old road is thought to have been an earlier church. The hill is still known as Church Hill. From this hill there was an old road that ran across Church swamp. From there one ran southerly toward Route 619, and one led easterly toward the vicinity of Bray's Fork. On this there was a still earlier church. A clue to its existence is found in a deed to land referred to as being on Church Road. This land was near Bray's Fork, perhaps back on the hill south of Route 360 and some distance west of Route 17. The first sheriff of Rappahannock County had a large tract of land on the north side of Route 17 on Piscataway, running down it about a mile.

The first churches were all located on bodies of water where travel by boat was convenient, and where the water was wide enough so that Indian arrows did not reach the boats. The other important thing was protection from Indians while at church. The fact that William Johnson was sheriff was an asset to the location of the church on his place near the open waters of Piscataway Creek. The community was comparatively thickly populated, and the creek wide enough for fairly safe travel. One of the early preachers had a patent about a mile below Johnson's plantation. It is probable that the first church was located up the creek from its mouth, a safer and more approachable site than that at the mouth.

Another interesting path started southeast from the Indian trail that came to the King's Highway. It began about two miles southerly from Dunbrooke where Route 620 meets Route 625. It went along the general direction of Route 625, through old Paul's Cross Roads. This segment of the trail was called Lizzard Tree path. From Paul's Cross Roads the trail continued southeasterly along the south side of what is called Mill Creek, crossing Route 17 near what has been known as

Ozeana, now the junction of Route 607 and Route 17. This trail ran comparatively straight to the vicinity of Montagues, the junction of Routes 601 and 17, and continued to the Middlesex County line near Laneview.

After the departure or the regulation of the Indians, white men ventured to move into the hills. They began to widen the Indian trails and to make new roads to suit their needs. The use of horses, oxen, and wheeled vehicles constantly increased; but it was just beginning in the latter years of Rappahannock County. From the earliest days even into the twentieth century overland travel was greatly handicapped in rural areas by roads deep in mud and full of ruts.

It was not at all uncommon for a man to drive from one to twenty miles along the beach at the river shore when the tide was not high. As a boy, on several occasions, I drove a horse hitched to a light buggy from my old home about seven miles below Tappahannock, going all the way along the firm sand beach to Middlesex County. In the winter season, it was usually better than the rough public roads.

In September 1632, the House of Burgesses enacted the following law: "Highwayes shall be layd out in such convenient places as are requisite accordinge as the Governor and Counsell or the commissioners for the monthlie corts shall appoynt, or accordinge as the parishioners of every parish shall agree."[88]

The Indian paths remained little disturbed, however, until after Berkeley was restored to power, and an act was passed in March 1661/2, that reveals the heavy task of the pioneers in creating the first highways, and their methods of accomplishing it, the future of the parish vestry in the project, and the penalties imposed for failure of duty. It follows in full:[89]

WHEREAS through the frequent alterations of the highwayes by falling of trees over them, and many times taking them into ffenced plantations to the great hindrance of travellers and traders: *Be it therefore enacted* that the justices doe yearely in October court appoint surveyors of the highwayes who shall first lay out the most convenient wayes to the church, to the court, to James Towne, and from county to county, and make the said wayes forty foote broad, and make bridges where there is occasion, and the wayes being once thus layed out, and the bridges made they shall cause the said wayes to be kept cleere from loggs, and the bridges in good repair that all his majesties subjects may have free and safe passage about their occasions; and to effect the same, the vestryes of every parish are upon the desires of the surveyors hereby enjoyned and impowered to order the parishoners every one according to the number of tithables he hath in his family, to send men upon the dayes by the surveighors appointed to helpe them in cleering the wayes, and making or reparaing the bridges according to the intent and purpose of this act, and if any court shall omitt the appointing surveyors, or

[88] Hening, Vol. 1, p. 199, September 1632, Act L.
[89] Hening, Vol. 2, p. 103, March 1661/2, Act LXXIX, Surveyors for highways.

they neglect the executing their office, or the vestry to order the worke, or any person to send helpe according to the said vestryes order, the said court, surveighor, vestry or person, shalbe amerced five hundred pounds of tobacco to the use of the county. And if any person shall contrary to this act fall trees upon the highwayes and not cleere the same, or incase any parte of the said highwayes within any ffence, the grant jury shall present the same as a comon nusance, and the inclosure shalbe thrown open, and the offender be fined one thousand pounds of tobacco to the use of the county; and if any countyes have creeke or swampe, lymitting the bounds betweene the said counties, It is enacted that both county's bounding upon such passage shall contribute to the makeing of the bridge or the way over it.

After the passage of this act, the roads of Rappahannock County were gradually developed. Paths going straight over the steep hills, as did the Indian trails, were not suited to the frequently heavily loaded wheeled vehicles, usually carts, of the settlers. Therefore, a new road usually detoured around a hill. Even on level ground, firm soil, fenced fields, and property lines helped determine the course of a road.

The courts gave first consideration to the owner of the land over which a road passed. The road bed was his property. Unless it caused the public serious inconvenience, the course of a road followed the wish of the land owner. (No wonder the old roads were crooked!)

It seems to have been the first desire of each justice of the court, as soon as he took office, to change the road to go by his place. This changing and twisting of roads followed the horse and cart through the centuries; and practically every old cross road of today indicates the spot where stood an ordinary or the home of some justice of long ago.

In this age of the automobile, road engineers are following in the footsteps of the Indians and are making roads as straight as practical.

As soon as white men settled back from the river, and something better than paths was needed, the courts began to set apart rolling roads for these plantations. They were so called because the hogsheads of tobacco were rolled over them from the back plantations to the landings on the rivers or creeks.

With the early court orders destroyed, the records establishing the first rolling roads in Rappahannock County are lost; but in 1688 the court entered this order [O2, pp. 103, 111]:

Ordered that the road leading through the plantation of John Wood beeing a rolling road for the back plantations and otherwise useful to them be from henceforth continued and that the said road do not prevent any person in the passage thereon.

Later other rolling roads were developed. By 1720 more than a score led to landings on the water front or to warehouses near them in which hogsheads of tobacco were often stored until shipped. All such roads became a care and charge of the county. A little later, the number of these private warehouses was greatly reduced, the county itself establishing in their stead public warehouses such as the one at Hobbs Hole.

From the earliest days the problem of road maintenance has been one of the most difficult and persistent with which the county government has had to deal. In 1684, at December court, Thomas Wheeler, who lived in the vicinity of Dunbrooke, had trouble keeping open to travel the roads under his supervision. They were in bad condition, and tithable citizens were slow in helping to fix them as was required by law. It was necessary for the court to enter an order drafting twelve men to work the roads for three days. Failure to do so would draw punishment by law [O1, p. 82].

The English soon gave the Indian paths new names. Lizzard Tree path led southeasterly from Mattaponi Indian town along the ridge to the south of Piscataway Creek; thence to what was Old Paul's Cross Roads about a mile southeast of what is not Route 360 where Route 615 and Route 695 meet. Route 695 here goes northerly to what was and still is known as Church Road, also called Route 572. See Chapter 11 on Parishes.

At old Paul's Cross Roads corner, early settlers developed a road southerly through the present Howertons, Bestland, and across to King and Queen County, passing near the courthouse in a southerly direction, crossing the Mattaponi River.

From the junction of Routes 695 and 615, the old road from Piscataway town, Route 615, continued southeasterly across Mussel swamp; thence up it toward its head. From Mussel swamp, running in a southeasterly direction, it was the main road down toward Middlesex County, the part of Lancaster County on the south side of the Rappahannock River. The old road continued approximately along the ridge on the south side of the main southeast branch of Piscataway, formerly known as Busby's Mill swamp, later as Webbs, Ritchies, Covingtons, and finally today as Essex Mill swamp. This old road passed near Ozeana and northeast of Montagues, and into Middlesex County.

Most of the heavy travel of the early days was by water. Grain was carried to mills by water and tobacco was shipped by water. Even in the later years of old Rappahannock County, the roads described above had very limited use.

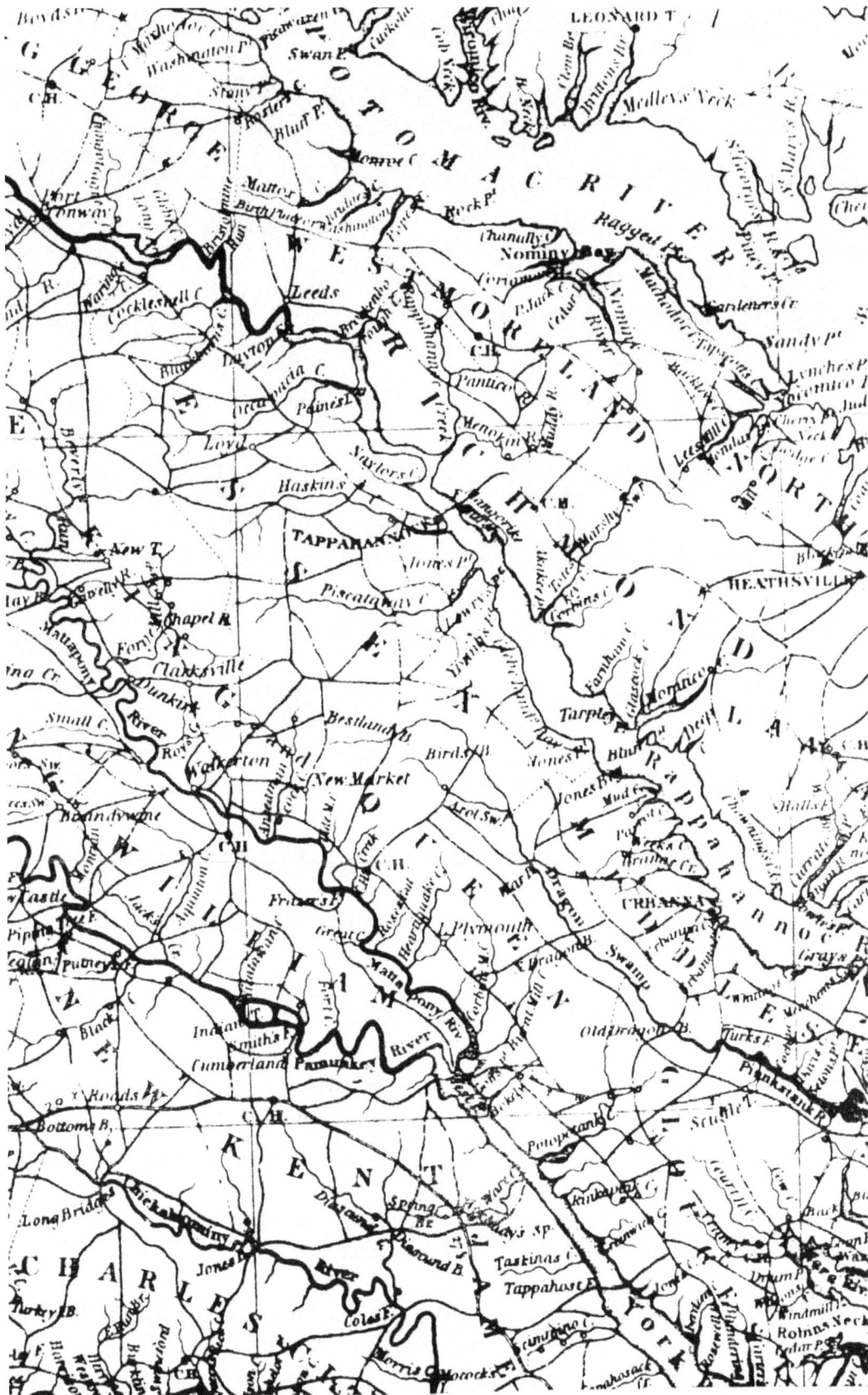

CHAPTER 14

Old Rappahannock County
Old Places and Streams

In this chapter are given the old names and locations of places and streams; and as far as possible, when the name has been changed, the present name for each.

Some men had several tracts of land in different parts of the county. Patents prior to 1651 were below Leedstown. Patents prior to 1654 were below Weir (Ware) Creek. Here the limit remained fairly constant, for, though there were a few patents in the vicinity of the falls, yet there was practically no habitation above Massaponax Creek until after Bacon's Rebellion.

In 1666, Robert Taliaferro and Lawrence Smith patented 6300 acres reaching from Nusaponucks (Massaponax) Creek southeast down river to within four miles of Weire (Ware) Creek. This patent was given by the governor to be free of taxes for a period of years in consideration of their pledge to establish a frontier town with fifty men ready to answer any call to arms to protect the white settlers at the head of the river.

In the upper part of the river, the stream is not only narrow, but the bluffs overlooking it are high; and a man in an open boat would be helpless in event of attack by Indians with guns from shore.

There is no evidence that the forts prior to this date were above the mouth of the Massaponax. The frontier patrol in the head of the river was at this time hardly any higher up than this vicinity, as the peninsula between the Rappahannock and Potomac rivers is about as narrow here as anywhere.

The names of a number of landholders on or near the various creeks are given that they may be of assistance in better coordinating the approximate location of various properties in the county. Some men had sons of the same name who patented land in the county.

The second tract a man took up was often up-river from his first patent because westward desirable, unpatented land was more abundant. There were frequent exceptions to this trend, as during the years just after Bacon's Rebellion when nearly all white persons were slain or driven out of the upper parts of the river.

The names of land owners here given were taken at random, and are in no sense supposed to represent the most prominent landholders prior to about 1692, nor to be all the land owners on the respective streams.

1. In the fall of 1692, two prominent men of the James River section, Richard Bennett, who was destined later to be governor of the colony, and William Durant, a man of but little less importance, took ship and sailed up the Rappahannock River. Thirty-five miles above the mouth, they were favorably

impressed by several beautiful open clearings where stood Indian villages. They were impressed by the fact that the hills were very near the river, and that they might, therefore, find good clay soil that would abundantly grow tobacco.

They landed on a small island, Neimcock Point, and there they marked the spot that should be the beginning of their patents. Durant was to get the lands lying just up-river, and Bennett was to get the lands lying down river. Soon they returned to Jamestown and filed their patents, which were recorded November 4, 1642; Richard Bennett taking up 2,000 acres of land, and William Durant taking up 800 acres [P.B. 1, p. 850; 2, p. 209]. Durant's was the first patent taken on the south side of the Rappahannock River in what was to become a part of old Rappahannock County. Their patents were preceded in the river only by that of John Carter, who took his a few months earlier on the upper side of Carter's Creek on the north side of the river.

2. Niemcock Point, now called Jones's Point, is located in the lower end of Essex County, at Latitude 37° 47' 10" and Longitude 76° 42' 5". About ½ mile up-river from Jones's Point was *Niemcock Point Farm*. By the many oyster shells it is evident that this was at one time the site of one of the Indian villages of Nimcock. The Nimcock Indians also accupied other places on the river, and patents for these lands are referred to as lands at Nimcock. The Niemcock (Nimcock) community extended almost to Bowler's.

   The lands of Durant became the old home place of Rice Jones in the early eighteenth century, hence the name Jones's Point.

   A spot below the creek mouth below this point was the original boundary point dividing old Rappahannock and Lancaster counties. A later survey established the county line on the top of Butylo bluff about ¼ mile lower down the river below the creek.

3. Bowlers, a trading post of lower Rappahannock County, was first owned by Thomas Bowler, merchant. It descended to his son, James Bowler, merchant. In Thomas Bowler's will of 1678, he referred to this place as his manor plantation. There still stands there today a very old plantation house, at least a part of which is thought to have been the manor house building to which Thomas Bowler referred. This place is still known as *Bowlers*.

4. Evans Mill swamp, flows into the Rappahannock at Longitude 76° 45' 30". The east branch was known as Poplar swamp. Near unto and on Evans swamp were lands belonging to Toby Smith, John Evans, Thomas Bowler, William Beale, and Thomas Pain.

Home of
Col Thomas Bowler
built before 1682

5. *Gore of the Smock*, was a place owned by Thomas Payne, and by him sold to Edward Adcock about 1694 [D7, p. 382]. It was the next place below the lands of Toby Smith and his son Henry [O1, p. 199]. This place is located between Adcock's and Evans' Creek about ¾ of a mile above Bowler's Wharf on the river. It was recently owned by W.S. Robinson, now deceased. The name of the place was derived from the similarity of the shape of the tract of land to the gore of a smock or dress.

6. Adcock Creek, also called Tobias Smith's Creek, and now known as Muddy Gut, flows into the Rappahannock one mile above Bowler's Wharf. It lies just west of the *Gore of the Smock*. On Adcock Creek were lands belonging to Toby Smith, Edward Adcock, Leonard Hill, William Hoskins, John Dobbins, Francis Slaughter and Ralph Paine.

7. *Rockingham*, was the name of the plantation of Lt. Col. Toby Smith. It was located above the mouth of Adcock Creek. Col. Smith's lands extended up river perhaps a thousand feet above the creek. Remnants of an old foundation were found, about 1950, washing into the river.

8. James Bagnall's plantation is now known as *Bellevue*.

9. Tuscarora Creek, a small creek formerly known as Tom's Creek, flows into the south side of the Rappahannock River at Latitude 37° 51' 56" north.

10. Beaverdam Creek, now known as Bellevue Creek, separates *Bellevue* and *Waterview*, early called Young's Plantation, about ½ mile below Ware's Wharf. The two main branches of this creek were known as the north and south branch of Beaverdam swamp. At one time here were the lands of Sir Henry Chicheley.

11. Covington swamp, also called Cheney Bridge swamp and Owen's swamp, is that swamp which is crossed by the present Cheney Bridge. Land owners on or near it were William Claiborne, William Ferth, William Covington, John Owen, and William Dudley. The creek is about a mile southwest of Upright.

12. White Marsh was a general expression that referred to any open grass marsh that looked white in winter; but there is one swamp often referred to as "The White Marsh." This swamp flows south into the Dragon at Longitude 76° 47' 45". Its head branch is south of Ozeana. Among those who patented land on or near this swamp were Richard Lawrence, William Baldwin, Richard Bredgar, James Green, Col. Richard Lee, John Smith, William Cheney and Richard Broocke.

13. Yorker's swamp flows south into the Dragon about ¾ mile below Bird's Bridge at the point where the meridian of Longitude 76° 46' 45" intersects the Dragon. The point just below the mouth of the creek was known as Kooper's Point. The highway from King and Queen to Center Cross crosses the Dragon above Yorker's swamp. Land owners on Yorker's swamp were Thomas Williamson, Thomas Meriwether, Richard Bridger, Leonard Hill, James Dyer, Robert Mann, John Harper, William Claiborne, Peter Mills, William Hudson and John Sharp.

14. Bryery Branch was a name used to refer to several different streams. The largest and best known of those so designated heads near lower Essex and flows through upper Middlesex into the Dragon swamp. Thomas Willis patented land there and on the Great swamp adjoining William Dudley, Thomas Pattison and Robert Chewning.

15. Dragon swamp was also known as the Great swamp, the Great pocoson, and Pianketank swamp. This swamp formed the western boundary of the lower end of old Rappahannock County. It was on the head of this swamp, in the vicinity of and including Bestland, that Col. William Claiborne planted a large colony after he failed in his efforts to secure abiding control of Kent Island. His holdings here were known as Col. Claiborne's quarter.

Other landowners on the Dragon were Dennis Conniers, Mrs. Elizabeth Brocas, Cuthbert Potter, Robert Davis, Thomas Puckett, Edward Hudson, Evan Davis, etc.

16. Piscataway Creek, with certain variations in spelling, has maintained its old name. It was originally named Piscatacon or Pascaticon for a certain tribe of Indians who apparently dwelt upon its south bank. This tribe departed before the coming of white men to the section. There is no direct reference to Piscataway Indians in old Rappahannock County, but there is mention of Indian fields on Piscataway Creek. It is known that in Maryland and on the James River were Indians called the Piscataways; but whether or not they had any connection with some tribe that once dwelt here is not known.

About a decade after the settling of this section, this creek was called Coxes Creek after John Cox, justice, whose lands extended from Piscataway up to Hoskins Creek, and up Piscataway about a mile. By early land owners this creek was sometimes called Crooked Creek.

Piscataway is a goodly, navigable creek with many streams flowing into it. Starting up the south side of Piscataway there comes first:

17. Peter Taylor's Creek or David Foxes Creek, at Longitude 76° 49' 30". Among those who owned land on it were John Beeby, John Busch, Dewell Prad (Dual Pead), David Fox, Richard Cauthorn, Ralph Pain, John Cable and Sam Parry.

There are a number of Beaverdam creeks, one of which flows into Piscataway at Longitude 76° 50' 27". Among those holding land on this creek were John Waters, Samuel Clayton and John Beeby.

18. There is a large branch that flows into Piscataway from the southeast. It was by many considered to be Piscataway. It took a ruling of the court to fix the name Piscataway as that of the west branch. The other large branch became known as the southeast branch of Piscataway or King's swamp.

On this swamp there have been five water grist mills, most of which were built before 1692. The south swamp was also called Green swamp, Beeby's swamp, Webb's Mill swamp, Covington's Mill swamp, Dunn's Mill swamp, and now Essex Mill swamp.

Landowners on or near this swamp were Alexander McKenny, John Lacy, Roscoe Overton, Capt. Josias Pickens, Thomas Bowler (Bowler's quarter), Peter Treble (Trible), Henry Woodnut, Edward Hudson, James Webb, Henry

Smith, John Harper, William Edwards, John Jones, John Gibbs, Richard Bush, Thomas Boughton, Raleigh Travers, Thomas Toseley, Henry Williamson, Ralph Pain and Samuel Parry.

19. Beeby's Mill, also called Bush's Mill, James Webb's Mill, etc., was the lower mill on this stream and is now called Essex Mill. It is located at Longitude 76° 50' 42" and Latitude 37° 53' 33". The next mill up this stream has fallen into decay, but it has lately been known as Ware's Mill, and is located about 1¾ miles above Essex Mill on the same stream.

20. Covington's Mill, also called Piscataway Mill or Old Piscataway Mill, was located at 76° 53' 3" on Piscataway swamp where the old highway, until lately, passed over the creek. The present new highway, Route 360, passes over what was the middle of the pond of Old Piscataway Mill on a west branch of Piscataway Creek.

21. *Marry Gold* [Merigold] was a quarter plantation named in the will of Thomas Bowler in 1678. It was at one time the quarter plantation of Lt. Col. Thomas Goodrich, and is now the home of Waring Lewis, located at Longitude 76° 48' 53" and Latitude 37° 49' 4".

22. Ralph's Creek, also called Parry's Creek and Perrin's Creek, was named after Ralph Payne, the first settler who made his home upon it. It was near Kilman's beaverdam swamp. It was later known as Fisher's Bridge swamp, and is today called Mussel swamp. It flows into Piscataway at Longitude 76° 51' 43".

    Among those who owned land on it were Ralph Payne, Samuel Parry, Thomas Harper, Robert Clement, Richard Bray, Thomas Meader Jr., William Young, Thomas Edmondson, Richard Jones, Oliver Segar, George Turner, John Cable, Richard Paine and James Henneygam.

23. Harry Land swamp flows into Piscataway at Longitude 76° 54' 45". It has been known as Brown's swamp and as Harry Hill swamp. Among those holding land on it were James Younger, Francis and William Brown, Richard Holt, William Denby, Thomas Gaines and William Wood.

24. Sturgeon swamp flows north to Piscataway at Longitude 76° 56' 6". Among those who owned land on or near it were Richard Haile, George Baughan, Col. Thomas Goodrich and James Baughan.

25. Western Branch flows north into Piscataway at 76° 57' 45". On this were the lands of Richard Burnett, George Wright, Benjamin Jones, Thomas

Goodrich, John Baker, Col. Thomas Brereton, Henry Cox, Theophilus Faver, William Aylett, R. Pickett, John Clark, William Ball and John Griggs.

26. Mirery Branch, entering Piscataway just east of Route 620, is thought to be what is now called Merry Branch, and flows into Piscataway at Longitude 76° 59' 43". Nearby dwelt William Ball. Below where this western branch flows into Piscataway was Pickett's Bridge, now called Haile's Bridge, on the road from Dunbrooke south.

27. Mariner's Branch flows from the north into Piscataway at Longitude 76° 56' 58". The lower west branch was known as Haile's spring branch. It heads up at Dunbrooke. This ran into the lands of Capt. Richard Haile and John Haile, not far from the lands of John Dix, Richard Awberry and Thomas Harris.

28. The mouth of Haile's old swamp is at Longitude 76° 56' 18". Not far from Haile's patent were the lands of Whitlock, David Thomas and Richard Macubins.

29. The mouth of Young's swamp is at Longitude 76° 52' 50". It is known as Baughan's swamp and as Robert Young's swamp. On or near it were the lands of Robert Young, Robert Armstrong, Major Baughan, Thomas Edmondson, Thomas St. John, Randall Chamley, William Tidner, James Baughan and William Young.

30. Merry Vayle Creek flows into Piscataway at Longitude 76° 51' 35". It flows through a marsh on the west side of Rogue Island, a tract of about an eighth of an acre in Piscataway Creek. On Merry Vayle were the lands of the St. Johns and the Baughans.

31. William Johnson's Creek is a goodly size creek running easterly into Piscataway at Longitude 76° 50' 15". Nearby were the lands of William Johnson, John Cox and Randall Chambers.

32. Black Duck Creek, at Longitude 76° 49' 53", flows south into Piscataway Creek and helps form the island at the mouth of Piscataway first known as Coxes Island, and now known as Jones's Island, sometimes called *Curlee Island Farm.* John Cox and John Smith held land on this creek.

33. Hoskins Creek, sometimes spelt Hodskins Creek, is a large stream that flows into the south side of the Rappahannock River just below the town of Tappahannock. This creek was named for Bartholomew Hoskins, burgess of Lower Norfolk County, who patented the land on which the town of Tappahannock now stands; his patent reaching back to Hoskins Creek. In

this creek there was at least one shipyard. Land holders on Hoskins Creek included Bartholomew Hoskins, Clement Thrush, Thomas Pettit, Thomas and James Williamson, Cyprian Bishop, John Gatewood, R. Gregory, James Taylor, Richard Awberry, Francis Gower and Robert Coleman.

34. Church swamp or Gregory's swamp flows into Hoskins Creek at Longitude 76° 52' 40". Land owners on it were John Gregory, Henry Awberry and James Gatewood.

35. Ticknor's Creek or Beaver Dam Creek lies two hundred yards north of Tappahannock High School. Among those who had land on it were Bartholomew Hoskins, John Green, Henry Reeves, Samuel Griffin, Thomas Goodrich and Benjamin Goodrich.

36. Mount Landing Creek has, from time to time, been given many names. They were, for the most part, names of prominent planters who dwelt upon it or who owned the mill on it.

   Its first name was Andrew Gilson's Creek, sometimes spelt Gelson or Jelson. It was next named for Richard Tignor. Later, it was called Parker's after Richard Parker; next Weir's, after John Weir; then Mill's, after John Mills who had a landing on the creek near the head of navigation for big boats. This came to be known as Mount Landing.

   This creek was for a time called Jones's Mill Creek, then Mill Creek, and after 1700 it was best known as Goldman's Mill Creek and as Waring's Mill Creek. Practically all for whom the creek was named at some time owned the mill whose dam may still be seen on the west side of the road where the county road crosses this swamp leading from Mount Landing to Caret.

   The point on the north side of the mouth of the creek was known as Cedar Point. The point on the outer end of the great marsh above it on the river was known as Troublesome Point. The point at and below the mouth of Mount Landing Creek was called Cooper's or Kooper's Point.

   Land owners on or near this creek were Col. Joseph Smith, Thomas Goodwyn, Stephen Lloyd, Robert Tomlin, Peter Byrum, Thomas Sthreshley, James Rennolds, William Dangerfield, Thomas Button, Thomas New, Thomas Gordon, Peter Ransome, John Dangerfield, William Axom, Thomas Goldman, Henry Reeves, James Reeves, William Allen, Samuel Bloomfield, Motrum Wright, John Pate, Christopher Wormley, Philip Ludwell, George Morris, John Long, Thomas Rayson, Alexander Robbins, Robert Pleyes, John Masters, Capt. Beverley, Thomas Wale, Francis Graves, Philip May and Thomas Pitts.

37. On Accokeek, near Troublesome Point, there stood an Indian town that passed out of existence about 1650. It was located at Longitude 76° 53' and

Latitude 37° 58'.   Here Robert Tomlin later lived, and thence the Rappahannock Indians were transferred up-river thirty-five miles. The bay northwest of here was called Brecknock or Tomlin's Bay. The small gut was called Devil's Mire.

38. Crow Island is not an island. It is only a cluster of trees in an open barren field on a point. Approaching it by water it looks from a distance as though it were an island. It got its name because of the fondness of crows for building their nests in the trees there. It is located at Longitude 76° 53' 30" and Latitude 37° 59' 5".

39. Breiknock or Brecknock Bay, or Robert Tomlin's Bay, is located at Latitude 37° 59' and Longitude 76° 55'. It may be seen in a northeasterly direction from the span of Route 17 four and a half miles above Tappahannock.

40. Ralph Warren's Creek is located at Longitude 76° 55' 47" and Latitude 37° 59'. Near unto it were the lands of Giles Bland, Humphrey Booth, Thomas Axum, Robert Tomlin, Thomas Goldman, Andrew Gilson and Ralph Warren.

41. Lewis's Creek, now called Beverley's lower creek, it at Longitude 76° 55' 30" and Latitude 37° 59' 25". Associated with it were the lands of Richard Lawson and Humphrey Booth, and later those of Robert Beverley.

42. Occupacia Creek still has the Indian name that is bore when white man first pushed his boat into its mouth. It was for a time, however, called Lawson's Creek after Richard Lawson, Gent., who had land thereon. It has been variously spelt Ocupaso, Occupaico, Occupated, Occupation, Occupace, Occupatia, and Occupache. On it were Lawson, Catlett, Hawkins and Waring.

43. The branch flowing southwest from the inner bay opposite Payne's Island was first known as Wassanasson, then as Little Occupacia, later as Brick House Landing Creek, and is today generally called Farmer's Hall Creek. Here lived John Foxall and others.

44. Today only the west branch of this creek, dividing a mile and a half up Farmer's Hall Creek, bears the old name of Wassanonson Creek.

45. The other branch of Occupatia is generally known as Occupatia. It is located at Latitude 38° 2' 25" and Longitude 77° 0' 40". At a joint just below Occupatia Mill dam is a branch that flows into the creek from a northwesterly direction. This branch was known as Poppoman or Popeman's Creek. On it were the lands of John Waring and Hawkins.

Associated with Occupatia Creek, were the lands of Richard Lawson, James Gaynes, Peter Johnson, William Lowry, George Morris, William Moseley, Peter Rucker, John Weir, Thomas Hawkins, Richard Coleman, Ralph Rowzee, Augustine Smith, [   ] Farmer, John Warren (Warring now spelled Waring), John Pyne, Robert Payne, George Eaton, John Gillett, John Phillips, John Watson, Philip Rowsey, John Johnson, George Pley, Henry Berry, William Gray, Henry Tandy, Alexander Newman, Valentine Allen, Cornelius Nowell and Hugh Owen.

46. Chestixent Creek or Chesituxent Creek was the principal southwest branch of Farmer's Hall or Little Occupacia Creek.

47. Cheavneck or Charvneck Creek is a branch of Occupacia. The plantation of Richard Goode was on the west side of its main swamp.

48. Grimes Creek, called the Island Neck Creek or Sharp's Creek, lies back of Payne's Island, which was also called Lawson's Island.

49. Cedar Creek flows east into the south side of the Rappahannnock River a little over half a mile below Layton's Wharf. There is also a cedar creek which flows into the Rappahannock River about a mile below Port Royal on the south side of the Rappahannock River. Land owners on these creeks were John Gillett, John Catlett, Thomas Hawkins, Robert Payne, Abraham Moon and Daniel Henry.

50. Coleman's Creek, called Coleman's Gut and Butler's Creek, is the first creek flowing into the Rappahannock River above Layton's Wharf on the south side of the river. It was above here that Richard Coleman planted his settlement and Rev. Amory (Embry) Butler had his home, and the school. Coleman planted his frontier town here about 1652. Arthur Ownlee owned land here.

51. Yarratt's marsh is a point of land about a mile above Leedstown and on the north side of the river.

52. Landrums or Landrun's Creek is a small creek that flows north into the Rappahannock River just east of Saunders' Wharf at Latitude 38° 5' 26" and Longitude 77° 1' 58". Associated with it are the lands of Thomas Lucas Jr., Robert Brooke and Thomas Hawkins.

53. Lucas Creek, later Blackburne Creek, was named after Thomas Lucas, burgess of old Rappahannock County. It has several prominent branches. Its most southern and principal branch came to be known as Blackburne Creek. The present state highway 17 crosses it a little distance above Vawters Church.

With this section are associated the Hoskins or Hodkins, Washington, Gray, Blackbourne, Brown, Winston, Garnett, Muscoe and other prominent families. On it were the lands of Thomas Purifoy, Thomas Fogg, Thomas and Mary Lucas, Thomas Page, Christopher Blackburn and Thomas Vicars.

54. Cockleshell Creek, also called Cock Hill Creek and Cockill Creek, is located at Latitude 38° 6' 30" and Longitude 77° 4', and flows into Lucas Creek through the lands of Richard Baylor. One of its branches is now called Baylor's Mill Creek. Land owners on Cockleshell Creek were John Washington, William Hodgson, Robert Pain, Thomas Page, Alexander Fleming, [   ] Brown, Simon Miller Jr., William Gray and William Mathews.

55. The Trysting Place (Calling Place) is located at the narrows on the north end of the point which lies on the east side of Green Bay. Down river from this point was *Port Micou*, the home place of Dr. Paul Micou, who was living there in the last year of the county. His grave is marked by a granite slab located about 100 feet back of the old dirt landing at Latitude 38° 7' and Longitude 77° 3' 25", where he was buried in 1736, aged 78. The slab is now at Vawters Church, having been recently removed from its original site.

56. Wickerquack Point is the large pocoson on the south side of the Rappahannock River lying between Portobago and Green Bay.

57. Portobago or Port Tobago Bay, also called Featherstone Bay, was given the latter name by Capt. John Smith after Dr. Featherstone (Fetherstone), one of his crew, who died and was buried there in 1608. It is located at Latitude 38° 9' and Longitude 77° 7'.

58. Portobacco Creek is a large creek that runs northeast into Port Tobacco Bay, not into Green Bay as the plat of the U.S. Geological Survey would indicate. Among the land owners on Port Tobacco Creek were Robert Payne, Alexander Fleming, John Ayres, and Major General Robert Smith.

59. Meaders or Meades Creek is a small creek that heads just east of Rappahannock Academy and flows northeast into the south side of the Rappahannock River opposite Nanzemun or Cleve Neck. There was also Meader Creek that flowed into the south side of Green Bay. A point in this creek is 300 poles north from Baylor's Mill pond, a branch of Cockleshell Creek. This Meades Creek became known as Lee Quarter Creek on the south end of Green Bay by Port tobago lower town.

60. Peumansend, Powmansend, or other similar spellings—even Pawamansee, is a large creek that flows into the Rappahannock River a little over two miles

below Port Royal. On this creek near the place known as Pin Hook is a mill known as Taliaferro's Mill. Today this creek is generally called Mill Creek and only the south branch is commonly known by the old name Peumonsand Creek. With this creek were associated the names of Francis Taliaferro, Warrick Cammack, John Meader and Simon Miller.

61. Golden Vale has held it name consistently from the beginning of white man's habitation. It flows into the south side of the Rappahannock about a mile above the town of Port Royal. At the mouth of this creek, on the river, the Rev. William White, an early preacher, had a patent.

   Other early settlers on or near this creek were Thomas Button, William White, John Gillett, Col. John Catlett, Richard Long, Andrew Harrison, Samuel Prosser, Thomas Hilliard, William Smith, Richard Buckner, John Buckner, Mr. Stanard and John Pattison.

62. Usensen is the old name of a creek located at Latitude 38° 12' and Longitude 77° 14', it being the most easterly of several creeks on the south side of the river that flows north into the river on the reach of the river where it is flowing almost east and west and over against the *Cleve Farm*.

63. Moon Creek, now called Mount Creek, was named after Abraham Moon. His home became known as *Moon's Mount*. This creek flows east into the south side of the Rappahannock River at Latitude 30° 11' 57" and Longitude 77° 15' 5". Rev. Charles Grimes had an early patent on the east side of Skinner's Neck just above this creek. Others who early had land on it were Abraham Moon, Thomas Cheetwood and Richard Buckner.

64. Ware Creek flows northeast into the south side of the Rappahannock River at Longitude 77° 18' 35" and Latitude 38° 14'. It passes just south of the present Moss Neck store. Lands on it were patented by John Weir (Wier), Robert Taliaferro and Henry Corbyn. Hazeltree Point was the next point west of Ware Creek.

65. Snow Creek flows into the south side of the Rappahannock River about ¼ mile below the Caroline and Spotsylvania county line.

66. Mussaponic, now usually called Massaponax Creek, is a large creek flowing northeast into the Rappahannock River at a point five miles or more below Fredericksburg. With it is associated Augustine Warner's vast patent.

Home of Colonel John Catlett   BUILT BEFORE 1690 ON CATLETT'S HILL SOUTH OF PORT ROYAL

67. Sandy Creek flows into the Rappahannock about four miles above the falls.

68. Muddy Creek or Mud Creek is an old name that still persists. It flows south into the Rappahannock River and forms the boundary between Stafford and King George counties on the Rappahannock River side. With it are associated the names of James Rennolds, George and John Mott, John Waugh, and William and John Moss.

69. Lamb Creek flows southeast into a small bay on the north side of the Rappahannock River at Longitude 77° 14' 30".

70. Jett's Creek flows south into Portobago Bay east of old Nanzatico Town. This creek was named after Peter Jett.

71. Keyes Creek is the northeast branch of Doeges Creek. It is sometimes called Keys Run. It was named for Peter Keyes who patented 200 acres on it in 1678.

72. Doeges Creek is so called for the Indian tribe that dwelt beside it. It flows into the Rapphannock at Latitude 38° 14' 30" and Longitude 77° 13' 15". It is sometimes called Dogue Creek. Enoch Doughty and William Berry had land on it.

73. Nanzimum Neck is located at Latitude 38° 12' and Longitude 77° 14' 30". It belonged to the Carter Family and is now generally known as the *Cleve*. Through the marsh lands on the outer or lower end of this neck is a small channel of the Rappahannock River called the *Slipe*. Running north into this neck is Lewis's Creek, which almost makes an island of the neck.

74. Guicotic or Guigateepe flows into the Rappahannock on the north side about 2½ miles below Port Conway at the narrows just above Port Tobago Bay. Here were the lands of John Cheetwood and John Russell, Chirurgeon.

75. Pepetick, now called Brockenbrough Creek, flows into the north side of the Rappahannock River. It is quite long, its branches extending over toward the head branches of Pope's Creek. It flows into the Rappahannock River at Latitude 38° 5' 25" and Longitude 76° 57' 35", across the river from and not quite two miles below Layton's Wharf. Pepetick has two large branches, one of which was known as the eastern branch and the other as the north branch. Associated with this creek were the names of Tobias Smith the Younger, Henry Smith, William Underwood, Thomas Whitlock, William Lane, John Payne, James Williamson's daughters, Alexander Fleming, John Barrow, Thomas Lucas and Arthur Spicer. This Brockenbrough Creek now serves part as the line between Richmond and Westmoreland counties.

76. *Ireland* was a farm named after a family called Ireland. It was located on the point above what is now called Leedstown.

77. Layne Creek flows into the Rappahannooock some two miles below Pepetick Creek.

78. Clift Creek or Cliff's Creek is a small creek flowing into the Rappahannock River between two high cliffs on the north side of the river and a short distance from Carter's Wharf. Here Charles Snead and John Weir had land.

79. Waterview Creek is a small creek flowing south into the north side of the Rappahannock just below Mulberry Island Point. With it were associated the names of James Ingoe, David Gwin and Peter Mills.

80. Doctor's Creek is the first creek above Naylor's Wharf. It is about sixteen feet wide with a marsh on the upper side and highland on the lower side. Here lived Robert Hopkins, Avery Naylor and William Moss.

81. Rappahannock Creek, known also as Fleet's Creek, Indian Creek, Great Rappahannock Creek, is now called Cat Point Creek. It is one of the largest creeks in the upper Rappahannock River valley. It flows into the north side of the river about three miles north of Tappahannock. It was named for the Rappahannock tribe of Indians, as was the Rappahannock River.

82. Its great branch running north toward Montross was often referred to as Great Hunting Creek. With Rappahannock Creek and Great Hunting Creek are associated the names of Lt. Col. Henry Fleet, John Bowin, Richard Webley, Henry Clark, Patrick Norton, William Moss, James Orchard, Motrum Wright, John Carr, John Simson, Edwin Thacker, Chicheley Corbin Thacker, George Brent, William Love, Richard Coleman, H. Sherman, Francis Furnes, Becket Burke, Col. John Walker, Thomas Hopkins, Henry, John and Peter Taylor, William Tayloe, William Stone, Capt. Richard Beale, John Stephens, John Carr and Avery Naylor.

In 1608, it may have been the conflict at the mouth of Rappahannock Creek, on the south side of the creek, at Latitude 37° 58' 25" and Longitude 76° 51' 7", that caused Capt. John Smith to be brought into the Rapahannock River for trial by the Indians.[90]

84. Clark's Run, which is thought to have been called Chesterton Run, is now known as Mt. Airy Mill swamp. It flows northwest into Cat Point Creek at Longitude 76° 48' and Latitude 37° 59' 25". With it were associated the lands of William Tayloe, John Clark, the Glebe, David Barrick, George Bryer, Richard Lawrence and Thomas Beale.

85. Menokin Creek was first known as Little Hunting Creek. It flows west into Rappahannock Creek at Latitude 37° 59' 50". On it or close to it were lands of John Willis, John Parsons, Col. William Pearce (Peirce), Richard Lawrence, James Orchard and John Clark.

86. The grave of Capt. Thomas Beale, who died in 1678, is located at Latitude 37° 59' 35" and Longitude 76° 47' 45", and is well marked.

---

[90] There is no number 83 in the original text.

87. Paddy's Creek, on lands formerly belonging to H.C. DeShields, dec., is a small creek running into the north side of the Rappahannock River, its mouth being located about a mile below Rappahannock Creek. It is also called Ferry Point and Marsh Creek.

88. Mangorite Creek was first known as Bushwood. In a short time, however, the name Mangorite was attached to it, and by that name it has been best known. It is frequently called Little Carter Creek. It flows into the Rappahannock River at Longitude 76° 47' and Latitude 37° 55' 30". There is a small creek that flows west into old Mangorite that now bears the name of Bushwood. It was at the mouth of old Bushwood Creek and on its east side that was located the first shipping point named in all of the upper Rappahannock River. This was called Bushwood in early 1652. Here, in 1656, was placed the upper courthouse of old Lancaster County. It was here that William Underwood lived when he made the Underwood treaty with the Rappahannock Indians regarding title to his lands.

It was but one and a half miles on the river front below the mouth of Mangorite Creek that Thomas Meader lived. At his place all the troops of all the counties of northern Virginia assembled when they marched against the Rappahannock Indians to demand peace in 1654.

It was but two and an eighth miles down the river shore that James Williamson lived. He named his large plantation *Cobham Park* after his ancestral home, *Cobham Hall*, in England. *Cobham Park* house was built in 1655, and lately burned.

Mangorite marsh was the name of the marsh across from Tappahannock.

89. Oatspekety was probably the name attached for a short time to Jugs Creek. In any event its head was in the vicinity of Warsaw.

90. James Williamson's Creek is what is now known as Ball's Creek. It is located at Latitude 37° 54' 30" and Longitude 76° 46' 36". Above this creek were lands of William Underwood, Thomas Meader and Thomas Brier. The home of Thomas Brier passed to Benjamin Rust early in the eighteenth century, and from that time to this has been known as *Islington*. The name of Thomas Meader is frequently spelled Meades.

91. Totuskey Creek was first called Willing Creek, and then named for an Indian town of the Rappahannocks called Totuskey, which was located on its north bank about two miles from the river. This is a large, deep and navigable stream. It has two principal branches.

92. The southeast branch was often called Cross Creek for the Chickacoon Indian trail that ran down and crossed it. (Chickakoon, Checkacoon, etc.)

93. At Longitude 76° 40' 40", Hogtown Branch flows south into Cross Creek.

94. The north branch of Totuskey is sometimes referred to as Little Totuskey, and sometimes as Herring Creek. It is given the latter name because of the abundance of fish caught here during the spawning season.

    The earliest planters to own land on or near Totuskey included John Overton, Thomas and Edward Lewis at the ferry, Thomas Robinson, Leonard Jones, Francis Gower, Quinton Sherman, John DeYoung, William Matthews whose farm was called *Lilly*, Arthur Etty whose land was known as *Wachford*, Capt. John Hull, Robert Bailie, Quintilian Harman, Thomas Robinson and Thomas Freshwater.

    Those who had land on or near Cross Creek were George Hasplock, John Alloway, John Cannida, Edward James, John Sherlock, Miles Reyley, William Barber and Robert Sisson.

95. Richard's Creek, sometimes called Jackman's, is the next large creek flowing into the river below Totuskey, on the north side of the Rappahannock River. It has two main branches. With it are associated the lands of Anthony Jackman, Thomas Dias, John Richards, William Cotton whose place is now called *Shandy Hall*, Robert Bayley, Luke Billington, John Webb, James Sampford, Dennis Swillivant and Will Barber.

96. Jackman's Folly. This peninsula below Totuskey was patented by Thomas Dias. Most of it was re-patented a little later in spite of the fact that Dias had a title ot it. The tract became involved in such a bitter law suit that the local justices of Rappahannock after several years notified the governor of the colony that they were unable to get a jury in the county that would go and review the disputed lands. The General Court finally decreed that it was the land of Thomas Dias. The peninsula has since been known as Anthony Jackman's Folly. The part next to the river is still called the *Folly Farm*.

97. Farnham Creek was named for *Farnham*, the plantation of Col° Moore Fantleroy. It is a goodly sized creek that flows into the north side of the Rappahannock River about a half mile below Sharps Wharf.

    The first branch of Farnham Creek, on the north side near its mouth, is called Hatter's Creek or Smith's Creek. The island near it and near the north shore of Farnham Creek is called Snake Island.

    The second branch that flows into Farnham Creek from its north side and a little over half a mile up was known as Pipe Makers Creek. Between Pipe Makers Creek and Smith Creek was the residence plantation of Col° Moore Fantleroy. On it there stands unto this day a very picturesque old brick house that is believed to have been the home of Col° Moore Fantleroy during his later years. Landholders on Farnham Creek included Samuel and Thomas

Griffin, John Williamson, Luke Billington and John Suckett, besides Col⁰· Fantleroy.

98. Morattico or Moratticon Creek has two principal branches. The eastern branch became the boundary line between Lancaster and Rappahannock counties; and to this day has remained the boundary line between Richmond and Lancaster counties. It is now called Lancaster Creek.

Early landholders on Morattico Creek were James Taylor, John Tarpley, Thomas Wright, John Scott, Thomas Madison, John Stott and his brothers, William Hanks, Charles Grimes, Thomas Stevens, David Mansell, Thomas Glascock, John Sharp, John Chinn, Mary Stevens, Paul Woolbridge, John Newman and Moore Fantleroy.

99. The folowing names of creeks and places are unnumbered, either because they do not lie on the route followed in nmbering those aforementioned or because their location is unknown.

- Whitlock's Creek, named for Thomas Whitlock, is one of the creeks lying between Green Bay and Leedstown on the north side. On September 20, 1661, Samuel Nickolls patented 688 acres lying on a small creek called Whitlock's Creek. Robert Bird, Sylvester Thacker, Richard Coleman and Thomas Whitlock had land on or near it.
- Prosser's Creek was named for John Prosser. On September 28, 1681, Edwin Conway patented 1200 acres on the northwest side of a small creek that issues out of the Rappahannock River on the southwest side next to Anthony Savage's plantation, the said creek being called Prosser's Creek.
- Peytresses, or Pey Creek, was a creek not far from Nanzatico Town, and probably was what is called Gincotic Run.
- Reedy Branch was on the south side near the head of navigation, location not exactly known. On it were located lands of Capt. Lawrence Smith, Capt. Robert Beverley, Augustine Smith and William Smith.
- Allin's Creek. On June 6, 1664, Lt. Col. C. Ellyot had 1400 acres of land granted him adjoining his former divident and Allin's Creek.
- Ekepaw Creek. On October 18, 1670, William Moseley had granted him 427½ acres on the south side of the Rappahannock River on the branches of Ekepaw Creek.
- Garland's Creek flows into the Rappahannock River between Jones's Creek and Carter's Wharf. It lies about in the center of the two hundred yard valley between the high cliffs.

CHAPTER 15

Old Rappahannock County
Men and Incidents

Col⁰· Moore Fantleroy was, without doubt, the most outstanding man in Rappahannock County from 1650 to 1662. He was in charge of all Indian affairs in the Rappahannock River valley. He was "maior" of the court. He owned and ooperated several extensive plantations, the larges of which was called *Farnham*. That he shared actively in the life of the church is manifest by the fact that, in spite of his political chastisement by Berkeley, the people, in tribute to him, kept the name of the lower parish of Rappahannock County as Farnham Parish. To this day the North and South Farnham parishes bear their names in his honor.

A burgess of distinction, it was under his leadership that the Rappahannock River valley gained its greatest impetus toward settlement. A scholar and a gentleman, he was the son of the clerk of the court of Nansemond County, who was for many years a resident of Virginia, but later returned to England.

Democratic in his thinking, a zealous commoner in politics, he was aligned against the party of the governor and marked for disfavor. As soon as the era of the Commonwealth was over the Berkeley was again governor, he pried into Col⁰· Fantleroy's past and trumped up a charge of very questionable credibility against him to depose from office and disfrancise this gallant leader of the frontier country.

The first court of Rappahannock County was composed almost entirely of Col⁰· Moore Fantleroy and men connected by marriage with his family. This may at first sight seem reprehensible, but it must be remembered that this was the first court after the organization of the county, that population was sparse and scattered, and that in the event of Indian trouble he needed men that he could reach quickly and trust implicitly with government secrets which should by no chance leak to Indian ears.

Both the spellings Fantleroy and Fauntleroy are used in old records.

Henry Awberry

Henry Awberry, burgess from Rappahannock County, justice of the court, high sheriff of the county, Indian interpreter, and first burgess of Essex County after its formation, was for years the most influential citizen in the county. Because of his kindness to Indians when they needed help, he may be fitly styled the friendly Mr. Awberry. With the massacre in the head of the river in 1675, with the crying out against all Indians by the white man, and with the murder of white people within a mile of their town, the Rappahannocks, whether alarmed for their safety or because there were those among them guilty of the murder, or for lack of counsel, slipped away from their town leaving the land deserted. The following June their lands were declared forfeited by their absence, and were at once taken up by Richard Lawrence and other active supporters of Bacon. Since this land was their reservation, the Rappahannocks thereby became a tribe without a home. In this emergency they found an advocate in Henry Awberry.

He had long lived in peace and harmony close by the Mattaponies. After the close of the hostilities of 1676, the Rappahannocks are thought to have besought his help. They settled themselves in his neighborhood, it is believed on part of his large patent that lay on the head branches of Piscataway and Hoskins creeks.

Eight years later, in 1684, when these Indians were being persecuted by the Susquehanna Indians, he acted as interpreter and mediator between them and the county court; visited them in behalf of the court; and after many conferences persuaded them to move up the river where they might unite forces and be near their friends and kinsmen on Port Tobacco Bay.

There are distinct traces and traditions of an old Indian town on the *Meadow Farm*, which was later the property of the Latane Family. It may be that this was the site of the fort of the Rappahannocks.

John Stone

Colonel John Stone was perhaps the ablest jurist in the history of old Rappahannock County. He seems rapidly to have risen to the position of senior justice, and in that position he served efficiently and well. He was a man of high literary attainments and a sound reasoner. He served his year as high sheriff and was then elected burgess. In 1684, as presiding justice, he issued the final order for the removal of the Rappahannock Indians out of the lower Rappahannock valley. In his latter years he lived quietly in Richmond County on or near Clark's Run, a branch of Rappahannock Creek.

Samuel Griffin

Samuel Griffin lived at the headwaters of Farnham Creek. Serving as a justice and as sheriff, and, after Bacon's Rebellion, as burgess, he lived to a ripe old age, spending the declining years of his life in Northumberland County. He stood high in the social life of his time.

Jacob Lumpkin

Captain Jacob Lumpkin of New Kent County, who also had land in Rappahannock County, was in 1690 accosted by a young officer and requested to give his reason for not saluting the governor of Virginia. His reply was, "I am as good as the governor," For this response he was brought to trial before the General Court at James City.

A Funeral Feast

Dinners at funerals were not uncommon in those days. In 1650, Mr. Hugh Lee served a big funeral dinner on the occasion of the death of Mr. Fanniger. For this he received 1000 pounds of tobacco from John Motrom, executor, by order of the court of old Northumberland County.

Slanderous Words

Elizabeth Herd, wife of Walter Herd, was tried by the court of Lancaster County in 1656 and found guilty of slandering the wife of Thomas Powell. For this she was required to appear at the next court with capital letters printed on her breast declaring her offence, and publicly to ask forgiveness [L1, p. 289]. In 1691, Alice Jones was ordered to be given three duckings on the public ducking stool for using slanderous words against another woman [O2, p. 290].

A Writing Challenge

To challenge an officer of the law was unlawful, even to challenge him to a writing contest, as Thomas Harding discovered to his sorrow when he challenged David Fox, a justice of the court. Even the man who delivered the challenge was fined [L1, p. 65].

King William Cursed

Roger Loveless drank to the health of King James on July 13, 1691, and cursed his majesty King William. He used other irreverent expressions. For this he received at the hands of the sheriff twenty lashes on his bare back. Symon Copnell, for a similar offence, suffered a like punishment [O2, p. 302].

Bootlegging Out of Maryland

In 1691, Hugh French, a bootlegger out of St. Mary's, Maryland, was selling rum to the "poor labouring men" of Rappahannock County [O2, p. 291].

Horse Race Winner Decided by County Court

Horse racing was a favorite sport; and on at least one occasion the county court handed down a decision as to the winner, for after an exciting race on August 6, 1684, with Thomas Harwar holding the stakes, much dispute arose as to which horse won the eleven pounds sterlling. The court settled the question, and awarded the money to George Parker [O1, p. 119].

Indenture Papers

In 1685, Capt. Richard Feversham, mariner, tried to conceal the indenture papers of his servants, but was detected and punished by the court [O1, p. 189].

John Alloway

Acknowledgement of the presence of a visiting celebrity was made when John Alloway appeared in court September 4, 1689, and upon the rising of the court, made notion that his presence be recorded. Court so ordered [O2, p. 169]. John

Alloway was a member of the General Court at Jamestown, and was paying this court a visit.

Lt. Col. John Walker

Justice to the Indians is revealed in a report by Lt. Col. John Walker, who had considerable land on Rappahannock Creek in the first years of its settlement. He was appointed in 1661 by Gov. Berkeley to settle a dispute between the heirs of Lt. Col. Thomas Ludlow, deceased, and the Chesquiack Indians. He reported to the Assembly that the lands of the Chesquiack Indians had been encroached upon; whereupon it was ordered by the Assembly that the said Indians enjoy the whole tract of land.[91]

Runaway Negroes

On August 5, 1691, there is an entry [O2, p. 301]: Whereas divers complaints are made to the court that several run-away Negro and Mulatto slaves are in company together and have & still continue to do great mischiefs." Action was taken to control then.

Informer Rewarded

One Berkenhead of Gloucester County discovered a plot to upset the government of Berkeley. He was given his freedom and 5,000 pounds of tobacco. September 13 was set apart to be kept annually holy to commemorate the saving of the country by God in his Infinite Mercy.[92]

Surgeons and Doctors

Thomas Roots, Chirurgeon (Surgeon), of Lancaster County, was about to marry Fra. Mansell, daughter of Mar. Grimes, widow. Witnesses Ed. Conway and Wm. White [L1, p. 212]. October 24, 1653.

Jno. Edwards, Chyrurgion, sued the estate of Elias Edmonds for Physic and services of attendance to him and his wife at the time of their sickess [L1, p. 145]. 1654.

Thomas Cheevers, chirurgeon, witnessed the oral will of Thomas Crowder onboard the ship *Richard and Benjamin* [L1, p. 87]. January 28, 1653.

Mr. George Davis, Physician [D4, p. 438]. October 1, 1667.

Dr. Gibson is referred to October 26, 1671 [D5, p. 136].

Dr. Peter Hopegood was an executor of the estate of John Curtis, November 29, 1677 [W2, p. 58].

Dr. Roger Waters sued for fees [O1, p. 98].

Dr. Roger Synock is mentioned June 4, 1684 [O1, p. 41].

Dr. Richard Pemberton appeared in court, August 6, 1684 [O1, p. 49].

---

[91] Hening, Vol. 2, p. 153, March 1661/2, At a Grand Assemblie.
[92] Hening, Vol. 2, p. 190, September 1663, Act XIV.

Dr. Reynolds is mentioned in 1683 [D6B, p. 10].

Dr. Godson's farm was on Piscaticon Creek in 1684 [D7, p. 111].

James Simons made Gerard Greenwood, alias the German doctor, his only executor, on February 24, 1686/7; will probated May 4, 1687.

Inventory of the estate of Dr. Nathan Allen was made by Samuel Bloomfield, November 16, 1687 [O2, p. 57].

Dr. Henry Willoughby, late of Rappahannock County, was deceased [O1, p. 211].

Dr. Moses Hubbart was asked to appraise the estate of Dr. Nathan Allen, February 1, 1688 [O2, p. 59].

Henry Wilson, of Farnham Parish, left his weights and instruments to William Brazir, Chirorigon [Old Manuscripts, 1686-9].

Dr. Robert Clark sued the estate of Robert Baylis, deceased, July 4, 1689 [O2, p. 158].

Dr. Paul Micou is mentioned November 1690 [O2, p. 262].

CHAPTER 16

Old Rappahannock County
Officers of the Crown

All men who served as officers of trust under the Crown were citizens of the county for which they served. They were landholders and housekeepers and were over twenty-one years of age.

Burgesses

The first burgesses representing this section at James City were from Northumberland County. They were John Mottram, 1645-6; William Presley, 1647-8; Capt. Francis Poythers and John Trussell, 1649-50; John Mottram and George Fletcher, 1651-2.

Burgesses from Lancaster County before Rappahannock County was formed were: Moore Fantleroy and Raleigh Travers of Northumberland and Lancaster counties, 1651-2; Henry Fleet and William Underwood, 1652; Moore Fantleroy and John Baldwin, 1653; John Carter and James Bagnall, 1654-5.

Burgesses from Rappahannock County were: Thomas Lucas, 1657-8; Moore Fantleroy and John Weyre (Weir), 1658-9; Thomas Lucas and John Weyre, 1660-7; Thomas Hawkins and Samuel Griffin, 1676-9 [O1, p. 23]; Thomas Goldman and William Lloyd (Loyd), 1680-2; Henry Awbrey and George Taylor, 1684; Henry Awbrey and John Stone [William Colston serving in Stone's stead in the second session], 1692-8.

After Essex County was formed, Col. John Stone served Richmond County as burgess.

Justices

As the first Order Books of Rappahannock County are lost, we do not have the names of all the justices and jurors who served there; but it seems most probable that some of the men who were or who had been justices of Lancaster County, and who, in 1656, were living in that part of Lancaster that was cut off to form Rappahannock County, became justices of Rappahannock. Among them were Toby Smith, James Bagnal, William Underwood, Andrew Gilson, Rawleigh Travers, James Williamson, Thomas Lucas, Thomas Brier, Moore Fantleroy and George Taylor.

November 7, 1661, justices serving at Rappahannock County court were Col. Moore Fantleroy, president, Mr. Thomas Lucas, James Bagnal, Mr. William Johnson and Mr. George Marsh [D7, p. 285].

Col. Moore Fantleroy was president of the court, November 7 1661. On September 28/9, 1664, Thomas Bowler was added to the commission for Rappahannock County and ordered to be sworn.[93]

October 23, 1665, Capt. Humphrey Booth was added to the commission of Rappahannock County by the governor's command [W&D1, p. 41].

On June 7, 1666, Maj. John Weir and Mr. Samuel Griffin were added to the court, and "Mr. John Cox was raised to the Comicon and the power of the Comiconds; one being of the Quorum to make a Court" [D3, p. 63].

October 4, 1667, Giles Cale and Robert Taliaferro were added [D3, p. 307].

On July 7, 1686, Col. Cadwallader Jones, Mr. William Tayloe, Capt. Sam. Travers, Mr. Henry Williamson, Mr. Thomas Harwar, and Mr. Thomas Edmondson took the oaths of allegiance and supremacy and were sworn justices of the peace of Rappahannock County [O1, pp. 230, 239].

On July 1, 1691, Mr. Francis Taliaferro, Thomas Edmondson and James Harrison took the oath as justice of the peace enjoined by the act of Parliament instead of oath of allegiance and supremacy [O2, p. 295].

May 19, 1686, the following justices in court included: Samuel Peachy, William Fantleroy and James Harrison [O1, p. 222]. The following justices were sworn as by dedimus directed to the court: Col. John Stone, Lt. Col. William Lloyd, Col. Leroy Griffin, Capt. Henry Awbrey, Capt. George Taylor, Mr. Samuel Bloomfield, Mr. James Harrison, Mr. William Fantleroy and Mr. Samuel Peachy [O1, p. 223].

In June 1691, Capt. Samuel Travers was sworn again as justice [O2, p. 293].

On August 5, 1691, Henry Williamson took the oath as justice as enjoined by act of Parliament instead of the oath of allegiance and supremacy [O2, p. 301].

On June 3, 1691, John Stone and Mr. Henry Awbrey administered the oaths of allegiance and supremacy to Capt. George Taylor, Capt. John Catlett, Capt. William Moseley, Capt. Bernard Thomas and Mr. Alexan. Doniphan, which being done these together administered the oaths to Col. John Stone and Henry Awbry [O2, p. 293].

Henry Awbery was president of the court in 1689 [O2, p. 175].

On February 3, 1691/2, Capt. Wm. Barber having taken the oaths appointed instead of the oath of allegiance and supremacy was admitted and sworn justice of the peace of Rappahannock County [O2, p. 336].

Other justices mentioned in Rappahannock County are:
Richard Awborie, June 9, 1669 [D4, p. 498]
Thomas Goodrich, June 22, 1666 [D3, pp. 27, 57]
Samuel Bloomfield, May 1684 and 1689 [O1, p. 26; O2, p. 156]
Col. John Catlett, August 20, 1669 [D4, p. 195]
Maxmillian Robinson, 1683 [O1, p. 5]

---

[93] Orders of the General Court at James City, p. 508; Rappahannock Co. Deeds Bk. 2, p. 403.

William Fantleroy, May 1684 [O1, p. 26]

Col. Leroy Griffin, March 5, 1685 [O1, p. 97]

Thomas Hawkins, August 20, 1669 [D4, p. 195]; and February 2, 1669/70 [D4, p. 216]

Col. Cadwallader Jones, 1685 [O1, p. 142] and July 4, 1688

Guliott [William] Travers, August 1, 1677

Col. William Lloyd (Loyd), August 1, 1677 and May 1684 [O1, p. 26]; President of the Court, October 10, 1686. His name was sometimes written Guliett or Guliott Lloyd.

William Moseley, February 16, 1666 [D3, p. 215]

Mr. Samuel Peachy, August 6, 1684 [O1, p. 43] and July 4, 1689 [O2, p. 156]

John Rice, 1688 [O2, p. 132]

Col. John Stone, President of the Court, May 1684 [O1, p. 26] to July 4, 1689 [O2, p. 156]

Henry Smith, February 7, 1677 [D6, p. 91]

William Slaughter, August 6, 1684 [O1, p. 43]

Thomas Goldman, 1682 [D7, p. 8]

William Barber, 1691 [O2, p. 350]

Capt. Alexander Swan, 1691 [O2, p. 350]

William Underwood, 1691 [O2, p. 350]

Capt. Edward Thomas, April 6, 1692 [O2, p. 352]

Henry Williamson, President of the Court, April 2, 1692 [O2, p. 352]

Coroners

Capt. Samuel Bloomfield and Mr. John Tavernor, after taking the oath of allegiance and supremacy, were sworn coroners of this county, in 1685 [O1, p. 231].

Mr. John Catlett was coroner in 1661 [D2, p. 202 (154)]

Sheriffs

Due to the loss of the earliest Order Books of old Rappahannock County, the names of some of the county sheriffs are not known. They were appointed by the governor.

Clement Herbert, sub-sheriff, is "ordered by the Governor to act as High Sheriff in place of the dead high sheriff until the new appointment can be made." April 6, 1663 [D2, p. 278 (215)]

By the Governor's order the 23rd of March 1664/5, Col. Thomas Catlett is "appointed sheriff of Rappahannock County, it being his term according to act, but in case his other duties prevent his acting then he hath the right to dispose of the said place of Sheriff to Major Andrew Gilson or whome soever he please." "I assign the place of High Sheriff and the profits thereunto to Major Andrew Gilson, under my hand this first day of April 1665. John Catlett." [D2, p. 427]

Mr. Samuel Griffin is found eligible by reason of his many years as justice and is appointed High Sheriff for the year 1670-1. June 2, 1670 [D4, p. 443]

Henry Clark, sub-sheriff, for the year 1670-1, did according to law "forewarn John Alloway from off the land in the Indian towne in Totuskey Creek, and further not to clear or fall any more timber or to commit any further respass, the said forewarding being made June 25, 1670." [D4, p. 227]

Leroy Griffin, High Sheriff of Rappahanock County, was selling land formerly belonging to Bagwell. November 4, 1679 [D6, p. 86]

Henry Smith was appointed sheriff of Rappahannock County, July 22, 1680, by the Council at *Green Springs*, 1680/1.[94] Henry Smith, deceased in 1684, was made sheriff in 1682. May 7, 1684. [O1, pp. 1, 26]

Ralph Gaydon was sub-sheriff of Rappahannock County, March 5, 1683 [O1, p. 6]. He was retiring in 1684. [O1, p. 76]

Col. Cadwallader Jones was High Sheriff of Rappahannock County on May 8, 1684 for the ensuing year [O1, p. 37]. He was bonded for 400,000 pounds of Tobacco, with William Colston and Arthur Spicer his lawful attorneys to act in his behalf and name. [O1, p. 37]

Mr. James Taylor was sworn under sheriff for the county of Rappahannock on the north side for the ensuing year. May 8, 1684. [O1, p. 37]

Mr. John Battaille was made under sheriff for the south side, May 8, 1684 [O1, p. 87]. John Battaile, sub-sheriff of the county, was in court December 16, 1685. [O1, p. 185]

"Mr. William Slaughter was this day sworn High Sheriff of this county for the insuing year" [O1, p. 131]. William Slaughter gave bond as High Sheriff for 100,000 pounds of tobacco, seal delivered April 7 last past, bond dated May 19, 1687. Signed Wm. Slaughter, Alex. Swan, Edward Thomas and Sam Bayly [Old Manuscripts]. William Slaughter gave bond as collector of public and county levies for the ensuing year. July 10, 1686. [Old Manuscripts]

Edward Jones gave bond as under-sheriff in 1686 [Old Manuscripts]. He was mentioned as under-sheriff on December 16, 1685. [O1, p. 185]

John Battaille gave bond as under sheriff of Rappahannock County, said bond being for 200,000 pounds of tobacco. May 19, 1686 [Old Manuscripts]. John Battail, deputy of the high sheriff, says that "hogsheads were taken and roled off from the plantation of William Jewell. [O1, p. 216]

William Tayloe gave bond as High Sheriff of Rappahannock for the ensuing year, May 4, 1687 and May 23, 1688 [Old Manuscripts]

Capt. Samuel Travers presented his commission for the office of High Sheriff of the county and prayed that by virtue of this fact he may be admitted in place of Capt. William Tayloe, but he objected to taking the oath, etc. [O2, p. 149]. Capt. Samuel Travers was High Sheriff, January 8, 1690 [O2, p. 274]

David Lloyd was sworn sub-sheriff, April 1, 1691 [O2, p. 289]

---

[94] *Executive Journals of the Council of Virginia*, Vol. 1, p. 10.

William Slaughter was High Sheriff, January 2, 1689 [O2, p. 139]

Robert Williams was deputy sheriff on the south side of the river, January 1, 1690 [O2, p. 196]

Edward Jones was sub-sheriff, 1690 [O2, p. 220]

John Battaille gave bond of 200,000 pounds of tobacco as Sheriff of Rappahannock County, 1690-1. Signed Henry Aubry and Sam Bloomfield. Witnesses George Taylor and James Harrison [Old Manuscripts]

Col. John Stone was admitted and sworn as high sheriff of Rappahannock County, July 1, 1691 [O2, p. 298]. His bond was endorsed by Henry Awbery and James Harrison, July 1, 1691 [Old Manuscripts of Court]

Mr. George Parke was admitted and sworn under sheriff of the lower side of the county, July 1, 1691 [O2, p. 298]. He gave bond July 1, 1691 [Old Manuscripts of Court]

Edw. Jones was admitted and sworn as under-sheriff of the north side of the county, July 1, 1691 [O2, p. 298]. He gave bond same date.

Henry Awbery gave bond as high sheriff of Essex County, July 11, 1692. The bond was endorsed by Wm. Moseley, Edw. Thomas and John Battaille [Old Manuscripts]

Mr. Malachy Peale, the High Sheriff of Stafford County, was at the court of Rappahannock County, September 2, 1691 [O2, p. 311]

Clerks of Court

Anthony Stephens was the first clerk of old Rappahannock County, 1656-8. He was sworn clerk and surveyor of Rappahannock County on February 19, 1656/7 [L1, p. 318]

Walter Granger was clerk, 1660-1 [D2]

Francis Kirkman was clerk, 1664 [W1, p. 49]

Robert Davis first appears as clerk of court, January 5, 1663 [D2, p. 323 (258)]. He signed as clerk in Will Book 1. In Deed Book 3, p. 104, we find that Robert Daves, sometimes spelled Davies and Davis, took his old name of Robert Pain. 1665.

Robert Sisson was clerk of court 1675 [D6, p. 7]

Edmond Crask was clerk of court from 1672 to 1683 [W2, D4-D6]

Thomas New was clerk August 1, 1683 to January 2, 1683/4 [D6]

William Colston was clerk 1683-1692 [D7-D8]

John Almons was deputy clerk, April 6, 1692 [O2, p. 352]

Attorney

Arthur Spicer was attorney of the crown in 1684 [O1, p. 45]

Land Surveyors

Anthony Stephens, first surveyor of Rappahannock County, February 19, 1656 [L1, p. 31]

John Catlett, before 1662 [D2, p. 267 (204); D3, p. 302]

Alexander Fleming, 1668 [D3, p. 399]

Edwin Conway, prior to 1678 [D6, p. 50]

William Moseley, January 1, 1683 [D7, p. 88]

Major George Morris, April 2, 1684 [O1, p. 16]

Capt. John Hayne, September 4, 1684 [O1, p. 54]

Mr. William Moseley, July 4, 1688 [O2, p. 99]

Edwin Conway, March 6, 1689 [O2, p. 144]

Edwin Thacker, March 5, 1689/90 [O2, p. 206]

Mr. Tomlin, January 1, 1690 [O2, p. 206]

Constables

Henry Arkeel in place and stead of Edward Taylor, May 8, 1684 [O1, p. 37]

William Clapham in place of William Jett, May 8, 1684 [O1, p. 37]

John Garton in place of James Orchard, May 8, 1684 [O1, p. 37]

David Pursall in room of Lewis Lloyd, May 8, 1684 [O1, p. 37]

Edward Jones in place of Alexander Newman, May 8, 1684 [O1, p. 37]

Thomas Wheeler in room of John [Gatewood], June 4, 1684 [O1, p. 42]

Tobias Ingram in room of John Grant, June 4, 1684 [O1, p. 42]

Richard Gregory in room of Henry Reeves, June 4, 1684 [O1, p. 42]

James Baughan in room of William Acres, June 4, 1684 [O1, p. 42]

Robert Rederford in room of Seth Tinsley, June 4, 1684 [O1, p. 42]

Joshua Mason [O1, p. 221]

Edward Rowsey [O1, p. 232]

Thomas Day in the precincts of Francis Browne [O1, p. 240]

Thomas Hine in the room and precincts of Daniel Dobins [O1, p. 240]

William Marshall in the room of Joshua Mason, June 1687 [O2, p. 31]

John Williamson in place of Rowsey, June 1687 [O2, p. 31]

Francis Thorne in place of Josiah Mason, February 2, 1688 [O2, p. 60]

William Starke in St. Mary's Parish in place of Francis Thorne, May 23, 1688 [O2, p. 76]

William Davis, May 2, 1688 [O2, p. 83]

Robert Halsey in place of John Diskin, May 2, 1688 [O2, p. 83]

John Phillips in place of Philip Henings, May 2, 1688 [O2, p. 83]

Anthony Carnaby in room of John Nichols, May 2, 1688 [O2, p. 83]

John Deane in room of Avery Naylor, April 4, 1688 [O2, p. 88]

John Stronge in place of Thomas Munday, June 6, 1688 [O2, p. 96]

Thomas Harris in place of Daniel Dobins, June 6, 1688 [O2, p. 96]

William Payne, in room of John Nicholls, July 4, 1688 [O2, p. 100]

Samuel Thacker in room and bench of John Stronge (Strange), August 7, 1689 [O2, p. 162]

William Dyer in room and precinct of Robt. Halsey, September 4, 1689 [O2, p. 167]

Samuel Sanford, May 7, 1690 [O2, p. 218]

Anthony Carnoby (Cannady) in the precinct of Chas. Snead, May 7, 1690 [O2, p. 218]

Jacob Nichols in the room and precinct of James Scott [O2, p. 218]

William Club in stead of William Dyer [O2, p. 219]

Daniel Browne in the precinct of Samuel Parrey [O2, p. 219]

Thomas Thorpe in place of Ralph Rowzy [O2, p. 231]

William Griffin in room and respect of Anthony Carnaby, June 3, 1691 [O2, p. 294]

Leonard Rowzee in room of David Wilson, June 3, 1691 [O2, p. 294]

Thomas Reyley to officiate as constable in the precinct of Xpher Ascaugh, June 3, 1691 [O2, p. 294]

Hugh Crabb in the precinct of Thomas Thorpe, June 3, 1691 [O2, p. 294]

Andrew Dew Jr. was ordered to officiate in the room and precincts of Samuel Samford and was ordered sworn, July 1, 1691 [O2, p. 298]

John Reynolds in the room and precincts of Thomas Grimsley, July 1, 1691 [O2, p. 299]

Collector
Richard Bray was a collector of county levys, December 1685 [O1, p. 181]

Listing of Tithables
On July 1, 1691, there were recorded in Order Book 2, pages 296-7, the names of the following men ordered to take the list of tithables in the assigned precincts:
    Capt. Bernard Gaines in the precincts of Samuel Bloomfield,
    Mr. Thomas Edmondson in his precincts as he formerly took them,
    Capt. Samuel Peachy from Farnham to Totuskey Creek as before,
    Capt. Samuel Travers between Farnham and Moratico Creeks,
    Capt. Wm. Lloyd from Totuskey to Rappahannock Creek,
    Capt. Thomas Catlett in the room and precinct of Anthony Savage

Grand Juries
June 4, 1684 [O1, p. 42]. Francis Slaughter, foreman, Robert Parker, John Evans, Jno. George [Gorge], Thomas Games, Thomas Cockin, Andrew Dudding, Robert Halsey, John Billington, Robert Cardin, John Willard and Leonard Chamberlaine.

June 4, 1690 [O2, pp. 230-1]. Arthur Forbes, Anthony Smyth, Richard Grimstead, Samuel Thacker, Jno. Griffin, Robert Brooke, William Ball, Thomas Wood, Daniel Diskin, Thomas Hinds, Jno. Gatewood and Thomas Cooper.

North Side

July 2, 1690 [O2, p. 233]. Edward Jeffries, John Garton, William Sims, Daniel Jackson, James Orchard, John Jennings, Jno. Wells, Peter Ellis, James Crutcher, John Hill, Wm. Bayly and Jno. Nicholls.

June 3, 1691 [O2, p. 295]. Samuel Green, Robert Thomas, Martin Johnson, Thomas Blanton, Richard West, Thomas Green, Robert Keyes, William Freeman, Henry Pickett, William Hudson, Edward Geffries, David Wilson.

July 1, 1691 [O2, p. 299]. William Brockenbrough, Thomas Walker, David Barwick, Robert Walker, Fran. James, Jno. Easter, Walt^r Anderson, Thos. Bryant, Wm. Browne, David Pursell, Rich. Apleby and Thos. Taylor.

Juries and Jurors

August 6, 1684 [O1, p. 45]. Edward Keeling, foreman, Andrew Dudding, John Billington, Christopher Chant, Wm. Bendry, Francis Browne, John Waggoner, Arthur Hodges, John Webbe, John Smythe, Wm. Leake, Robert Halsey.

September 4, 1684 [O1, p. 54]. Denis Carty, foreman, John Alloway, James Trent, Andrew Harrison, John Phillips, Angel Jacobus, Edward Geffreys, Henry Burdit, Francis James, George Southing, Alex. Newman, Thos. Chitty.

October 5, 1684 [O1, p. 62]. Joseph Goodrich, foreman, John Taliaferro, Richard Hale, Robert Parker, Thos. Jarvas, Wm. Moss, Giles Mathews, John Dike, Jno. Dangerfield, John Smith, Wm. Bendery, and John Meadors.

October 5, 1684 [O1, p. 57]. Thos. Edmondson, foreman, Richard Hale, John Smith, Andrew Duding, Joseph Goodrich, John Meadors, Wm. Ackres.

December 5, 1684 [O1, p. 81]. Edward Keeling, foreman, Joseph Goodrich, Richard Hail, Thos. Greene, Daniel Dobins, John Hale, Henry Longe, Ralph Whitton, Humphrey Perkins, Wm. Ackres, Henry Duding, Edward George.

March 4, 1685 [O1, p. 95]. Francis Settell, foreman, John Jacobs, Richard Lawson, John Richards, Henry Williams, Jno. Ford, Thos. Chitty, Richard Jasper, Avery Naylor, Jno. Halloway, Ed. George, James Jackson.

May 7, 1685 [O1, p. 124]. Angell Jacobus, foreman, Robert Clark, John Diston, Edward Keeling, Edward Jones, Robert Young, James Jackson, Paul Woodbridge.

April 14, 1690 [O2, p. 217]. Elizabeth Lawson was tried by a jury of women. The questions put to and answered by her are listed.

April 4, 1688 [O2, p. 81]. Martin Johnson, John Graves, John Diskin, Thos. Games, Ja. Baughan, Wm. Johnson, Jno. Stockley, Arthur Forbes, Jno. Waters, Ed. George, Thos. Garbett, Daniel Diskin.

July 4, 1688 [O2, 100]. Samuel Bayley, Wm. Barber, Angel Jacobus, Francis Gowre, Charles Dodson, John Browne, Arthur Forbes, Wm. Smythe, Thos. Dew, Robert Brooks, John Dangerfield, Martin Johnson.

March 7, 1688 [O2, p. 72]. Jno. Dangerfield, Jno. Willis, Elias Yates, Richard Carter, John Jones, Wm. Coghill, Rich. Mathews, Jno. Sherlock, Danl. Diskin, Wm. Hasle, Thos. Monday, Ed. George.

April 2, 1688 [O2, p. 86]. Wm. Barber, Jno. Orchard, Adam Woofendall, John Alloway, Jacob Nicholls, Jno. Dangerfield, Thos. James, Martin Johnson, Philip Henning, John Jones, Thos. Colley, Wm. Marshall.

October 4, 1688 [O2, p. 117]. Arthur Forbes, Edward Thomas, Robert Halsey, Martin Johnson, John Dangerfield, Xpher Blackburne, John Catlett, Jno. Waters, Wm. Johnson, Henry Picket, Nich. Bennett, Thos. Wheler.

November 7, 1688 [O2, p. 123]. Martin Johnson, Xpher Blackburn, Wm. Clapham, John Gray, David Stern, Robert Brooks, Giles Matthews, Wm. Underwood, Henry Pickett, Jno. Deane, Alex. Doniphan, Thos. Swinburne.

December 9, 1688 [O2, p. 130]. Arthur Forbes, James Bowler, Wm. Almond, Philip Hennings, Ralph Rowzey, Walt. Anderson, Angel Jacobus, James Trent, Thos. Hine, Thos. Swinburne, Abraham Hop, John Kitching.

July 3, 1689 [O2, p. 154]. Wm. Browne, Henry Willis, Elias Yates, Geo. Bruce, Fran. James, Daniel Browne, Ralph Whitting, Davis Roper, Walt. Anderson, Jno. Jones, Joshua Lawson.

September 4, 1689 [O2, p. 168]. Jno. Waters, Fran. Gowre, Hen. Lewis, John Browne, John Jones, Jno. Deane, Phill. Henning, Jno. Griffin, Henry Austin, Geo. Bruce, Rich. White, Wm. Tomlin.

August 7, 1689 [O2, p. 164]. Alex. Swan, Jno. Dike, Henry Picket, Jno. Jones, Thos. Wood, Henry Johnson, Jno. Griffin, Rich. Gorge (George), Robert Coleman.

April 3, 1689 [O2, p. 148]. Edward Thomas, Francis Stone, Saml. Bayly, Richard Henlie, Arthur Forbes, John Smyth, Dan. Dobyns, Jno. Waters, Nicholas Franklin, Jno. Dangerfield.

December 5, 1689 [O2, p. 194]. Wm. Young, Mr. Antho. Smyth, Sam. Parry, Wm. Covington, David Pursell, John Hill, Ralph Noel, James Baughan, Thos. Gaines, Henry Williams, Danl. Diskin, Wm. Markes.

March 5, 1690/1 [O2, pp. 289-90]. Thos. Monday, Thos. Coggin, Hugh Crabb, John Suttle, John Cheeke, John Harper, Wm. Harwood, Henry Woodnut, Thos. Wheeler, Henry Austin, John Ratcliff, Wm. Hudson.

A jury of neighbors for settling a land dispute, the second Monday in February 1690 [O2, p. 190]. Francis Thorne, Wm. Strodder, Hugh French, John Goss, Xpher Blackburne, Wm. Gunnock, Martin Johnson, Hugh Crabb, Nich. Copeland, Silvester Thatcher, Wm. Underwood, Francis Sterne, David Sterne, Wm. Clapham, Roger Richardson, or any twelve of them.

A jury of neighbors for trying land disputes, March 5, 1690 [O2, p. 201]. Arthur Forbes, Jno. Waters, Thos. Parker, Robert Brooke, Anthony Smythe, Wm. Younge, Robert Coleman, James Baughan, James Scott, Ja. Taylor, Wm. Johnson, Ja. Orchard, Alex. Doniphan, Wm. Payne, Jno. Burkett, Thos. Arnold.

April 2, 1690 [O2, p. 209]. Alexander Doniphan, Thos. Monday, Edward Jeffreys, Arthur Forbes, John Dangerfield, Wm. Bendry, Saml. Thacker, Antho. Smyth, Ja. Bowler, Rich. Haile, Ja. Baughan, Jno. Gatewood.

April 3, 1690 [O2, p. 212]. A land jury. John Dangerfield, Rob. Brooks, Rob. Plea, Thos. Monday, Jno. Wells, Anthony North, Jno. Waginer, Jno. Evans, Wm. Bendree, Ed. Pagett, Jno. Waters, Richard Stoakes, Thos. Barber, Robt. Mills or any twelve of them.

April 3, 1690 [O2, p. 213]. Alex. Doniphan, Rich. Haile, Rich. West, Danl. Diskin, Wm. Bendry, Jno. Dangerfield, Edward Jeffries, David Wilson, Robt. Payne, Robert Coleman, Wm. Marshall, Philip Henings.

April 9, 1690 [D8, p. 210]. Land Jury. Thos. Parker, John Dangerfield, Robert Brooks, Richard Stoakes, Thos. Monday, Wm. Bendry, Arthur North, John Wells, John Hines, John Baughan, John Waginer, Robert Mills.

July 3, 1690 [O2, p. 238]. James Jackson, Josh. Lawson, Wm. Carter, Jos. Beckley, Jno. Ingol, John Thomas, James Gilbert, Walt. Anderson, Jno. Alloway, James Orchard, Wm. Harwood, David Pursell.

May 7, 1690 [O2, p. 222]. John Phillips, Ed. Jeffries, John Hill, Jno. Morgan, Francis Settle, Geo. Bruce, Jno. Ingoe, Luke Thornton, James Gilbert, Henry Wms., James Orchard.

August 7, 1690 [O2, p. 249]. David Wilson, Saml. Sanford, Wm. Hancock, Wm. Morgan, Wm. Carter, Jno. Jones, Henry Lewis, Jno. Cheek, John Gatewood, John Tarcliff, Henry Goring, Wm. Leake.

September 3, 1690 [O2, p. 254]. Edward Jeffries, Xpher Ascaugh, Giles Mathews, Wm. Smyth, Jno. Foushee, Ja. Mariott, Nich. Copeland, Wm. Hanks, Wm. Browne, Richd. Shipway, Robt. Mayfield, Richard Mathews.

January 7, 1690 [O2, p. 265]. Francis Taliaferro, Francis Settle, Wm. Haile, Wm. Lynes, Hen. Lewis, Avory Naylor, Thos. Bayly, Angel Jacobus, Wm. Hanks, Wm. Brockenbrough, Jno. Nikols, Henry Puckett.

October 8, 1691 [O2, p. 327]. Xpher Blackburn, Wm. Dyer, Hugh Crabb, Thos. Blanton, Samuel Perry, Thos. Green, Jno. Williamson, Richard Shipway, Jno. Dangerfield, Jno. Hailes, Leo. Chamberlain, Jno. Brener.

February 5, 1691 [O2, p. 347]. Rob. Coleman, Thos. Wheeler, Wm. Johnson, Davis Wilson, Phill. Parr, Jno. Mills, Jno. Williamson, Wm. Dyer, Richard Lackland, Jno. Brazier, Ja. Baughan, Sam. Parry.

February 19, 1691 [D6, p. 142]. John Gatewood, Thos. Wheeler, Richard Gregory, Richd. Haile, James Bahun, Thos. Coggin, Thos. Greene, Thos. Wood, John Waters, Fra. Browne, Thos. Edmondson, Wm. Johnson.

April 1, 1691 [O2, p. 291]. Thos. Monday, Thos. Coggin, Hugh Crabb, Jno. Suttle, Jno. Cheek, Jno. Harper, Wm. Harwood, Henry Woodnot, Thos. Wheeler, Hen. Austin, Jno. Ratcliff, Wm. Hudson.

February 6, 1693 [O1, p. 8]. Samuel Bayley, foreman, John Alloway, Walter Pavey, James Jackson, Isaac Webb, Anthony Carnaby, Roderick Jones, Henry Austin, Henry Fleet, Bryan Hodgson, Robert Henley, Wm. Brokenbrough.

CHAPTER 17

Farnham and North Farnham Parish Register

Preserved by the Circuit Court of Richmond County, at Warsaw. A photostat is in the Library of Virginia. The records prior to 1692 were made in old Rappahannock County, and are here listed as follows:

Births and Marriages

A

Born Anne daughter of John and Anne Arnolds, Dec. 17, 168-	Arnolds
" John the son of John and Helena Aspall, Feb. 4, 1687	Aspall
" Mary daughter of Thomas and Alicia Algar, Aug. 2, 1692	Algar
" John son of John and Anne Arnolds, Dec. 25, 1677	Arnolds
Married John Answorth to Sarah Bridger, July 15, 1678	Answorth
" John Allen to Catherine Major, Nov. 15, 1678	Allen
" Richard Apleby to Ann Arnolds, July 4, 1680	Apleby
Born Gabriel son of John and Dorothy Alloway, May 28, 1672	Alloway
" Priscilla daughter of John and Dorothy Alloway, 1672/3	"
" Richard son of Richard and Anne Appleby, June 14, 168-	Appleby
" Alex. son of John and Mary Adams, May 10, 1686	Adams
" Catherine daughter of John and Mary Adams, April 30, 1684	"

B

Married David Burk (or Burt) to Mary Read, Oct. 19, 1673	Burk
Born David son of David and Mary Burk, Mar. 7, 1673/4	Burk
" John son of Wm. and Elizabeth Bendoll, May 10, 1677	Bendoll
" Sarah daughter of David and Charity Barrick, Aug. 5, 1688	Barrick
" Elizabeth daughter of Dominick and Elizabeth Berneham, Mar. 29, 1692	
	Berneham
" Samuel son of Samuel and Sarah Bayly, Mar. 20, 1691	Bayly
" Elizabeth daughter of Wm. and Elizabeth Bendall, 1671	Bendall
" Jane daughter of Wm. and Elizabeth Bendall, 1674	Bendall
" Joyce daughter of Samuel and Joyce Bailey, Jan. 17, 1677	Bailey
Married Richard Brasser to Elizabeth How, July 7, 1678	Brasser
Born Jane the daughter of John and Jane Bowles, Feb. 25, 1675	Bowles
" Elizabeth daughter of Wm. and Mary Barber, Jan. 11, 1665	Barber
" Charles son of Wm. and Mary Barber, June 19, 1676	"
" Thomas " " " " " " ", Jan. 19, 1678/9	"
Born William son of Wm. and Mary Barber, Aug. 7, 1679	Barber
" John son of John and Jane Bowls, April 15, 1680	Bowls
" Phillis daughter of John and Mary Battin, Sept. 6, 1680	Battin
" Thomas son of John and Jane Bowls, Feb. 1, 1681	Bowls
" Anne daughter of Thomas and Anne Beal, Aug. 10, 1672	Beal
" Thomas son of Thomas and Anne Beal, Jan. 29, 1675	Beal
" Charles son of Thomas and Anne Beal, Oct. 20, 1678	Beal
" Joseph son of Thomas and Catherine Brad, Aug. 10, 1679	Brad

Born John son of John and Jane Bowls, April 15, 1680   Bowls
"   Thomas " " " " " " ", Feb. 1, 1681/2   "
"   Charles " " " " " " ", Jan. 5, 1683/4   "
"   William son of Robert and Jane Baylis, Sept. 16, 1684   Baylis
"   Henry son of John and Jane Bowles, July 6, 1687   Bowles
"   Lucy daughter of Wm. and Mary Barber, Jan. 16, 1681   Barber
"   Thomas son of Thomas and Isabell Bradley, Dec. 11, 1687   Bradley
"   Catherine daughter of John and Elizabeth Bonner, Aug. 23, 1686   Bonner
"   Amadine daughter of Thomas and Catharine Baylis, Jan. 18, 1684   Baylis
"   Robert son of " " " " " " ", Sept. 7, 1686   "
"   Frances daughter of " " " " " " ", Sept. 23, 168-   "
"   Thomas son of Thomas and Elizabeth Bryant, July 12, 1688   Bryant
"   William son of Wm. and Mary Brockenbrough, Nov. 10, 1687   Brockenbrough
"   John son of Richard and Deborah Bramham, Sept. 20, 1690   Bramham
"   Catherine daughter of Thomas and Catherine Bailis, Mar. 28, 1691   Baylis
"   Mary daughter of Henry and Mary Bruse, April 3, 1692   Bruse
"   Margaret " " Thomas and Eleanor Bryant, July 22, 1693   Bryant
"   Eliz. daughter of David and Charity Barrick, Jan. --, 1690   Barrick
"   Anne " " " " " " ", Nov. 11, 1694   "
"   Mary " " John and Elizabeth Bennett, Sept. 5, 1682   Bennett
"   Elizabeth " " " " " " " ", Feb. 12, 1683/4   "
"   John son " " " " " " " ", April 2, 1689   "
"   William son " " " " " " " ", Oct. 16, 1691   "
"   Margery daughter of " " " " ", May 11, 1694   "
"   Elizabeth daughter of Dominick and Elizabeth Branham, May 29, 1692   Branham

C

Married Thomas Collee to Ann Fann, July 23, 1673   Collee
Born Sarah daughter of John and Sarah Canaday, Oct. 3, 1673   Canaday
Married Samuel Conserve to Elizabeth Killingsby, Jan. 22, 1675   Conserve
"   William Creswell to Anne Allin, June 18, 1677   Creswell
Born Anne daughter of Joseph and Frances Creswell, Feb. 18, 1675   "
"   Walter son of Giles and Elizabeth Cole, Mar. 5, 1677   Cole
"   Mary daughter of John and Sarah Canaday, Oct. 11, 167-   Canaday
"   Samuel son " " " " " " ", Sept. 16, 1684   "
"   Reubin son of Christopher and Ann Colvert, Nov. 5, 168-   Covert
"   Charles son of Wm. and Ann Colston, April 17, 1691   Colston
"   Cicely daughter of John and Jane Crutcher, July 17, 1692   Crutcher
"   Hannah daughter of John and Sarah Canaday, Oct. 15, 1678   Canaday
"   Robert son of Robert and Mary Cole, Sept. 30, 1677   Cole
"   Mary daughter of Hezekiah and Mary Colewick, Nov. 27, 1681   Colevick
"   Richard son of Wm. and Elizabeth Cooper, Sept. 3, 1680   Cooper
"   John son of Henry and Jane Clark, Feb. 13, 1666   Clark
"   John son of John and Jane Crutcher, Oct. 3, 1682   Crutcher
"   Susanna daughter of Wm. and Anne Colston, Dec. 8, 1686   Colston
"   Jane daughter of John and Jane Crutcher, June 15, 1686   Crutcher

D

Born Arthur son of Martin and Margaret Dye, May 18, 1673   Dye
Married Wm. Davis to Elizabeth Thrift, April 23, 1677   Davis
"   Edward Davis to Mary Maxen, Nov. 16, 1677   "
Born Ralph son of Ralph and Honor Downing, April 15, 1688   Downing
"   James " " " " ", Jan. 25, 1690   "
"   Mary daughter of Thomas and Dorothy Durham, June 5, 1686   Durham
"   Thomas son " " " " " ", June 27, 1690   "
"   Jane daughter of William and Elizabeth Davis, Nov. 20, 1680   Davis
"   Robert son " " " " ", March 25, 1682   "
"   Richard " " " " " ", Sept. 5, 1687   "
"   William " " " " " " ", March 15, 1677   "
Married Richard Draper to Elizabeth Man, Sept. 12, 1680   Draper
Born Thomas son of Charles and Anne Dodson, May 15, 1681   Dodson
"   Elizabeth daughter of Joseph and Elizabeth Dukeshell, Dec. 10, 1686   Dukeshell
"   Ruth " " Ralph and Honor Downing, Sept. 5, 1686   Downing
"   Jeremiah son of Jeremiah and Joane Dalton, July 9, 1693   Dalton
"   Rawleigh " " Wm. and Million [Downman], Dec. 14, 1681   Downman
"   Million daughter of " " " " ", May 21, 1683   "
"   William son " " " " ", Oct. 19, 1685   "
"   Robert " " " " " ", Jan. 2, 1686/7   "
"   Elizabeth daughter " " " " "m Jan. 26, 1688/9   "

E

Born Anne daughter of Peter and Frances Elmore, Aug. 29, 1674   Elmore
Married Francis Elmore to Anne Allen, Dec. 2, 1677   "
Born Richard son of Peter and Diana Evans, Aug. 5, 1688   Evans
"   Daniel son of Francis and Ann Elmore, Dec. __, 1689   Elmore
"   Thomas son of Richard and Jane Elliott, Sept. 29, 1692   Elliott
"   Peter son of Peter and Elenor Ellis, April 21, 1670   Ellis
"   Richard son of Richard and Anne Ellit, Sept. 22, 1686   Ellit
"   Elizabeth daughter of Francis and Catharine Elmore, July 6, 1693   Elmore
"   John son " " " " " ", Nov. 25, 1685   "
"   Wm. son of Daniel and Anne Everet, Mar. 15, 1692   Everet

F

Born Martha daughter of David and Mary Fowler, Sept. 19, 1673   Fowler
"   Michael son of Thomas and Johanna Freshwater, Jan. 2, 1672   Freshwater
Married Robert Fristow and Jane Sherman, Aug. 1, 1675   Fristow
"   William Fann to Alicia Samford, Jan. 23, 1675   Fann
Born Mary daughter of Edward and Mary Fryar, Sept. 11, 1676   Fryar
"   Robert son of Robert and Jane Fristow, May 2, 1676   Fristow
"   Frances daughter of David and Mary Fowler, June 4, 1677   Fowler
"   Catherine daughter of George and Mary Fristow, June 14, 1683   Fristow
"   William son of " " " " , October 1687   "
"   John son of Alexander and Sarah Fleming, Mar. 23, 1690   Fleming
"   Joanna daughter of Thomas and Joanna Freshwater, Oct. 30, 1677   Freshwater
"   Jane daughter of Robert and Jane Fristow, Mar. 23, 1678   Fristow

Born Anne daughter of Edward and Mary Fryar, May 21, 1680	Fryer
" John son of David and Mary Fowler, Sept. 30, 1679	Fowler
" Mary daughter of John and Mary Fristow, June 25, 1682	Fristow
" Mary daughter of Thomas and Mary Fuller, June 28, 1687	Fuller
" Charlott daughter of James and Mary Foushee, June 5, 1692	Foushee

G

Married John Green to Dorothy Benjamin, Aug. 24, 1673	Green
Born Jean daughter of Thomas and Anne Glascock, July 10, 1673	Glascock
" Mary and Anne daughters of Gregory and Mary Glascock, Nov. 10, 1673	"
" John son of John and Barbara Grimston, Dec. 20, 1672	Grimston
" John son of Gerard and Elleanor Greenwood, Sept. 20, 1676	Greenwood
" Ralph son of Ralph and Joanna Gayton, Oct. 2, 1680	Gayton
" George " " " " " ", Dec. 22, 1682	"
" John son of Ralph and Joanna Gayton, Sept. 14, 1684	"
" Isaac son of George Green and Anne Bodkin, Aug. 12, 1688	Green
" Edward son of Thomas and Catharine Gladman, Nov. 24, 1688	Gladman
" Mary daughter of Thomas and Ann Glascock, Jan. 22, 1690	Glascock
" John son of William and Constance Glen, Jan. 11, 1688	Glen
" Elizabeth daughter of Edward and Eliz[a.] Geffrys, Aug. 4, 1679	Geffrys
" Frances daughter of Thomas and Anne Glascock, July 14, 1680	Glascock
" Corbin son of Leroy and Winnefred Griffin, April 12, 1679	Griffin
" Winnefred daughter of Leroy and Winnefred Griffin, October 1682	"
" Gerrard son of Gerrard and Eleanor Greenwood, Feb. 19, 1681	Greenwood
" Stanley son of Francis and Anne Gower, Nov. 17, 1679	Gower
" Francis " " " " " ", April 15, 1682	"
" Thomas son of Leroy and Winnefred Griffin, Sept. 20, 1684	Griffin
" William son of William and Constant Glen, Jan. 5, 1682/3	Glen
" Simon " " " " " ", Aug. 15, 1686	"
" Jane daughter of William and Jane Goare, Dec. 25, 1687	Goare
" Elizabeth daughter of David and Catherine Gwin, Dec. 31, 1692	Gwin

H

Born Richard son of William and Grace Hammock, May 4, 1674	Hammock
" Robert son of Andrew and Thomasin Harrison, Oct. 23, 1674	Harrison
Married Thomas Holland to Joyce Johnson, Aug. 2, 1675	Holland
Born Elizabeth daughter of Henry and Elizabeth Hartley, Nov. 14, 1672	Hartley
" Anne " " " " " ", May 4, 1675	"
" Job son of Job and Elizabeth Hammond, July 10, 1677	Hammond
" William son of Andrew and Thomasin Harrison, May 14, 1677	Harrison
" Leonard son of Thomas and Elizabeth Hart, Jan. 7, 1688	Hart
" Sarah daughter of Richard and Sarah Harman, Sept. 23, 1688	Harman
" William son of William and Alice Hammock, Mar. 15, 1688	Hammock
" Edward son of Martin and Mary Hammond, Nov. 22, 1689	Hammond
" Thomas son of Thomas and Elizabeth Hart, April 17, 1691	Hart
" Mary daughter of William and Anne Hazell, April 3, 1692	Hazell
" Thomas son of Martin and Mary Hammond, July 17, 1692	Hammond
" Elizabeth daughter of Richard and Judith Hinds, Mar. 30, 1678	Hinds
" Anne daughter of Andrew and Thomasin Harrison, June 21, 1679	Harrison

Born Elizabeth daughter of Henry and Elizabeth Hartley, July 22, 1679   Hartley
"   Elizabeth daughter of Daniel and Mary Hargrove, Feb. 6, 1678   Hargrove
"   Elizabeth " " Job and Mary Hammond, Mar. 10, 1680   Hammond
"   William son of William and Sarah Hanks, Feb. 14, 1679   Hanks
"   Hannah daughter of Richard and Elizabeth Hudnell, Sept. 3, 1682   Hudnell
"   William son of Job and Elizabeth Hammond, Sept. 3, 1682   Hammond
"   John son of John Hawford, Feb. 25, 1676   Hawford
"   Elizabeth daughter of John and Elizabeth Hawford, Oct. 20, 1680   "
"   Mary daughter of Brian and Mary Hodson, Oct. 24, 1682   Hodson
"   Joyce daughter of Zachariah and Mary Hawford, Jan. 14, 1686   Hawford
"   Mary daughter of Martin and Mary Hammond, April 24, 1687   Hammond
"   Thomas son of John and Catharine Hawford, June 5, 1687   Hawford
"   John son of George and Dianna Howell, Nov. 18, 1686   Howell
"   Anne daughter of Randolph and Charity Homes, Aug. 22, 1686   Homes
"   Marin son of Martin and Mary Hammond, July 3, 1683   Hammond

I and J

Born Christopher son of Christopher and Joyce Johnson, Aug. 24, 1673   Johnson
"   John son of John and Mary Inger [Ingoe], Feb. 7, 1675   Ingoe
"   John son of Rotherwick and Mary Jones, May 16, 1689   Jones
Married Edward Jones to Alicia Lunn, Aug. 27, 1679   "
"   John Jacobs to Mary Cary, Nov. 8, 1680   Jacobs
Born James son of John and Mary Ingoe, April 26, 1680   Ingoe
"   Elizabeth daughter of Angel and Elizabeth Jacobus, Nov. 14, 1680   Jacobus
"   Anne daughter of Richard and Sarah Jesper, Oct. 8, 1682   Jesper
"   Mercy daughter of Edward and Alicia Jones, May 13, 1682   Jones
"   Samford son " " " " , April 13, 1684   "
"   John " " " " " , Aug. 20, 1680   "
"   Austin son of Edward and Priscilla Jones, May 10, 1682   "
"   Hannah daughter of " " " " , June 16, 1685   "
"   Anne daughter of Rotherwick and Mary Jones, June 16, 1685   "
"   Richard son of Richard and Sarah Jasper, April 21, 1687   Jasper
"   Thomas " " " " " ", Oct. 2, 1689   "

K

Born Mary daughter of Edward and Elizabeth King, Mar. 9, 1692   King

L

Born Roger son of William and Alicia Lun, Feb. 28, 1676   Lun
"   Henry son of Henry and Jane Lucas, Mar. 23, 1677   Lucas
"   Johanna daughter of Edward and Mary Lewis, Sept. 8, 1676   Lewis
"   Mary daughter of William and Alicia Lun, Sept. 12, 1673   Lun
"   Francis son of Henry and Jane Lucas, Sept. 1, 1680   Lucas
"   Benjamin son of Thomas and Mary Lewis, Sept. 10, 1685   Lewis
"   Thomas son of Thomas and Mary Lewis, Dec. 5, 1692   Lewis

M

Born Winnefred daughter of John and Jane Mercy, July 2, 1677   Mercy
"   Michael son of Edward and Margaret Massings [Mozingo], Sept. 6, 1687   Massings
"   Elizabeth daughter of Edward and Elizabeth Morris, Aug. 5, 1688   Morris

Born Elizabeth daughter of William and Anne Morgan, Mar. 20, 1691	Morgan
" Catherine daughter of Dennis and Elizabeth McCarty, Apr. 16, 1678	McCarty
Married John Marsy to Anne Canes, July 11, 1680	Marsy
Born Elizabeth daughter of William Mills, Jan. 26, 1679	Mills
" Daniel son of Daniel and Elizabeth McCarty, Mar. 19, 1680/1	McCarty
" William son of William and Patience Marks, June 25, 1682	Marks
" Elizabeth daughter of John and Esther Mills, Aug. 9, 1682	Mills
" Bridget daughter of Anthony and Elizabeth Morgan, Sept. 14, 1682	Morgan
" Charles son " " " " " " , Sept. 28, 1680	"
" Andrew son of James and Elizabeth Mathews, Feb. 24, 1683/4	Mathews
" Anny daughter of Anthony and Elizabeth Morgan, Mar. 14, 1684	Morgan
" Anne daughter of John and Anne Marsy, Dec. 28, 1681	Marsy
" Anthony son of Anthony and Elizabeth Morgan, Nov. 20, 1686	Morgan
" William son of William and Elizabeth Marsh, Feb. 15, 1683	Marsh
" John " " " " " " , June 19, 1687	"
" Barbara daughter of John and Barbara Morgan, July 23, 1686	Morgan
" John son " " " " " " , July 19, 1687	"

N and O

Born John son of John and Mary Nethercutt, Sept. 2, 1687	Nethercutt
" Robert " " " " " " , Aug. 6, 1686	"
Married Daniel Oneal to Elizabeth Harding, May 10, 1674	Oneal

P

Born Robert son of Eliza and Samuel Peachy, Mar. 21, 1673	Peachy
Married Simon Polling to Jean Wade, Oct. 19, 1673	Polling
Born Elizabeth daughter of Edward and Mary Pool, 1671	Pool
Married Joseph Polley to Joanna Ken, May 4, 1677	Polly
Born Tobias son of John and Elizabeth Phillips, July 12, 1687	Phillips
" Henry son of David and Billender Pursell, April 20, 1682	Pursell
" John " " " " " " , Jan. 29, 1683/4	"
" David " " " " " " , June 30, 1686	"
" William " " " " " " , Aug. 25, 1688	"
" Tobias " " " " " " , Dec. 23, 1691	"
Married John Partridge to Frances Creswell, April 6, 1678	Patridge
" Jeremiah Phillips to Anne Brooks, June 3, 1678	Phillips
Born William son of James and Anne Pritchard, Mar. 31, 1680	Pritchard
" Elizabeth daughter of John and Elizabeth Phillips, Dec. 3, 1674	Phillips
" John son " " " " " " , Dec. 23, 1676	"
" Bryant " " " " " " , Feb. 13, 1678	"
" Mary daughter of John and Elizabeth Phillips, Oct. 7, 1681	"
" Thomas son " " " " " " , Oct. 27, 1684	"
" Tobias " " " " " " , Jan. 12, 1687	"
" Anne daughter " " " " " , Sept. 23, 1690	"
" Samuel son of James and Mary Phillips, Nov. 30, 1689	"
" Mary daughter of John and Michall Powell, Jan. 4, 1690	Powell
" John son of " " " " " , Jan. 26, 1692	"

R

Married John Russell to Alicia Billington, Sept. 11, 1673	Russell

Married William Rolls to Margaret Reeves, June 8, 1674	Rolls
" John Reynolds to Sarah Grimes, Aug. 5, 1674	Reynolds
Born Mary daughter of William and Mary Richardson, July 28, 1688	Richardson
" William son of Lewis and Jane Richards, Aug. 13, 1691	Richards
" Elizabeth daughter of Elias and Hannah Robinson, Sept. 13, 1691	Robinson
" Anne daughter of William and Anne Robinson, Aug. 25, 1679	"
" Elizabeth " " " " " " , Dec. 4, 1681	"
" Barbara " " " " " " , Dec. 4, 1683	"
" Frances " " " " " " , Nov. 10, 1684	"
" Simeon son of John and Grace Rider, Mar. 14, 1691	Rider
" Hannah daughter of Elias and Hannah Robinson, Dec. 1688	Robinson

S

Born Martin son of Quintilion and Jean Sherman, Oct. 4, 1673	Sherman
" Thomas son of John and Sarah Suggett, Mar. 7, 1677	Suggett
" John son of Timothy and Sarah Swindall, Mar. 20, 1676	Swindall
" Margaret daughter of Mary and Thomas Sampson, 1663	Sampson
" John son of " " " " " , 1674	"
" William son of William and Ann Smith, May 13, 1688	Smith
" Thomas " " Samuel and Elizabeth Sanford, Mar. 20, 1687	Sanford
" Samuel " " Samuel and Jane Steel, Jan. 4, 1690	Steel
" John " " Alexander and Judith Swan, Jan. 22, 1691	Swan
" Elizabeth daughter of John and Mary Smith, Mar. 20, 1691	Smith
" Richard son of Thomas and Mary Smith, July 27, 1690	Smith
" Thomas son of Thomas and Mary Sanford, 1674	Sanford
" Anne daughter of " " " " " , April 16, 1676	"
Married Alexander Swan to Judith Hinds, Nov. 15, 1678	Swan
Born Elizabeth daughter of Tobias and Anne Stevens, Oct. 31, 1679	Stevens
" William son of Thomas and Mary Sampson, Feb. 28, 1678	Sampson
Married William Shaw to Margaret Holland, Nov. 22, 1680	Shaw
Born Margaret daughter of Alexander and Judith Swan, 1680	Swan
" Francis Settle son of John and Mary Settle, Dec. 6, 1681	Settle
" John son of John and Judith Stewart, Mar. 15, 1686	Stewart
" Thomas " " William and Ann Smith, Oct. 30, 1683	Smith
" Elizabeth daughter of John and Jane Stewart, Mar. 5, 1692	Stewart
" Margaret " " John and Judith Stewart, Aug. 20, 1685	"
" Anne " " " " " " , Aug. 10, 1690	"
" Elizabeth " " " " " " , Dec. 27, 1692	"
" Mary " " William and Jane Smoot, April 1693	Smoot
" Mary " " Robert and Abigal Sisson, July 31, 1692	Sisson
" John son of William and Frances Smith, Mar. 11, 1681	Smith
" Elias " " " " " " , Nov. 10, 1683	"
" Gabriel " " " " " " , Mar. 10, 1692	"
" Hannah Bower daughter of Richard and Rachel Smith, Nov. 1689	"
" William son of Samuel and Elizabeth Samford, Sept. 12, 1692	Samford
" Mary daughter of Thomas and Eleanor Southern, Aug. 1689	Southern
" Susanna " " " " " " , Mar. 19, 1691	"

T

Married Hezekiah Turner to Elizabeth Hugell, Nov. 7, 1674	Turner
" Henry Tillery to Mary Wasscole, Nov. 7, 1675	Tillery
Born William son of Nathaniel and Elizabeth Thrift, Jan. 30, 1675	Thrift
" Thomas " " Luke and Ann Thornton, April 5, 1688	Thornton
" Ester daughter of Robert and Ester Tomlin, June 27, 1688	Tomlin
" John son of William and Ann Tayloe, Feb. 15, 1687/8	Tayloe
" Mark " " Luke and Ann Thornton, Sept. 23, 1686	Thornton
" Richard son of Charles and Eleanor Tillery, Aug. 12, 1688	Tillery
" John " " James and Mary Tarpley, Feb. 21, 1690	Tarpley
" John " " John and Elizabeth Taverner, Mar. 7, 1682/3	Taverner
" Richard " " " " " " , July 30, 1685	"
" James " " James and Mary Tarpley, May 8, 1692	Tarpley
" Rebeccah daughter of Samuel and Frances Traverse, Oct. 15, 1692	Traverse
" Sarah " " John and Elizabeth Taverner, Jan. 7, 1679	Taverner
" Henry son of Henry and Mary Tillery, Nov. 12, 1679	Tillery
Married James Tune to Mary Jackman, Sept. 6, 1680	Tune
Born Elizabeth daughter of Walter and Mary Thompson, Oct. 19, 1680	Thompson
" Elizabeth " " John and Elizabeth Taverner, Mar. 25, 1681	Taverner
" Mary " " John and Sarah Trock, May 29, 1681	Trock
" Mary " " Henry and Mary Tillery, Nov. 23, 1685	Tillery
" Roger son of Henry and Ann Thornton, June 17, 1686	Thornton
" Elizabeth daughter of William and Anne Tayloe, July 26, 1686	Tayloe
" Richard son of John Thomas, Aug. 8, 1686	Thomas
" Sarah daughter of Simon and Elizabeth Taylor, Sept. 28, 1692	Taylor

U

Born Mary daughter of Thomas and Sarah Underwood, Oct. 22, 1687	Underwood
" Rachell " " Shadrack and Mary Ungwin, Sept. 23, 1679	Ungwin

W

Married John Webb and Mary Samford, July 14, 1673	Webb
Born Shadrack son of Roger and Jean Williams, Feb. 1, 1673	Williams
Married Thomas Warring to Alice Underwood, Oct. 5, 1673	Warring
Born James son of John and Mary Webb, Aug. 9, 167-	Webb
" Thomas son of Robert and Mary Wood, Nov. 15, 1673	Wood
" Thomas " " Henry and Sarah Wilson, May 2, 1674	Wilson
" Giles " " John and Mary Webb, April 15, 1677	Webb
Married Stephen Wells to Alce Howard, Dec. 3, 1677	Wells
Born John son of John and Mary Woollard, April 14, 1685	Woollard
" Rebeccah daughter of John and Mary Woollard, Sept. 9, 1687	"
" Rachell " " Thomas and Anne Walker, Aug. 5, 1688	Walker
" Luke son of Luke and Anne Williams, May 13, 1692	Williams
" Richard " " John and Mary Woollard, Oct. 22, 1691	Woollard
" Elizabeth daughter of Charles and Sarah Walker, Oct. 29, 1691	Walker
Married Isaac Webb to Mary Bedwell, April 6, 1678	Webb
Born Rebeccah daughter of Roger and Jane Williams, June 20, 1675	Williams
" Elizabeth " " Paul and Bridget Woodbridge, Dec. 24, 1677	Woodbridge
" Robert son of Robert and Mary Wood, Sept. 25, 1679	Wood

Born Isaac   "   "   John and Mary Webb, Dec. 18, 1681   Webb
 "   William   "   "   Paul and Bridget Woodbridge, July 14, 1668   Woodbridge
 "   Elizabeth daughter of Thomas and Anne Walker, Nov. 8, 1679   Walker
 "   Anne   "   "   "   "   "   "   , Nov. 4, 1681   "
 "   Thomas son of Charles and Isabella Wilson, Nov. 1, 1678   Wilson
 "   Henry   "   "   "   "   "   "   , July 1, 1681   "
 "   Aaron   "   "   Henry and Charity Webster, April 7, 1687   Webster
 "   Mary daughter of Thomas and Anne Walker, Dec. 28, 1683   Walker
 "   Sarah   "   "   "   "   "   "   , Feb. 15, 1685   "
 "   Mary   "   "   John and Mary Woollard, Oct. 1, 1682   Woollard
 "   Samuel son of Samuel and Ann Wharton, Nov. 19, 1684   Wharton
 "   John   "   "   "   "   "   "   , Dec. 24, 1686   "

                                          Y

Born Priscilla daughter of Ellias and Mary Yeates, Feb. 9, 1681   Yeates
 "   Dorothy   "   "   Thomas and Mary Yeates, Oct. 31, 1686   "
 "   William son of Thomas and Mary Yeates, Mar. 15, 1689   Yeats

BIBLIOGRAPHY

Court records of Rappahannock, Essex, Richmond, Lancaster and Northumberland Counties, including deeds, wills, orders, and miscellaneous loose papers.

Virginia Land Office Patent Books, Library of Virginia

Farnham and North Farnham Parish Registers

Beverley, Robert, *The History and Present State of Virginia* (Chapel Hill, N.C.: The University of North Carolina Press, 1947)

Hening, William Waller, *The Statutes at Large; being a collection of all the Laws of Virginia, from the First Session of the Legislature, in the year 1619.* Vols. 1-3.

Mcilwaine, H.R., *Minutes of the Council and General Court of Colonial Virginia*

Smith, John, *The General History of Virginia, New-England and the Summers Isles*

Winder, F.A., *Transcripts concerning the Colony of Virginia made from original papers in the Public Records Office, London.* 2 Vols. State government records collection, Library of Virginia (barcode 1140023)

Colonial papers at the Library of Virginia, and others named where the reference occurs.

INDEX

[ ]: Alice, servant, 69; Robert, 70; William, 106

A.P. Hill Camp, vii

Abbott: Nicholas, 106

Accokeek, 139

Ackres: William, 162

acorns, 88

Acres: William, 160

Act of Assembly, 27, 78, 82, 104

Act of Parliament, 156

Adams: Alexander, 165; Catherine, 165; George, 68; John, 165; Mary, 165

Adcock: Edward, 99, 134

Adcock's Creek, 134

Aikens: John, 69

Algar: Alicia, 165; Mary, 165; Thomas, 165

Alger: Alitia Kennedy, 76; Thomas, 76

Allawaye: William, 68

Allen: Anne, 167; Catherine Major, 165; Jo:, 70; John, 165; Margaret, 68; Nathan, Dr., 154; Nathen, Dr., 154; Valentine, 86, 141; William, 139

Allerton: Isaac, Col., 19

Allin: Anne, 166

Allin's Creek, 149

Allison: James, 68; Thomas, 69

Allistree: Paul, 123

Alloway: Dorothy, 165; Gabriel, 165; John, 79, 85, 86, 148, 152, 158, 162, 163, 164, 165; John, Col., 21; Priscilla, 165

allum, 9

Almond: Jo:, 99; William, 163

Almons: John, deputy clerk, 159

American Revolution, 66

ammunition, 39, 48, 62

Amoroleck, 7

Anderson: Walt, 163, 164; Walter, 162

Andry: Elinor, 67

Answorth: John, 165; Sarah Bridger, 165

Apleby: Ann Arnolds, 165; Richard, 162, 165

Appamatuck, 1

appeals, 19, 121

Appleby: Anne, 165; Richard, 165

Appleton: Abraham, 70; Elizabeth, 70

apprentices, 72, 73, 87

apprenticeships, 78, 79

Argall: Samuel, Sir, 9, 10, 13, 62

Arkeel: Henry, 160

Arlington: Lord, 46

Armstead: John, 118; Mary Browne, 118

Armstrong: Robert, 30, 138

Arnold: Anthony, 58; Benjamin, 106; Thomas, 163

Arnolds: Ann, 165; Anne, 165; John, 165

Arnoll: Margarett, 70

arrow heads, 36

arrows, 4, 5, 6, 7, 29, 35, 127

Ascaugh: Christopher, 161, 164

Aspall: Helena, 165; John, 165

Atkins: Francis, 69

Atlantic coast, 1

Attapaugh, 31

attornies, 159

Aubry: Henry, 159

Austin: Henry, 163, 164; William, 162

Austing: Henry, 64

Austing's Landing, 64

automobiles, 129

Awberry: Henry, 34, 139, 150; Richard, 138, 139

Awbery: Henry, 92, 159

Awborie: Richard, 156

Awbrey: Henry, 56, 155, 156; Henry, Capt., 156

Axacon, 1

axes, 43, 62

Axom: William, 139

Axon: Margery, 70

Axum: Thomas, 140

Ayers: Robert, 13

Aylett: William, 138

Aylett Family, vi

Aylmer: Justin, clerk, 113

Ayres: John, 142

Bacon: Nathaniel, 17, 45, 50, 53, 56, 151; Nathaniel Jr., 49, 57, 106; died, 52; Nathaniel, capture ordered, 50

Bacon's army, 127; charged with treason, 57

Bacon's Assembly, 106

Bacon's forces, 60

Bacon's Rebellion, 24, 33, 34, 43, 44, 45, 83, 106, 109, 118, 119, 120, 132, 151; blame for, 97

Bacon's troops, 51

Bagnal: James, 155

Bagnall: A., 6; Anthony, 3, 25; James, 25, 69, 155; John, 135; Mr., 25

bags, 92

Bagwell: James, 58; John, 113; Mr., 158

Bahun: James, 164

Bailey: Joyce, 165; Samuel, 165

Bailie: Robert, 148

Bailis: Catherine, 166; Thomas, 166

Baker: John, 138

Goodrich: Benjamin, 58, 97, 99, 119, 139; Col., 30, 123; Joseph, 162; Lt. Col., 30; Thomas, 39, 42, 58, 59, 115, 138, 139, 156; Thomas, Col., 29, 41, 58, 59, 82, 97, 119, 137; Thomas, Lt. Col., 114, 137; Thomas, Maj., 70
Goodrich Family, 97
Goodrich's quarter, 58
Goodridge. *See* Goodrich
Goodwyn: Thomas, 139
Gookin: Daniel, Capt., 13
Goose: Thomas, 76
Gordon: Thomas, 139; Thomas, clerk, 59, 118; Thomas, Rev., 58
Gore: Samuel, 120
Gore of the Smock, 134
Goring: Henry, 164
Goss: John, 163
Gostell: Jo:, 69; Stephen, 69; William, 69
governors, 40, 44, 45, 59, 122, 128, 132, 148, 151, 157; attempted murder, 38; message to, 48, 50
Gower: Anne, 168; Francis, 68, 139, 148, 168; Stanley, 168
Gowre: Francis, 162, 163
grain, 62; carried to mills, 130
granaries, 61
Grand Assembly, 12, 24, 38, 46, 48, 54, 84, 92, 96, 97, 114
grand juries, 22, 161
Granger: Walter, clerk, 101, 159
Grant: John, 160
grave markers, 61, 142
Graves: Francis, 139; John, 162
Gray: James, 106; John, 163; Miss, 79; William, 78, 87, 91, 141, 142
Gray Family, 142

Great Hunting Creek, 33, 146
Great pocoson, 136
Great Rappahannock Creek, 146
Great swamp, 135, 136
Green: Anne Bodkin, 168; Dorothy Benjamin, 168; George, 168; Isaac, 168; James, 135; John, 76, 139, 168; Samuel, 162; Thomas, 76, 162, 164
Green Bay, 5, 25, 34, 126, 142, 149
Green Springs, 45, 52, 158; hangings at, 57
Green swamp, 85, 136
Greene: Thomas, 162, 164
Greenfield, 76
Greenwood: Eleanor, 168; Elleanor, 168; Gerard, 154, 168; Gerrard, 168; John, 168
Gregory: John, 139; R., 139; Richard, 160, 164
Gregory's swamp, 139
grievances, 46, 54, 57, 106
Griffin: Corbin, 168; John, 161, 163; Leroy, 158, 168; Leroy, Col., 156, 157; Samuel, 139, 149, 151, 155, 156, 158; Thomas, 82, 149, 168; William, 161; Winnefred, 168
Griffing: John, 87
Griffith: Thomas, 69
Griggory: John, 115
Griggs: John, 138
Grigory: John, 114
Grilles: Jonathan, 106
Grimes: Benjamin, 120; Charles, 111, 114, 116, 149; Charles, clerk, 110; Charles, Rev., 104, 109, 116, 143; Edward, 39, 116; Margaret, 39, 153; Sarah, 171

Grimes Creek, 141
Grimes Family, 124
Grimes Point, 110
Grimes' land, 63, 95
Grimshaw: Frederick, 87
Grimsley: Thomas, 161
Grimstead: Richard, 161
Grimston: Barbara, 168; John, 168
grist mills, 44, 111, 136
guardianships, 74
Gudloe: George, 70
Gudlow: Margaret, 70
Guicotic Creek, 145
gunners, 43
Gunnock: William, 163
gunpowder, 24, 38, 39, 56, 73; given to Indians, 48; value of, 94
guns, 24, 43, 50, 52, 61, 73, 93, 112; in exchange for furs, 48; to Indians, 38; value of, 91, 94
gunshot, 24, 39, 73; given to Indians, 48; value of, 91
gunsmiths, 87
Gunstacker: Edward, 52, 60
Gunston: Thomas, 85
Gunston's Mill, 85
Gwin: Catherine, 168; David, 146, 168; Elizabeth, 168
Hail: Richard, 162
Haile: John, 138; Joseph, 106; Richard, 137, 164; Richard, Capt., 138; William, 164
Haile's Bridge, 138
Haile's old swamp, 138
Haile's spring branch, 138
Hailes: John, 164
hailstones, 42
Hale: John, 162; Nicholas, 39; Richard, 162
Haling: James, 68
Hall: Thomas, 57
Halloway: John, 162

Halsey: Robert, 160, 161, 162, 163
Hamilton: Anthony, 58
Hamlin: Peter, 69
Hammock: Alice, 168; Grace, 168; Richard, 168; William, 168
Hammond: Edward, 168; Elizabeth, 168, 169; Job, 168, 169; Martin, 168, 169; Mary, 168, 169; Thomas, 168
Han: Susan, 68
Hancock: William, 164
Handerson: John, 70
Hanes: William, 106
hangings, 57
Hanks: Nancy, 66; Sarah, 169; William, 149, 164, 169
Hanks Family, 67
Hanover Co., Va., 127
Hanover Parish, 120
Hanrauly: Darby, 68
Hansford: Thomas, 57
Harding: Elizabeth, 170; Thomas, 152; William, 77
Hardinge: William, 68
Hardis: Thomas, 88
Hardridge: James, 58
Harford: Christopher, 68
Hargan: Cornelia, 69
Hargrove: Daniel, 169; Elizabeth, 169; Mary, 169
Harker: John, 69
Harley: Henry, 78
Harman: Quintilian, 148; Richard, 106, 168; Sarah, 168
Harper: John, 135, 137, 163, 164; Thomas, 137; William, 39, 106
Harris: Ann, 123; Baro., 69; E., 26; Thomas, 68, 138, 160
Harrises Creek, 26
Harrison: Andrew, 143, 162, 168; Anne, 168; James, 156, 159;

Robert, 168;
Thomasin, 168;
William, 168
Harry Hill swamp, 137
Harry Land swamp, 137
Harrys: John, 70
Hart: Elizabeth, 168; Leonard, 168; Thomas, 168
Hartley: Anne, 168; Elizabeth, 168, 169; Henry, 168, 169
Harwar: Thomas, 93, 152, 156
Harwood: Elizabeth, 68; William, 163, 164
Hasle: William, 163
Hasplock: George, 148
Hassininga, 6, 7
hatchets, 8
Hatter's Creek, 148
Hawes: Nicholas, 9
Hawford: Catharine, 169; Elizabeth, 169; John, 169; Joyce, 169; Mary, 169; Thomas, 169; Zachariah, 169
Hawkes: Mary, 70
Hawkin: Thomas, 115
hawking, 71
Hawkins: John, 76; Mr., 140; Thomas, 53, 69, 77, 141, 155, 157; Thomas, Maj., 51, 76
Hawsman: David, 86
Hayne: John, Capt., 160
Hazell: Anne, 168; Mary, 168; William, 168
Hazeltree Point, 143
headrights, 65, 67, 83
hemp, 82
hemp and silk grass, 5
hemp seed, 92
Hening: William Waller, 122, 174
Henings: Philip, 160, 164
Henley: Robert, 164
Henlie: Richard, 163
Henneygam: James, 137
Henning: Philip, 163
Hennings: Philip, 163

Henrico Co., Va., 49, 79
Henry: Daniel, 141; Patrick, 117
Herbert: Clement, 157; William, 10
Herd: Elizabeth, 152; Walter, 152
Herring Creek, 148
hides: taxes on, 47
high sheriffs, 21
highways, 137; to be laid out, 128
Hill: Col., 53; Edward, Col., 30; John, 162, 163, 164; Leonard, 134, 135
Hilliard: Thomas, 143
Hind: Thomas, 68
Hinds: Elizabeth, 168; Judith, 168, 171; Richard, 168; Thomas, 161
Hine: Thomas, 160, 163
Hines: John, 164
Hobbs His Hole, 58, 59, 81, 97, 101, 102, 119, 130, *See* Tappahannock, Va.; courthouse at, 101; port purchased, 97; prison at, 102; seat moved to Lloyds, 124
Hockaday Family, vi
Hodges: Arthur, 162
Hodgson: Bryan, 164; William, 87, 142
Hodson: Brian, 169; Mary, 169
hog keepers, 41
Hoge: Jeremiah, 68
hogs, 27, 38, 40, 88; killing of, 88; stealing of, 39
hogsheads, 55, 129, 158; making of, 87; of tobacco, 83; shipped to England, 47
Hogtown Branch, 148
Holcomb: William, 106
Holden: Robert, 58

Jugs Creek, 147
Julian calendar, 97
July: Thomas, 70
juries, 20, 148, 162
jurists, 151
jurors, 21, 155, 162
jury rooms, 20
justices, 20, 36, 65, 66, 95, 96, 98, 136, 148, 150, 151, 152, 155, 156; for each parish, 21
Keale: George, 68; Richard, 2, 3
Keck: W.F., 113
Kecoughtan, 2
Keeling: Edward, 124, 162
Keene: Mary, 70; Susanna, 70; Thomas, 70; William, 70
Kelly: John, 74
Ken: Joanna, 170
Keney: Edmond, 70
Kennedy: Alitia, 76; John, 76
Kenny: William, 53
Kent Island, 136
Kenyan: Abraham, clerk, 113
Key: Francis Scott, 67
Keyes: Peter, 145; Robert, 162
Keyes Creek, 145
Keys: Sarah, 68
Keys Run, 145
Killingsby: Elizabeth, 166
Killman: John, 53
Kilman's beaverdam swamp, 137
King: Edward, 169; Elizabeth, 169; Mary, 169; Sidney E., vii; William, 70
King and Queen Co., Va., 35, 75, 105, 119, 126, 130, 135
King George Co., Va., 19, 37, 66, 109; boundary change, 102; boundary line, 144
King James, 8, 152
King of Denmark, 10

King William, 123, 152
king's grant, 46
King's Highway, 29, 51, 119, 126, 127
King's swamp, 85, 136
Kinge: Jo:, 70
kings, 5, 6, 7, 8, 9, 13, 28, 29, 31, 38, 39, 41, 46, 47, 50, 152; arrested and bound, 40; killed, 48
Kinloch, 102
Kirby: Philip, 70
Kirk: Elizabeth, 53
Kirkaldie, Scot., 112
Kirkman: Ann, 64; Francis, clerk, 60, 101, 159
Kitching: John, 163
Knight: Peter, 120
Knights of the Horseshoe, 127
Knowles: Sands, 58; Thomas, 70
Kooper's Point, 135, 139
Lackland: Richard, 164
Lacy: John, 136
Lamb Creek, 144
lambs, 33; value of, 90
Lamory: Mary, 70
Lancaster Co., Va., 18, 24, 38, 42, 43, 63, 66, 78, 87, 108, 122, 130, 152, 153, 155; army raised, 50; boundary line, 133, 149; boundary of, 113; company raised, 39; courthouse, 96, 147; courthouse location, 95; divided into two parishes, 110; dividing of, 110; early colonists recorded in, 67; early courts, 95; established, 18; first ferry, 63; formation of, 109; formed in 1652, 108; line, viii; parishes in, 108; wills recorded in, 53
Lancaster Parish, 108

land: acquiring large tracts, 65; apportionment of, 24; clearing of, 27; escheating, 83; fifty acres, 71, 74, 78, 97, 98; glebe, 113
Land: Thomas, 68
land certificates, 68, 69
land grants, 46; on the Rappahannock River, 13; to Arlington and Culpeper, 46
land patents. *See* patents; early, 13
land values, 83; 26 pounds per acre, 83
landholders, 76, 132, 155
landings, 33, 129; Austing's, 64; Daingerfield's, 64, 101
Landrum's Creek, 141
lands: clearing of, 39; escheated, 46; fifty acres, 83
Lane: William, 145
Laneview, Va., 128
Latane Family, 151
Lathbury: John, 69
Lawrence: Richard, 50, 59, 135, 146, 151
Lawson: Elizabeth, 162; Epaphroditus, 61; John, 59; Josh., 164; Joshua, 163; Mr., 25; Richard, 140, 141, 162; Rowland, 69; Rowland, Dr., 25
Lawson Family, vi
Lawson's Creek, 140
Lawson's Island, 141
Layne Creek, 145
Layton's Wharf, 111, 124, 141, 145
Leake: William, 162, 164
leather: tax on, 47
Lee: Bridget, 69; Hugh, 74, 151; Mr., 122; Richard Henry, 66; Richard, Col., 53, 135; Robert Edward, 67

Markes: William, 163
Markmun: James, 68
Marks: Patience, 170;
    William, 170
Maroughan: Katharine,
    68
Marracassick Creek, 30
Marracossick Creek, 30
Marraughtacum, 1
marriage licenses: prior to
    1660, 107
marriages, 75; after
    apprenticeship, 87;
    fees to minister, 109;
    list annually to
    governor, 108
Marry Gold, 137
Marsh: Elizabeth, 170;
    George, 70, 155; John,
    170; Mr., 30; William,
    170
Marsh Creek, 147
Marshall: William, 160,
    163, 164
Marshesell: John, 69
Marsy: Anne, 170; Anne
    Canes, 170; John, 170
Martin: John, 77; John
    Sr., 77; Mrs., 77
Maryland, 38, 48, 56, 117,
    136; immigrants from,
    13; in supremacy of
    tobacco, 47; land in, 77
Maryland Indians, 41, 47;
    trade in Virginia, 47
Mason: George, Col., 56;
    Joshua, 160; Josiah,
    160
massacres, 48, 49, 62, 78,
    111, 119, 120; of 1644,
    13, 24, 26, 37, 38, 103;
    of 1675, 83, 150; of
    1675/6, 48, 60;
    protection from, 45
Massaponax Creek, 44,
    132, 143
Massawomeck Indians, 3,
    5
Massawomek Indians, 6
Massawtecke, 5

Massings: Edward, 169;
    Margaret, 169;
    Michael, 169
Masters: John, 139
matchcoats, 28, 29, 38
Matchymop Quarter, 32
Mathews: Andrew, 170;
    Elizabeth, 170; Giles,
    162, 164; James, 170;
    Richard, 163, 164;
    Samuel, Capt., 45;
    William, 142
Mathews Co., Va.: army
    raised, 50
Mattaponi, 39
Mattaponi Indian town,
    29, 130
Mattaponi Indians, 29,
    31, 39, 40, 41, 151;
    king, 29; paths, 29
Mattaponi path, 126
Mattaponi River, viii, 1,
    16, 29, 30, 37, 51, 126,
    130
Mattaponies, 25
Matthews: Giles, 163;
    William, 148
Mattoponi upper path,
    126
Maxen: Mary, 167
Maxy: Joseph, 69
May: Philip, 139
Maydox: Hugh, 69
Mayfield: Robert, 164
McCarty: Catherine, 170;
    Daniel, 170; Dennis,
    170; Elizabeth, 170
Mcilwaine: H.R., 174
McKenny: Alexander,
    136
Meader: John, 143;
    Thomas, 39, 147;
    Thomas Jr., 137
Meader Creek, 35
Meaders Creek, 142
Meades Creek, 142
Meador. *See* Meader
Meadors: John, 162
Meadow Farm, 151
meats, 9
Melbeck Creek, 39

Menendez de Aviles
    Pedro, 1
Menokin Creek, 33, 146
Menokin Run, 85
Menokin Swamp, 32
merchandise, 62
merchants, 47, 62, 76, 87,
    111, 113, 133; of
    England, 88
Merchants of Monodas,
    47
Mercy: Jane, 169; John,
    169; Winnefred, 169
Merigold, 137
Meriwether: Thomas, 135
Merriman's land, 95
Merry Branch, 138
Merry Vayle Creek, 138
Mexican War, 67
Micou: Paul, Dr., 142,
    154
Middle Plantation, 50, 51,
    52
Middlesex Co., Va., 53,
    128, 130; army raised,
    50; boundary line, 13,
    128; boundary of, 113,
    118; line, viii; road
    toward, 130
Middleton: Beale, 117;
    John, 106
Miles: Ann, 69; Anne, 70
Milford, Va., vii
military: office held, 40
military activities, 24, 37
military commanders, 65
militia, 73
militia officers, 22
Mill Creek, 60, 127, 139,
    143; mill on, 86
Mill's Creek, 139
milled lumber, 87
Millenbeck, 43
Miller: Mary, 70; Mrs.,
    60; Simon, 87, 143;
    Simon Jr., 142; Simon,
    Capt., 56; Simon, Maj.,
    52, 60
millers, 84; to take 1/8 of
    grain, 84
Millers Tavern, Va., 126

Millessent: Jo:, 70;
Robert, 70
mills, 30, 44, 78, 84, 111,
136; Barber's, 85;
Beeby's, 85, 137;
Bowler's, 85; Bush's,
137; Bushby's, 130;
Cheduxon, 85;
Chestoon, 85; Combs',
85; Covington's, 130,
137; Essex, 85, 130,
137; Fauntleroy's, 84;
Gilson's, 84, 85;
Goldman's, 139;
Gunston's, 85;
Moore's, 126;
Morattico, 85;
Nichols', 85;
Occupace, 86;
Occupatia, 140; on
Morattico swamp, 85;
Parker's, 85; Payne's,
85; Piscataway, 85,
137; produce from, 85;
Ritchie's, 130; Stone's,
85, 99; Taliaferro's, 86,
143; Tandy's, 86;
Tomlin's, 85;
Underwood's, 85;
Ware's, 137; Waring's,
139; Webb's, 130, 137;
Weir's, 85; Wilson's,
85
Mills: Elizabeth, 170;
Esther, 170; John, 93,
139, 164, 170; Peter,
53, 135, 146; Robert,
164; William, 170
mineral rights, 92
minerals, 92
Minfrey: George, 69
ministers, 54, 64, 109;
fees for services, 108;
importation into
colony, 107
Minshaw: Constant, 70;
Eliza, 70
Mirery Branch, 138
Mohaskahod, 6
Moineichrom, 39
Momford: Thomas, 2, 3

Monacan Indians, 6
Monday: Thomas, 102,
163, 164
Monroe: Andrew, 70
Montagues, Va., 128, 130
Montross, Va., 146
Moon: Abraham, 141,
143
Moon Creek, 143
Moon's Mount, 143
Moone: Abraham, 68;
An, 68
Moore: Anne, 70
Moore's Mill, 126
moorish point, 7
Moratacond, 26
Moraticco Creek, 19
Moratico Creek, 161
Moraticon, 26
Moraticond, 27
Moraticond Creek, 25
Moraticond Indians, 28
Moratiquond, 26, 28
Morattaco, 31
Morattico, 25, 26
Morattico Creek, 26, 79,
93, 110, 111, 114, 116,
117, 149
Morattico Indian town,
28
Morattico Indians, 25
Morattico Mill, 85
Morattico swamp, 85
Moratticock Creek, 18
Moratticoes, 26, 28
Moratticond, 27; king of,
28
Moraughlacuds, 3
Moraughtacun, 3
Moraughtacund, 8
Moraughtacund Indians,
5
Moraughtacunds, 8
Morell: George, 67
Morgan: Anne, 170;
Anny, 170; Anthony,
170; Barbara, 170;
Bridget, 170; Charles,
170; Elizabeth, 170;
John, 102, 164, 170;
William, 86, 164, 170

Morill: Daniel, 68
Morratico Indians, 37
Morris: Edward, 169;
Elizabeth, 169; George,
139, 141; George, Maj.,
76, 78, 97, 160
Morrison: Francis, 46;
Francis, Col., 54
Morton: Ralph, 2
Mosco, 1, 5, 6, 7, 8, 26
Moscoe, vii
Moseley: Edward, 86;
Mr., 28; W., 115;
William, 65, 141, 149,
157, 159, 160; William,
Capt., 120, 156
Mosko, 3
mosquitoes, 112
Moss: Bridgett, 98; John,
144; William, 86, 98,
100, 114, 144, 146, 162
Moss Neck store, 143
Motley: John L. Jr., vii;
Vivien Farish, vii
Motram: John, 38
Motrom: John, 152
Mott: George, 144; John,
53, 144
Mottram: John, 155
moulding planes, 87
Mount Creek, 143
Mount Landing, 33, 85;
road to, 102
Mount Landing Creek,
85, 97, 101, 113, 118,
139
mountains, 1, 6; Blue
Ridge, 127
Mozingo: Edward, 169;
Margaret, 169;
Michael, 169
Mt. Airy Mill swamp, 146
Mt. Airy pond, 85
Muddy Creek, 144
Muddy Gut, 134
Mulatto slaves, 153
Mulberry Island Point,
146
Munday: Thomas, 160
Munro: Edmond, 70

Orchard: James, 100, 146,
160, 162, 163, 164;
John, 163
orchards, 88, 99
ordinaries, 63, 129
ordinary licenses, 86
orphans, 22, 74, 76, 78,
107; as vagrants, 76;
indentured, 74
orphans court, 72
Osterson: Mary, 68
Oswald: Henricus, 112;
Thomas, 112
otter skins: value of, 94
Otterburn, 111
Overton: John, 148;
Roscoe, 136
Owen: Hugh, 141; John,
68, 135; Richard, 106
Owen's swamp, 135
Ownchowlue, 39
Ownlee: Arthur, 141
oxen, 38, 128; value of, 89
Oxford, Eng., 45
oyster shells, 36, 133
oysters, 36, 39, 86
Ozeana, Va., 119, 128,
130, 135
Paddy's Creek, 147
Page: Henry, 57; John,
Maj., 53; Thomas, 53,
142
Pagett: Edward, 119, 164
Paggett: Edward, 70
Pain. *See* Payne; John,
111; Ralph, 136, 137;
Robert, 142, 159;
Thomas, 133
Paine: Elizabeth, 68; John,
62, 69, 70, 96, 115;
Penelope, 67; Ralph,
134; Richard, 137;
Robert, 92; Thomas,
67
Painter: Valentine, 70
Pamauncke River, 1
Pamaunke River, 1, 2
Pamunkey Indians, 35
Pamunkey Neck, 19
Pamunkey River, 14, 51
Pannell: Thomas, 53

pardons, 59
parish levys, 104
parish taxes, 47
parishes, 102; clerk of the,
107; court of, 22;
divided into precincts,
22; establishment of,
108; forty eight, 122;
recordkeeping, 107;
two justices each, 21
Parke: George, 159
Parker: Elizabeth, 85;
George, 152; John, 78;
Richard, 139; Robert,
78, 85, 92, 161, 162;
Thomas, 163, 164;
William, 106
Parker's Creek, 139
Paropatank Swamp, 52
Parot's Creek, 25
Parr: Philip, 164
Parray: Ralph, 69
Parrey: Samuel, 161
Parry: Sam, 136; Samuel,
137, 163, 164
Parry's Creek, 137
Parson's case, 117
Parsons: John, 146
Partridge: Frances
Creswell, 170; John,
116, 170
Passapatancy, 126
passengers, 62, 65
Pastancie, 9
Pastancy, 10
Pastancy Indians, 37
Patawomeck Indians, 3
Patawomecke River, 3
Patawomek Indians, 7
Pate: John, 139
patented land. *See* patents
patents, 19, 22, 26, 28, 30,
35, 36, 37, 38, 39, 47,
60, 74, 77, 78, 84, 98,
100, 101, 104, 109,
110, 111, 112, 113,
114, 118, 132, 133,
135, 138, 143, 145,
148, 149, 151; Town of
Tappahannock, 138

paths, 81, 129;
Chicacoon, 124;
Chickacoon, 126;
Lizzard Tree, 127, 130;
Mattaponi, 126;
Mattoponi upper, 126;
Port Tobago, 126;
Rappahannock, 126;
school-house, 111, 124
paths and roads, 126
Patowomeck, 9, 10
Pattersley: Michael, 86
Pattison: John, 143;
Thomas, 135
Patuxom, 38
Paul's Cross Roads, 127,
130
Pavey: Walter, 86, 164
Pawamansee Creek, 142
Payankatank River, 1
Payantank River, 3
Payne. *See* Pain; John, 85,
86, 87, 145; Ralph, 137;
Robert, 141, 142, 164;
Thomas, 87, 134;
William, 160, 163
Payne Family, vi
Payne's Island, 140, 141
peach trees: to make cart
axles, 86
Peachy: Eliza, 170;
Robert, 170; Samuel,
156, 157, 161, 170
Peacock: Mrs., 123
Peade: Dual, 104
Peale: Malachy, 87, 159
Pearce: Mr., 124;
Thomas, 70; William,
Col., 146
peas, 93; value of, 91
Pedee Creek, 121
Peeters: Anthony, 68;
Henry, 69
Peeterson: Elnor, 68
Peirce. *See* Pearce; Mary,
67; William, Capt., 16
Peksbury: Charles, 69
Pells: Timothy, 53
Pemberton: Richard, Dr.,
153
Pembroke River, 9, 10

172; Roger, 172;
Thomas, 172
Thorpe: Thomas, 161
Thrift: Elizabeth, 167,
172; Nathaniel, 172;
William, 172
Thrush: Clement, 67, 123,
139; Frances, 123;
Francis, 68
Thyreld: Richard, 69
Ticknor's Creek, 139
Tidewater Virginia, 66
Tidner: William, 138
Tigner: William, 68
Tignor: Richard, 139;
William, 86
Tignor's Creek, 139
Tillery: Charles, 172;
Eleanor, 172; Henry,
172; Mary, 172; Mary
Wasscole, 172;
Richard, 172
timber, 92
Tinsey: Samuel, 82
Tinsley: Seth, 87, 160
tithables, 12, 45, 64, 92,
128; persons taking
lists, 161
tobacco, 15, 38, 39, 43,
46, 58, 59, 62, 63, 64,
77, 79, 88, 91, 92, 133,
152, 153; American
crop, 73; art of raising,
80; as a drug, 47; as
salary, 113, 114;
bonded in amount,
158; crops destroyed,
46; failure of prices,
92; four pence per
pound, 82; hogshead
worth 30 shillings, 83;
in hogsheads, 47;
merchantable, 59;
monetary commodity,
82; not planted 1667,
82; not planted in
1667, 47; Oranoco, 82;
over production, 82;
production, 16;
regulating production,
82; sealed measures,

81; shipped by water,
130; tax on, 56; value
limitation for court
cases, 21; warehouses,
81; weights, 81; worth
50 shillings, 83
tobacco bags, 7
Tobicock Indian town, 29
Todkill: Anas, 2, 3, 4, 5,
25
Tom's Creek, 135
tomahawks, 35
Tomlin: Ester, 172; Mr.,
160; Robert, 33, 34, 62,
85, 139, 140, 172;
William, 163
Tomlin's Bay, 140
Tomlyn: Thomas, 70
Tompson: Ann, 69
tools, 10, 87
Toone: James, 53
Topahanock River, 1
Topahanocke, 1
Topahanocke River, 1
Topmanahocks, 1
Toppahannock River, 2, 3
Toseley: Thomas, 137
Totuskey bridge, 28
Totuskey Creek, 22, 25,
26, 27, 28, 31, 32, 33,
61, 64, 93, 115, 116,
117, 126, 147, 148,
158, 161
Totuskey Indians, 31, 37
Totuskey reservation, 28
Totuskey town, 147
town lots: sold at New
Plymouth, 97, 101
towns: establishing on
Rappahannock, 16;
ordered to be built, 95,
96; Rappahannock
Indian, 126; Richard
Coleman's, 111; to be
erected, 56
tradesmen, 72
trading posts, 111, 133
Tramer: Thomas, 68
transportation: difficult
for court, 95
Trapley. *See* Tarpley

trapping, 93
travel, 19, 45, 127, 128,
130
Travers: Raleigh, 137,
155; Rawleigh, 68, 155;
Rebecca, 88; Samuel,
Capt., 156, 158, 161;
William, 157
Traverse: Frances, 172;
Rebeccah, 172;
Samuel, 172
treaties, 14, 31, 34, 36, 39,
40, 147
Trent: James, 162, 163
Trible: Peter, 136
Trock: John, 172; Mary,
172; Sarah, 172
troops, 16, 54, 62, 147
Troublesome Point, 139
Trussell: John, 155
Trysting Place, 142
Tune: James, 172; Mary
Jackman, 172
turkey eggs, 42
Turner: Elizabeth Hugell,
172; George, 137;
Hesekiah, 53;
Hezekiah, 124, 172;
John, 58; Sarah, 69
turtles, 30, 36
Tuscarora Creek, 135
typhoid fever, 74
U.S. Army, vii
U.S. Geological Survey,
142
underwear, 73
Underwood: Alice, 172;
Mary, 172; Mr., 25, 40;
Sarah, 172; Thomas,
172; William, 24, 25,
70, 95, 96, 145, 147,
155, 157, 163; William
Sr., 85
Underwood's patent, 39
Ungwin: Mary, 172;
Rachell, 172; Shadrack,
172
universities, 73
Upper Piscataway
Church, 119
Upright, Va., 135